Physical Disability and Social Policy
Jerome E. Bickenbach

In Canada, as elsewhere, social policy addressing the needs of people with physical disabilities is at an impasse. There may be a vast array of legislative initiatives that target this population, but as a whole the policies are fragmented, incoherent, and uncoordinated. Moreover, the historical evidence is clear that piecemeal reform will only worsen the disincentives and other policy anomalies that already exist. What is needed is an understanding of the conceptual character of physical disability as well as a consistent account of what, if anything, society owes people with physical disabilities.

Bickenbach seeks to clarify disability and to survey the philosophy behind the moral and political positions underwriting its social policy. The impasse in social policy is shown to be the result of muddling three very different models of disability: the biomedical, the economic, and the social-political. Each model may capture a genuine aspect of disability but none offers an integrated solution, and each passes on its bias to the social policy based on it. Moreover, each model suggests a different account of society's obligations to people with disabilities.

Bickenbach concludes that only a suitable theory of political equality can do justice to the complex notion of disability, and so provide a coherent foundation for social policy. He proposes a potential theme for development of normative social policy through what he terms the equality of capability.

JEROME E. BICKENBACH is a member of the Department of Philosophy at Queen's University. He is co-author, with C. Ian Kyer, of *The Fiercest Debate: Cecil Wright, the Benchers, and Legal Education in Ontario.*

*Physical Disability
and Social Policy*

Jerome E. Bickenbach

UNIVERSITY OF TORONTO PRESS
Toronto Buffalo London

© University of Toronto Press Incorporated 1993
Toronto Buffalo London
Printed in Canada

ISBN 0-8020-2914-0 (cloth)
ISBN 0-8020-7419-7 (paper)

Printed on acid-free paper

Canadian Cataloguing in Publication Data
Bickenbach, Jerome Edmund
Physical disability and social policy

Includes index.
ISBN 0-8020-2914-0 (bound) ISBN 0-8020-7419-7 (pbk.)

1. Physically handicapped – Social conditions.
2. Physically handicapped – Government policy.
3. Sociology of disability. I. Title.

HV3011.B33 1992   362.4'04561   C92-095724-2

This book has been published with the help of a grant from the Social
Science Federation of Canada, using funds provided by the Social Sciences
and Humanities Research Council of Canada.

Contents

Acknowledgments

Many people inspired and helped to shape this book. First of all, David Lepofsky, the lawyer with whom I articled at the Crown Law Office in Toronto in 1982, brought my attention, not merely to the legal and political issues involved in disability, but also to the need to develop in this country policy that genuinely reflects, not just the rhetoric, but the reality of a social commitment to equality. Although we do not always agree, there is no doubt that but for his guidance and inspiration this book would not have been written.

The research for this book was done during my tenure as the recipient of the Bora Laskin National Fellowship in Human Rights Research for 1989. It is my hope that this book lives up to the aspirations of this award, and to the great Canadian teacher, scholar, and jurist who gave it its name.

Among the many others who helped me in a variety of ways in the preparation of this book, I would like to mention the following: Patrick Fougeyrollas, Consortium de recherche en réadaptation de l'Est du Québec; Adele Furrie, Statistics Canada; Nancy Lawand, Status of Disabled Persons Secretariat; Neil MacCormick, University of Edinburgh; Patricia Minnes, Department of Psychology, Queen's University; Patti Peppin, Faculty of Law, Queen's University; Marcia Rioux and her learned cohorts at the Roeher Institute, York University; Gary Woodhill, Ryerson Polytechnic; and William Young, Library of Parliament.

Finally, I would like to thank my partner, Jackie MacGregor Davies, who on countless occasions helped me to focus my research and formulate my thoughts in ways which would have been impossible without the benefit of her keen philosophical acumen.

Physical Disability
and Social Policy

1 Introduction and Overview[1]

Disablement and the Perspective of Policy Analysis

During the late 1970s and 1980s the cause of people with disabilities gained considerable attention in Canada and throughout the world. A catalyst of this awakening of concern and interest was the establishment of the International Year of Disabled Persons by the United Nations in 1981. The success of the International Year led to the International Decade of Disabled Persons, running from 1983 to 1993. Although there had been considerable study and advocacy in Canada before 1981, the symbolic act of the United Nations mobilized many disparate forces.

The federal government's response to the International Year of Disabled Persons took the form of a report tabled in Parliament by the Special Committee on the Disabled and the Handicapped.[2] *Obstacles* remains an important and remarkable document, not merely because of the wealth of detailed recommendations it contains, but also for its clarity of purpose and vision. For a public either inured to or ignorant of the concerns of people with mental and physical disabilities, *Obstacles* spoke eloquently of the three interlocking aspirations sought by these individuals:

1 that people with disabilities be treated with respect and dignity – that they not be victims of prejudice, stereotyping, and other forms of stigmatization, and that they be empowered to participate in decisions involving their own lives and futures, and that they be granted the right as autonomous individuals to control their fate and help themselves through their own service and advocacy organizations;

2 that they have the same opportunities as other Canadians to participate fully in the educational, employment, consumer, recreational, community, and domestic activities that characterize everyday Canadian social life; and in particular that they not be discriminated against or otherwise prevented from participating by virtue of their disabilities, and that they be provided with the means – educational, financial, and physical – to participate freely and fully in normal social activities; and

3 that society respond to the needs created by disabilities and accommodate those needs, both in the sense of providing medical and rehabilitative services, prosthetic and other assistive aids and devices required by the disability, and in the sense of structurally and organizationally altering the workplace and other social environments so as to remove impediments to full participation.

By highlighting respect, participation, and accommodation *Obstacles* expressed a consensus evident in Canadian society and elsewhere, a consensus about the legitimacy of a range of demands made by and on behalf of people whose needs and concerns could no longer be ignored.

Obstacles also performed another, more subtle, function. It transformed the aspirations of respect, participation, and accommodation into social goals. In effect, *Obstacles* called for the recognition of a discrete branch of social policy and the transformation of disability issues from an ill-defined collection of social problems to the object of social policy analysis.

As a general matter, an area of social policy develops in three stages.[3] First there is a public recognition of a cultural or political commitment to, and consensus about, general goals that guide policy formation and provide the mandate and motivation for reform. This recognition in turn initiates a process of identifying, in light of these goals and actual social conditions, objectives for social planning. Finally, the major practical task of policy development begins when concrete policy solutions are proposed which seek to satisfy these objectives, thereby furthering accomplishment of the general goals. The complex and interlocking tasks represented by these stages constitute social policy analysis.

By their nature policy goals are statements of principle invariably linked to substantive values that characterize the legal and political culture of the society, values such as liberty, equality, autonomy of the individual, and the rule of law. Policy analysis is therefore, in the first instance, a process of interpreting and clarifying policy goals in light of these dominant values.

Policy objectives, however, are wholly instrumental policy aims which have social significance only to the extent that they lead to the achievement, furtherance, or protection of one or more of the policy goals. Policy analysis explores this relationship between goals and objectives, and seeks out objectives that are at once truly representative of the fundamental values inherent in the goals and consistent with well-grounded objectives in other areas of social policy.

Finally, policy solutions are precisely defined courses of governmental action (including, if appropriate, inaction) that manifest concretely what is instrumentally valuable in the chosen objective. Policy solutions are moulded to existing conditions and subject to continuous review. Should the law, regulation, guideline, program, or initiative be found no longer to further the objectives for which it was designed, or if conditions change, the policy solution must be revised, rethought, or abandoned. Policy analysis at this level, therefore, must be rigorously sensitive to consequences:[4] to ignore the actual social consequences of policy solutions, or to entrench them as ends in themselves, is to make the fundamental blunder of confusing ends and means.

Policy on disability issues has long been recognized to be in need of focused analysis of this sort. Yet the prospect of unifying and integrating this policy seems impossibly daunting. For although there is in Canada, as elsewhere, a vast array of legislative provisions, programs, and other initiatives designed for, or otherwise benefiting, people with disabilities, the bulk of this policy takes the form of ad hoc exceptions to or special provisions of social programming not addressed to people with disabilities. Policy in this area is thus fragmented, incoherent, and uncoordinated.

Policy for people with disabilities is also extraordinarily diverse. Consider the following, partial list of the areas of current Canadian social policy in which disability issues and concerns are addressed, in one manner or another:

1 Biomedical services (preventative, diagnostic, research, therapeutic, nursing, chronic care, palliative, and epidemiological)
2 Rehabilitative and institutional care (vocational and occupational therapy and short- and long-term institutional care)
3 Independent living (attendant care, group homes, and deinstitutionalization)

4 Income security (social assistance, Canada/Quebec pension plans, old age security, and guaranteed income supplement)
5 Compensatory schemes (workers' compensation plans, disability insurance, and tort damages)
6 Health and safety legislation (disease control, public health, and employment safety)
7 Education ('special' education and integrative, educational programming)
8 Employment (training programs, counselling, affirmative action schemes, grants in aid, and employment equity)
9 Autonomy protection (competency and guardianship, informed consent, rights of the people who are institutionalized, and reproductive autonomy)
10 Housing (zoning restrictions for group homes, financial assistance for retrofitting, and other forms of accommodation)
11 Physical accessibility legislation (transportation, public buildings and facilities, and sports activities)
12 Communication and access to information (broadcasting and media, telecommunications, information resource centres, and print handicap)
13 Research, development, and provision of assistive aids and devices (supplementary aid and assistance for special needs)
14 Human rights (antidiscrimination and equality guarantees, rights to vote and to hold office, access to the legal system, and immigration)

Because of this range of diverse policy areas, the various ministries, departments, and administrative agencies that each have some aspect of the policy under their purview assume that their contribution is modest and tightly circumscribed and that some other ministry, department, or agency is responsible for overseeing disablement policy as a whole. However, this has never been true. Social historians agree that this policy is characteristically reactive and piecemeal: governments of the day establish programs and initiatives in direct response to particular events – especially returning soldiers injured in wars – but once the emergency has passed they move on to other issues.

From the perspective of policy analysis, the root problem with this policy is clear. There has never been focused and sustained policy analysis of disability issues as such. This area of social policy has historically suffered from basic ambiguities and confusions about its goals and, in consequence, uncertainties about the proper objectives to be pursued.

It is therefore the purpose of this book – in the spirit of *Obstacles* – to begin the task of creating a distinct, integrated, and coherent social policy for people with disabilities. I should emphasize that I hope to *begin* this task, not complete it. For my focus here is exclusively on the policy-analytic endeavours of goal clarification and formulation of objectives. I am concerned to explore what may be called the conceptual and normative foundations of social policy for, and on behalf of, people with disabilities. No new theory of disability or fully worked-out model for formulation of social policy is being proposed. There is far too much preliminary work to do. In particular, we need to find a way out of the current impasse in policy.

The Impasse in Disablement Policy

The present state of policy for and on behalf of people with disabilities was recently described by the House of Commons Standing Committee on Human Rights and the Status of Disabled Persons in its report *A Consensus for Action: The Economic Integration of Disabled Persons.*[5] The report speaks of the gap between expectation and action, the lack of consistent and coordinated policy resulting in 'add-on' programming and disincentives, the lack of accountability, and the apparent absence of the political will to put all of such policy on a firmer footing. The report also makes it clear that the problem is 'not that anybody says the wrong thing but [that] nobody does the right thing.'

A Consensus for Action is a very frank document and its tone of exasperation is warranted by the conditions it describes. Whether it be social insurance or social assistance programming, workers' compensation, employment policy, health care servicing, employment equity, or antidiscrimination legislation, in each aspect of policy the report points to glaring anomalies, inconsistencies, disincentives, and ambiguities of aim.

The report highlights a prominent policy anomaly about which much ink has been spilled, namely, that while some programs discourage people with disabilities from working, other programs aim to foster their employment. This is a major worry and may be responsible for the persistent linkage between disablement and poverty. But other anomalies, potential anomalies, and controversies are easy enough to spot. Consider the following, more or less random, sampling:[6]

1 In November 1990 groups representing people with disabilities complained to the Canadian minister of employment that people who wear glasses, have a minor speech impediment, or suffer lower back pain are being counted as disabled by companies seeking to improve their hiring record under the federal employment equity law. One of the offending companies had relied on a questionnaire that asked its employees if they perceived themselves as having any 'persistent physical, mental, psychiatric, sensory, or learning impairments.'

2 A woman writes of the anger she feels when able-bodied people rely on euphemisms to describe her 'condition': 'It is not fun to be disabled. Being disabled is not a "challenge" we voluntarily undertake. Nor is it that we are merely "differently-abled." We are disabled; there are just some things we can't do ... Even if the larger community would adopt totally fair and appropriate attitudes toward people with disabilities, this would still not eliminate the sense of loss, the frustration, and indeed the anger we feel just because we are disabled.'

3 A spokesman for a U.S. quadriplegic advocacy group complains that the far-reaching antidiscrimination provisions of the Americans with Disabilities Act will have almost no effect on the people he represents since, lacking affordable and reliable attendant care, quadriplegics are utterly powerless to take advantage of those protections.

4 In a 1988 judgment of the United States Supreme Court it was held that the Veteran's Administration was correct to presume, irrebuttably, that anyone granted a disability discharge on the basis of alcoholism could be denied educational benefits because the condition was the result of 'wilful misconduct.' In dissent, Mr Justice Blackmun insisted with such a presumption was just the kind of stereotype that section 504 of the Rehabilitation Act was designed to overcome.

5 In April 1990 the Thalidomide Victims Association objected to a Department of Health and Welfare proposal that a total of $7.5 million be divided up among its members in equal shares. The association argued for varying payment according to the severity of the deformity. A spokesman for the department replied that the

association's argument was not applicable, since the plan was a 'compassionate payment,' part of an 'extraordinary assistance program' that is not based on liability.

6 Both the Canadian and Ontario Human Rights commissions have adopted a definition of 'disability,' in terms of which a person who is perceived by others to associate with individuals who are perceived to be members of 'high risk' groups for HIV infection is disabled, even though such a person may be completely healthy.

Each of these situations signals tensions and inconsistencies that lie at the heart of some area of policy. None of them, however, are the result of carelessness or can be attributed to lack of administrative accountability, the absence of a coordinating agency, or even a failure of political will. Instead, they suggest that as a culture we are labouring under basic confusions about the point of the policy. The problem is not that of enunciating policy goals, but of being clear what these goals mean and what they oblige society to do. The impasse in policy is thoroughly normative and deeply theoretical.

But to point to confusions about social values or to speak about a problem of theory does not mean that the impasse concerns abstract and arcane philosophical controversies. Quite the contrary, it is my contention that the impasse in policy is a reflection of the fact that as a society we have not satisfactorily answered two straightforward, almost childishly simple questions:

• What does it mean to have a disability?
• What, if anything, is society obliged to do for people with disabilities?

Let us be clear about this: it is not that we have not addressed these two questions; the problem is rather that we have answered them in radically different ways at different times for different purposes and for different groups of people. As a result we do not have one, comprehensive policy toward people with disabilities; we have dozens of policies that presume sometimes profoundly different answers to these questions. Different aspects of policy are grounded in different dimensions of the problem, focus on different interpretations of the goals of respect, participation, and accommodation, and presuppose different normative accounts of the nature and scope of entitlements for and on behalf of people with disabilities.

The need to answer the first question has been recognized for some time. The task of defining and operationalizing terms like 'disability' and 'handicap' was for several decades during and after the Second World War a well-known epidemiological challenge, since policy could not be formulated or costed without a clear idea of who qualified as a person with a disability. As this increasingly interdisciplinary work progressed, it became obvious that there were several concepts involved, which applied differently to demographic, epidemiological, biomedical, rehabilitative, economic, and social contexts.

This work culminated in 1980 with the publication by the World Health Organization of its *International Classification of Impairments, Disabilities and Handicaps* (ICIDH).[7] Although it was a document with several aims, the principal contribution of the ICIDH was to characterize three distinct dimensions of disablement and to caution against confusing them. According to the ICIDH, an impairment (the recommended French term is *déficience*) is any abnormality of physiological or anatomical structure or function. A disability (*incapacité*) is any limitation (resulting from an impairment) in the ability to perform any activity considered normal for a human being or required for some recognized social role or occupation. And, finally, a handicap (*handicap*) is any resulting disadvantage for an individual that limits the fulfilment of a normal role or occupation. (To avoid confusion, the artificial term 'disablement' is commonly used to refer, inclusively, to all three dimensions. I will be following this practice in what follows.)

Although the ICIDH and its successors have been widely accepted, the point of the three distinctions can be easily misunderstood. The ICIDH is not making a linguistic recommendation; it is insisting instead that complex social forces have created a composite notion, disablement, rich in scientific and political meaning that, at once, embodies three distinct, though intricately related, conceptual structures. Thus, the ICIDH points out that some impairments are so trivial (say, being slightly under 'normal' height) that they are probably not disabling, in that they do not limit most people's repertoire of capabilities. In certain social settings, roles, or occupations, however, non-disabling impairments (say, a minor facial scar) may be handicapping, in the sense that the bearer of the scar may be made fun of, stigmatized, or subjected to disadvantageous discrimination.

Increasingly, researchers and policy analysts have argued that some of the confusions in disablement policy are the result of mixing up these three dimensions. For example, while it makes sense to base antidiscrimination law on the concept of handicap, it makes no sense to allocate medical resources or award workers' compensation on that basis. Perhaps, then, the impasse can be overcome and policy anomalies resolved once we correctly align each dimension with the relevant component parts of our policy.

Unfortunately, this suggestion is not merely optimistic, it is profoundly mistaken. The three conceptual dimensions of disablement are not detachable component parts of a single concept; they have evolved together as *competing perspectives* on a manifestation of human difference. If integration is possible it will only be by virtue of a complex synthesis in which each dimension will be altered. Moreover, the impasse in policy, as the examples given above suggest, involves normative disputes that cannot be prised away from our understanding of disablement.

One observation, frequently made but less frequently appreciated, reinforces this last point. Handicaps are not empirical phenomena or observable consequences of disabilities and impairments; instead they embody a normative basis for policy, that is to say an answer to the question: What does society owe people with disabilities? The mere act of identifying some social disadvantage *as a handicap* (as opposed to a misfortune one must put up with) implicitly makes the moral or political judgment that that disadvantage is unfair or unjustifiable.

Because of this it is wrongheaded to think that what disablement policy analysis requires is to get the 'facts' right and then decide what our social commitment is. It is far more complex than this. Our judgments about our social commitment will influence our analysis of disablement, and our analysis – what differences in social treatment we are prepared to call 'unfair' – will shape the normative basis we rely on to identify policy objectives and concrete solutions.

Thus, the impasse in disablement policy arises from a failure to appreciate the multidimensional character of the concept of disablement, a failure to address the normative question of what society owes to people with disabilities, and a failure to appreciate that these two issues are inextricably linked. The impasse in policy for people with disabilities stands, therefore, in need of a conceptual and normative investigation, guided by the philosophical standards of conceptual analysis as well as moral and political theory. These analyses are essential preconditions to the policy-analytic tasks of goal clarification and formulation of objectives.

While an analysis of disablement is a precondition to any satisfactory resolution of the impasse in policy, so too is a sensitivity to the social history of this policy. When one surveys this history one notices that the policy of the day focuses on one dimension of disablement to the exclusion of the other two. The assumption is made that, at bottom, disablement is really a matter of impairment, or disability, or handicap. This suggests that the three conceptual dimensions of disablement have, over time, initiated three, seemingly self-sufficient, models of disablement.

The Models of Disablement

The American political scientist Harlan Hahn has been responsible for developing this insight.[8] Hahn notes that, perhaps because of the human tendency to reduce the complex to the simple, the long history of disablement policy can be characterized as an ongoing battle between three models of disablement, each of which purports to capture what disablement *really is*. Each model has generated an expertise – usually a science – a class of experts, a canonical language or discourse that purports to get to the bottom of disablement, and a representational image of people with disabilities.

If one believes, therefore, that when all is said and done disablement is really a matter of impairment, one will be attracted to what might be called the biomedical model of disablement. To understand the 'problem' of disablement in this model one must turn to biomedical scientists. Their expertise defines varieties of disablement with precision and provides us with a clear agenda for social action, namely, prevention, cure, containment, pain management, rehabilitation, amelioration, and palliation. A person with disabilities, in this model, is one who is sick or injured, one with a medical problem, or a victim of personal misfortune or ineluctable bad luck.

If one believes that what is socially significant about disablement is the effects of impairments on a person's repertoire of capabilities, then the focus is on disability. Since employment-defined capabilities are of intrinsic interest to labour-market analysts, a disability focus lends itself to the adoption of the economic model of disablement. On this model, work-based disability is understood as the product of the interaction of an impairment and the existing supply-side conditions of the labour market. Disablement is thus conceived as a limitation of a worker's repertoire of productive capacities, abilities, and skills. Disablement policy tends to be understood as a regulatory instrument, subject to a cost-benefit rationale. In this model, a person with disabilities is a person who embodies an economic cost that must be factored into society-wide economic policy decisions.

Although the biomedical and the economic models are implicit in much of present-day disablement programming, and as such can justifiably be called the standard models, the third model is the one responsible for the current revolution in disablement theory, and it is the one that has brought about many of the political developments in this area in the past two decades. This is the social-political model, a model which, by focusing on handicapping phenomena, views disablement as a form of social injustice attributable to the stigmatizing attitudes and discriminatory practices of society at large.

The social-political model is more complex than the other two, since it arises from two main sources, sociological and social-psychological theories about handicapping, on the one hand, and an explicit civil rights political agenda, on the other. Only the first of these sources can be said to have stabilized, and even here controversies rage between sociological deviance theorists of various sorts, somatopsychologists, minority-group theorists, and advocates of other competing accounts. As a result there is no single coherent expertise that is called on. Adherents of the model agree, though, that handicaps are socially constructed phenomena brought about by attitudes toward people with disabilities which, once embedded in social practices and institutions, sustain the disadvantageous social condition of people with disabilities.

The political side of the social-political model is still very much in flux, as befits a social movement in the process of creating its agenda, rationale, and ideology. In the United States the political agenda has been dominated by self-empowerment (as evidenced by the very successful independent living movement) and strengthened legal protection against discrimination (the recent Americans with Disabilities Act). The rights approach is also animating the Canadian scene, although there are some suggestions of a more novel, and more contentious, collective rights approach. In either case, the social-political model offers us a representation of people with disabilities as an oppressed class, a marginalized non-ethnic minority group.

There is no doubt that each of these models has left its mark on disablement policy. It is not difficult to show how the biomedical model has influenced the disability evaluation process used in workers' compensation assessment and eligibility criteria for various forms of social assistance. One can also see how the economic model has provided both the rationale and the administrative structure for a wide variety of social assistance and social insurance programs. And, lastly, the social-political model has motivated nearly all of the critiques and calls for reform of the past two decades.

When these models are scrutinized, one can see why they have become entrenched in our thinking. Each highlights salient features of the social problems posed by disablement. The biomedical model makes it clear that the concept of disablement, however socially complex, is rooted in biomedically explainable phenomena. The economic model shows why it is crucial from the point of view of policy to highlight the effects of impairments in socially significant contexts; and the social-political model awakens us to the social phenomena of handicapping and the political need to challenge stereotypes, misperceptions, and institutionalized obstacles that make the experience of disablement what it is.

At the same time, though, each model deceptively reduces a complex and multidimensional phenomenon to a single dimension. Thus, notoriously, the biomedical model is almost wholly insensitive to the social character of disablement, whereas the economic model effectively reduces disablement to its economic consequences. The social-political model, moreover, as a result of its radical critiques of the standard models, oversteers and detaches disablement from its biomedical foundations and its economic consequences.

There is more. Each model gives a different priority to, and interpretation of, the policy goals of respect, participation, and accommodation. The biomedical model focuses on accommodation, understood as the provision of professional health services; the economic model ranks participation highest, and understands it as across-the-board economic integration; and, finally, the social-political model, stressing the need for destigmatization and securing rights, insists that the goal of respect is the crucial one.

This suggests that the three models have served yet another function. In addition to stressing one of the three dimensions of disablement, each answers the normative question of what society owes to people with disabilities and answers by reference to different *normative bases*, that is, fundamental moral and political principles that, systematically and coherently, provide conclusive normative grounds for a social obligation with respect to people with disabilities.

In our political tradition, only a few general moral and political principles are applicable to this normative question. The principle with the longest continuous history is that of beneficence or charity. Alternatively, one may claim that society owes people with disabilities compensation for any disadvantage caused by another. Or society might be thought to have a primary duty to satisfy the reasonable and legitimate needs of people with disabilities. Or again, it may be obliged to provide people with disabilities with any and all advantages and benefits that will secure welfare maximization for everyone. Finally, the source of society's obligations to people with disabilities might be argued to flow directly from a social commitment to equality.

As a matter of social history, once our culture left behind the primitive notion that people with disabilities deserve their fate because they must be sinners, charity was the dominant normative basis for social policy. In our era, the economic rationale of welfare maximization has occupied the field, although the political rhetoric of the welfare state relies on the principle of need. The compensatory or corrective justice basis, which usually augments rather than supplants the welfare maximization basis, is implicit in our tort law. Finally, the rise of the social-political model, and the politicization of disablement issues, have shifted the normative centre of gravity of disablement policy so that it is now common to view it as a response to inequality in the form of discrimination and marginalization.

Given all of this, it is hardly surprising that our disablement policy is at an impasse. The notion of disablement is conceptually complex and is linked to three competing models that have shaped our policy in often dramatically different ways. These models, though each is faithful to a dimension of disablement, are ultimately distortive because they ignore or radically reinterpret the other two dimensions. Moreover, the models embody different normative bases for policy and so generate very different accounts of why society has an obligation to people with disabilities.

Strategy and Caveats

What disablement policy requires, both theoretically and practically, is a complete and coherent theory of disablement. Such a theory would provide an analysis of the notion and a fully worked out normative basis appropriate to the policy goals; that is, the theory would answer the two, childishly straightforward questions mentioned above. Such a theory would describe a model that resolved the theoretical contradictions implicit in the social history of our understanding of disablement and the practical contradictions that have led to the impasse in policy.

Since models of disablement are social artefacts with complex, and highly contingent, social-historical and social-psychological antecedents, it is beyond the capacity of anyone to *create* such a model. None the less, it is possible to describe the models and inherent normative bases that mould policy and diagnose the source of the confusions and anomalies that have resulted. It is also possible to outline what an adequate theory of disablement would achieve, and, in particular, what normative basis would help to secure a consistent and coherent model. These are social-policy analytic endeavours of goal clarification and objective formulation, which, as suggested, involve a philosophical exploration of the conceptual and normative foundations of social policy for people with disabilities. That is the strategy of this book.

In Chapter 2 I begin with the question of language and the concept of disablement, as analysed in the 1980 ICIDH and its successors. The internal logic of the three dimensions of disablement is explored in some detail. The analysis that is offered departs from the ICIDH in the area of handicaps. On my account, to identify a social inequality of treatment as a handicap is (typically implicitly) to make the political judgment that that inequality is invidious, discriminatory, or unjustifiable.

In Chapters 3, 4, and 5 I describe the three models of disablement that have dominated our thinking on and policy about disablement for several hundred years. Following Harlan Hahn, I call these the biomedical, the economic, and the social-political models of disablement.

For each model I follow the same expository pattern. First the model is described in terms of the conception of disablement it embodies; second, and by way of reinforcing the point that these models are cultural artefacts and not abstract conceptions, I trace the intellectual history of the model, highlighting the forces that have gone into its creation and continue to sustain it. I then explore some of the virtues of each model, the problems and ambiguities each helps to resolve, and the insights about disablement each has brought to our cultural attention. I then turn to more concrete matters and show the effects of the model on actual policy concerning people with disabilities.

These preliminary discussions lead to a critique of the models. At one level, the critique in each case is the same, namely, that the model emphasizes one dimension of disablement to the exclusion of the other two, thereby distorting disablement in ways that profoundly affect the lives of people with disabilities and helping to create and sustain the policy anomalies and ambiguities of aim to which disablement policy is notoriously prone. Finally, each chapter ends with a discussion of the normative consequences of the model for disablement theory. The aim here is to show the linkage between the analysis of disablement each model presumes and the normative bases that analysis suggests. Each model is an alternative characterization of disablement as well as an incomplete and faulty account of society's obligations to people with disabilities.

In Chapter 6 I turn to the normative bases. After a preliminary look at the preconditions for an appropriate normative basis for disablement policy, and a look at our culture's earliest normative response to disablement, I briefly survey the four predominant normative bases that have shaped our policy: charity, need, compensation, and welfare maximization. This survey is compressed because elements of each of these normative bases, embodied as they are in the models of disablement, have already been considered. In each case it is not difficult to show how the background normative principle or theory is inadequate as a complete answer to the normative issue.

This leads me to the final chapter and the discussion of equality as a normative basis for disablement theory and policy. This chapter is divided into three parts. I first bring together the strands of earlier discussions and set out and explain four conditions of adequacy for a normative basis. These conditions constitute the normative challenge for disablement theory and policy. I then make the argument, by pulling together earlier conclusions, that the political value of equality, under some interpretation, is our best option for such a normative basis. The last section – 'Which Equality?' – reviews the current contenders for a theory of equality and shows the drawbacks and limitations of each, in the context of the kind of normative account that is patently required to complete disablement theory and avoid the impasse in policy.

The aims of this chapter are limited, being consistent with my overall strategy to explore the conceptual and normative foundations of disablement theory and policy. Still, at this point enough has been said to make two conclusions with confidence. First, the account of equality that is needed must be a substantively powerful one, since the 'weaker' principles of equality (and in particular, the highly influential equality of opportunity) cannot engage the social problems of disablement in any meaningful manner. Second, a suitable understanding of equality will identify as the object of policy that value that lies at the core of disablement itself, namely, positive freedom.

That this study is a preliminary one concentrating on the conceptual and normative foundations of theory and policy is the substantial caveat concerning this book. There are, however, three other caveats, and it is best to get them out of the way at the outset.

First of all, any general discussion of disablement ought to be independent of the kind of disability at issue, and in particular whether the disability is physical or mental. Yet, although a persuasive argument could be made that this distinction is overly drawn and artificial, there does seem to be a difference between the two that should make a difference in what a social commitment to equality requires. That crucial factor is mental competence.

Needless to say, as a culture we are still very far from understanding what ought to flow from incompetence; perhaps in the end, incompetence should make no substantial difference to our policy at all, other than to point to a different set of needs that must be accommodated. Still, the controversy involving how best to characterize competence and the appropriate social and legal responses to incompetence is far too extensive to be dealt with here. Therefore although the account of disablement suggested here ought in principle to apply to both physical and mental forms of disablement, only the case of physical disablement will be explicitly considered.

Second, although policy concerning the prevention of preventable disabling conditions is arguably a part of disablement policy in the broadest sense, the focus of this study is on the social aspects of disablement and the status of being a person with disabilities. Issues in the area of prevention are primarily issues of public health and epidemiology and cannot be done proper justice here.

Finally, as is hinted at various places in the text, a theory about disablement is a specific application of a far more extensive account of human difference – the ways in which people differ and when these ways are transformed, legitimately or not, into grounds for differential treatment. The demands of people with disabilities are, as we shall see, similar to those of other isolated, disadvantaged, and marginalized groups in society. Moreover, the social-psychological, political, and legal dynamics of all forms of difference – be they racial, sexual, religious, age-based, or disablement-based – are probably parallel, although it can be argued that people with disabilities confront a range of disadvantageous attitudes that have stigmatized them in unique ways. All of these insights may well contribute to a general theory of difference, of which disablement is but one manifestation. But that is not for me to say.

2 The Analysis of Disablement

The Question of Language

We unselfconsciously use terms like 'disability' and 'handicap' when talking about blindness or multiple sclerosis, and unthinkingly refer to people with these physical conditions as 'disabled people,' 'the disabled,' or 'the handicapped.' Confronted by challenges to our use of language by advocacy groups we may think that very little depends on semantic issues: handicapped people need job training, not language reform. Recently, too, newspaper columnists and other public pundits have dismissed such concerns as yet another example of oppressive and silly 'political correctness.' None the less, it has long been felt that there are at least three important reasons why we should be sensitive to the ways we label and describe those who are different from the norm.

First, it is no longer a matter of controversy, if it ever was, that the words we use to describe people have consequences that impinge upon their lives. Racial, sexual, cultural, and religious epithets insult and offend, that is obvious enough. Such expressions can also perpetuate stereotyping that contributes to a variety of unfair social practices. But it terms such as 'nigger,' 'bitch,' or 'kike' are offensive for this reason, surely so too are 'cripple,' 'retard,' and 'geek.'

At the same time, though, an obsession with 'correct' language may undermine efforts to avoid stereotyping by focusing attention on clever euphemisms. Recently, readers of *The Disability Rag* reported being 'remarkably consistent' in rejecting as demeaning and trivializing terms such as 'handicapable,' 'differently abled,' and 'physically challenged,' and similar terms used to describe them.[1]

To avoid both traps – ignoring the importance of language and obsessively dwelling on it – I will resort to the artificial but, so far, relatively neutral term 'disablement' to denote what is described by 'impairment,' 'deficiency,' 'medical problem,' 'dysfunctioning,' 'physical disability,' 'physical inability,' 'physical incapacity,' 'handicap,' and related terms.

Finding appropriate ways of referring to people is more contentious. There is some agreement that the phrase 'person with a disability' is unobjectionable. 'Disabled person' and 'handicapped person' (or worse, 'the disabled' or 'the handicapped'), however, are objectionable, some argue, because they leave one with the impression that the physical condition totally engulfs the person, which can only be prejudicial to the individual. In what follows, therefore, I will speak of 'people with disabilities' (or 'people who are blind,' 'people in wheelchairs,' and so on).

The second reason why terminology is important is that there is a need for a uniform vocabulary to describe different aspects of disablement, and so different components of policy. A uniform terminology might help to improve accountability and communication between different agencies, ministries, and departments, as well as different levels of government. It would also ensure comparability of statistical material through a common characterization of condition and individual.

Finally, and most fundamentally, it has been appreciated for decades that disablement is not a univocal notion but possesses a conceptual structure of considerable complexity. A successful account of disablement must take great care to define the terms it uses so as not to muddle important distinctions. Since disablement is not one thing, but many, we must take care to preserve rather than obscure distinctions.

As it happens, epidemiologists and rehabilitation therapists have long been conscious of the imprecision of their vocabulary and the need to mark off clear distinctions. They have professional experience of the interaction between a physical condition of some sort, the medical 'problem' so to speak, and the environmental and social conditions under which the person with that condition lives.

In the years following World War II , when the number of young and healthy people with disabilities dramatically increased, various attempts were made to define 'disability' for scientific and administrative purposes. Those who ran rehabilitation and retraining programs for veterans recognized the folly of making judgments about an individual's employability on the basis of a simple, routine physical examination. What was needed, they believed, was a separate system of disability evaluation, one that would assess the consequences of medical conditions for people's lives.

By far the most influential of these systems was devised by Dr Henry Kessler.[2] Kessler believed that it was essential to distinguish the medical from the non-medical dimensions of disability. By 1970, when he published his final word on the subject, Kessler was more convinced than ever that the legitimacy of the disability evaluation process as an administrative tool could only be ensured if non-medical considerations involving the personal, social, and economic consequences of physical conditions were kept distinct from purely biomedical considerations. Building on this intuition, but reflecting the more exacting standards of epidemiological research, in 1969 Dr Saad Z. Nagi identified three components of disablement. He distinguished active pathology and impairment, the two levels of medical involvement, from disability, an inability to perform socially expected roles and tasks.[3] Like Kessler, Nagi argued that a conflation of the medical and the social facets of disablement can only confound government policy, interfere with the practice of vocational rehabilitation, and profoundly distort the scientific study and measurement of disablement.

Although, as scientists, these researchers assumed that the problem they were tackling was an empirical one that could be resolved by the precise definitions they proposed, they were not unaware that something deeper was involved. For they saw that people with the same physical condition could manifest very different forms of disability. Impairments are not identical to disabilities, thus there must be a conceptual difference between the two aspects of disablement. In other words, they recognized that the medical or, more broadly, the biomedical fact of blindness or chronic disease constitutes a different dimension of disablement than the social fact of being unable to perform tasks, or fulfil social roles, by virtue of these physical conditions. They also saw that though these are different dimensions, each is intrinsic to a single complex notion, namely, 'disablement.'

Therefore, the task of defining 'disability' or 'impairment' or any other term in the vocabulary of disablement is, at bottom, not a factual matter at all. What one is doing by making these terms precise is exploring a historically developed notion that is rich in cultural and normative significance and that possesses a complex internal structure. Thus, the project of defining or operationalizing 'disability,' vigorously pursued for decades by researchers representing various health and social-scientific disciplines, set the stage for the more fundamental project of conceptual clarification.[4] Questions of lang-uage shaded imperceptibly into questions about the analysis of disablement.

The International Classification of Impairments, Disabilities, and Handicaps

In the early 1970s, responding to the need for an international standard for the evaluation of health care systems, researchers at the World Health Organization pondered how to assess the effectiveness of the provision of health care. Resolving questions of the efficiency and equality of distribution of health care resources seemed to require data on resource provision and utilization, which were readily forthcoming. But the issue of effectiveness was different, since it raised the difficult question of how we are to identify, let alone measure, a *beneficial change* in an individual's situation as a consequence of a contact with the health care system. How can we tell when a health care system improves a person's health?

What was needed was a way of describing the health status of an individual before and after contact. Although the *International Classification of Diseases* (ICD)[5] provided the basic vocabulary for describing disease conditions, it was of limited assistance. Since the ICD classifies states of pathology by their causal histories and specific manifestations, it only recognizes prevention, recovery, and death as possible changes in health status. Yet in practice most disease conditions are controlled rather than cured, and the more common health experience is that of coping with a variety of incapacitating effects of disease conditions and pathological abnormalities. In order to take account of the perceived health problems that lead people to make contact with a health care system, a classification of all consequences of diseases was needed.

By this somewhat indirect route the World Health Organization was led to the question of the conceptual clarification of disablement. A preliminary conceptual taxonomy was proposed by Philip H. N. Wood in 1975 and discussed at the International Conference for the

Ninth Revision of the International Classification of Diseases held that year.[6] Reworked with the assistance of Elizabeth M. Badley, this document was adopted and published in Geneva in 1980 as the *International Classification of Impairments, Disabilities, and Handicaps: A Manual of Classification Relating to the Consequences of Diseases* (ICIDH).

Since the aim of the ICIDH is to provide a framework for the identification and collection of data relevant to the effectiveness of health care systems, it has an epidemiological rather than clinical or diagnostic focus. What an epidemiological study of disablement requires, and what the ICIDH offers, is a conceptually coherent, classificatory scheme for the three dimensions of disablement, understood as levels of consequences flowing from an identifiable physical event. A classificatory scheme of this sort is the preliminary step to a complete evaluation, understood as a multidisciplinary process that scales degrees of disablement at each level. The ICIDH accomplishes this by means of three classificatory schemes, called codes.

Over the years the ICIDH has attracted a great deal of professional attention and criticism.[7] The ICIDH international network has, through its conferences and publications, provided a forum for continuing refinements and revisions to the manual. In particular, the Quebec Committee on the ICIDH (QCICIDH), founded in 1986, and the Canadian Society of the ICIDH (CSICIDH), founded in 1988, have been active in refining the conceptual boundaries of disablement and revising the manual in line with a broader vision of its role in clarifying interdisciplinary research. The 1991 proposals of the CSICIDH, which focus on the handicap-creation process, constitute a significant improvement over the original version.[8]

Unfortunately, the aim of the ICIDH, to provide a conceptual framework for epidemiological investigation, is not always grasped by critics. Some complain, for example, that it fails as a diagnostic tool, a use for which it was never intended. Others object that, by marking out conceptual distinctions within the overall discourse of disablement, the ICIDH is in effect offering a verbal recommendation about how best to use the words 'impairment,' 'disability,' and 'handicap.' Put plainly, the point of the manual is to draw conceptual boundaries by means of stipulative definitions that in no sense constitute endorsements of all the connotations and nuances associated with these three terms in ordinary language. Or, putting the point differently, nothing at all depends on which *words* are used to denote the three conceptual dimensions of disablement the ICIDH identifies.

Still, to insist that the ICIDH is an attempt to clarify the conceptual dimensions of disablement is not to deny that it makes significant theoretical assumptions about disablement. Specifically, both the original ICIDH and the 1991 CSICIDH version insist that, although the consequences, for particular individuals, of disease conditions and other physical disorders will vary with the social environment, and so be subject to a host of social and social-psychological forces, still the objective nature of the physical conditions themselves can (and must) be ascertained independently of all of these consequential, socially contingent phenomena. I call this the *assumption of the biomedical grounding of disablement.*

The assumption can take two forms, depending on how one interprets the scope of the background intuition. On the stronger interpretation, that adopted by the ICIDH and the 1991 CSICIDH, every particular manifestation of disablement, that is to say, every actual instance of an impairment, a disability, or a handicap, can (in principle) be traced back to an originating, physical state existing in that individual. The weaker interpretation holds that this strong claim is false, since it is perfectly possible for a handicap to have no biomedical grounding whatsoever. The weaker version states instead that the concept of disablement, as a whole, has an intrinsic biomedical dimension, which is an important fact about disablement.

There is no mystery why the ICIDH and its successors have adopted, without comment, the stronger interpretation of the assumption of biomedical grounding: the ICIDH was designed to be fully integrated with the *International Classification of Disease*, a document that embodies the so-called medical model of disease. As it is commonly understood, this model holds that for a condition to qualify, medically speaking, as a disease, it must have a clinically ascertainable causal history (its etiology) that explains the mechanisms by which changes in the structure or functioning of the body (the pathology) are manifested in specific ways (symptoms or signs). Much of the predictive and explanatory power of this biomedical model derives from its capacity to generalize about disease conditions by disassociating pathological phenomena from the individual people in whom they occur. None the less, there are good philosophical reasons for rejecting this understanding of disease (and health).

In any event, this link to a strongly realistic and non-normative conception of disease made it possible for Wood and Badley to motivate their conceptual distinctions in a manner particularly intuitive for epidemiologists. Impairments, disabilities, and handicaps are represented as successively removed levels of consequences flowing 'outward' from an objective state located in a particular human body. As these 'ripples in the pond' expand, the phenomena of disablement become more and more influenced by the background environment (becoming more and more interactive). But, as we are told, the first and most elemental 'plane of experience' of disablement is an 'intrinsic situation' within the body of an individual that gives rise to changes in the structure or functioning of that body. It is upon this physical event that all subsequent manifestations of disablement are grounded.

In the 1991 CSICIDH version, a level of phenomena prior to the intrinsic state is identified. This is the level of risk factors, or causes of impairments, grouped under four headings: social and environmental, individual behaviour, accidents, and biology. Though this level or dimension of disablement is an important addition to the overall scheme – since it brings prevention programming under the rubric of disablement policy – it has no effect on the theoretical point that all disablement consequences must flow from an initiating physical event.

Epistemologically, this first event may seem somewhat paradoxical. On the one hand, it cannot itself be experienced, since it constitutes what is 'really happening,' independently of any human interaction. Eventually, perhaps, the individual affected, or others, will experience manifestations of the event, but never the event itself. Once manifested, this first event ends, and we enter into the next plane of experience. On the other hand, what is 'really happening' is not some unintelligible jumble of random physical changes; quite the contrary, it turns out to be an event structured not only by the biomedical model, but by implicit standards of 'normal' human anatomical form and organic functioning.

Needless to say, there is no real paradox here, merely an unexpressed, ideological assumption about the nature of disease, namely, that a purely biomedical understanding of a disease condition accurately and directly mirrors the way the world really is. This is what I mean by the strong interpretation of the assumption of biomedical grounding.

Continuing the image of ever-expanding consequential circles, the authors of the original ICIDH tell us that the second event in the development of disablement involves the 'exteriorization' of the structural abnormality or organic disfunctioning. At this point, someone has become aware of the manifestations of abnormal or pathological changes. These manifestations are either symptoms, the qualitative changes experienced by the individual, or signs, the quantitative manifestations of disease conditions as observed and measured by others.

Thus, at this stage, the individual may feel pain, a friend or relative may draw attention to a change in appearance, a physician may identify a disease sign through questioning, or a random screening program may show the presence of an antibody or other indication of a disease process. In whatever form exteriorization occurs, and whether or not a direct causal link can be made to an identifiable disease condition, the individual becomes or is made aware of a change in status, a change from presumptive health to suspected or confirmed ill health.

Awareness of abnormality is next objectified through changes in the performance or behaviour of the individual. Physical changes, or psychological responses linked to physical changes, alter and limit the range of the individual's activities. Now the individual must react to, and interact with, the fact of an abnormality or disfunctioning, disease, or disorder. The individual is affected: if there is a disease, he or she is ill, and acts sick; activities are curtailed or modified; expectations of capacity are altered; and the requirements of social roles are either not met or are adjusted to accommodate the activity restrictions.

Lastly, at the outermost circle of consequences, the overt manifestations of a disease condition, abnormality, dysfunction, or other disorder are socialized. Family, friends, and society at large notice the individual's awareness of the disorder, the changes in behaviour and performance, and respond in a variety of ways. Most notably, changes in attitude and expectation, coupled with the implicit value attached to normalcy in appearance, range of activities, and competences, may place the individual at a disadvantage with respect to others.

Each process in this progression – exteriorization, objectification, and socialization – is, according to the ICIDH, ultimately linked to a physical event, the 'intrinsic situation' that grounds the whole sequence. Although the CSICIDH version sets out a far more sophisticated model of the socialization process, it follows the original ICIDH on this basic point.

In both versions, the sequence of events is not causal, at least in the sense of being inevitable, since once we move into the outer circles the interaction between exteriorized event and social environment produces consequences that are not predictable or regular. Thus, not every exteriorized disease condition will become objectified or socialized, nor does objectification invariably lead to socialization.

In short, the image that Wood and Badley appeal to, ever-expanding circles of consequences, is intended to capture a progression from one kind of health experience to another, a progression that commonly occurs, in one form or another, throughout the world. When people are made aware of a disorder they become 'sick' or 'infirm'; this alters how they present themselves to others, and this in turn alters how others, and society at large, respond to them.

In addition to the assumption of biomedical grounding, there are two features of the ICIDH that help to shape the conceptual taxonomy it offers. First, the progression starts with intrinsic states and moves on to increasingly interactive phenomena. Exteriorization brings an intrinsic situation, the presence of a disease condition or other abnormality, to someone's attention, although the condition itself can be understood without reference to any external phenomena in the individual's environment. However, objectification and socialization are processes that alter this intrinsic state by means of an interaction with other phenomena in the individual's environment. These phenomena are, broadly speaking, psychological and social, and by means of the standards and expectations they embody they produce new and more dynamic consequences of the original intrinsic condition. The CSICIDH version makes this point explicit by positing a separate dimension of disablement, obstacles, which identifies environmental factors which, in interaction with impairments and disabilities, produce handicaps.

The second, closely related, feature of this progression is that it travels from biomedical fact to social phenomenon, and so, as it is popularly put, from the hard to the softer sciences. Since each of these three processes takes an intrinsic, physical state further away from its grounding in biomedical fact, the possibility increases for 'distortion' from the same environmental obstacles which, through interaction with the physical occurrence, produced the consequences in the first place. Thus, the further removed from the physical grounding the more the environmental interaction and the greater the distortion.

With this model in place, the ICIDH sets out its conceptual taxonomy by associating each of the three processes that produce the consequences of disease conditions with a term that, in ordinary, non-technical discourse, more or less captures the implications of each process. Hence the conceptual distinctions between the 'externalized' impairment, the 'objectified' disability, and the 'socialized' handicap. Disablement thus has three dimensions, related yet independent. Each dimension is grounded in physical fact, though each is yet further removed from this fact inasmuch as it is more and more the product of an unpredictable interaction between physical condition and social environment.

Needless to say, the background theory of the ICIDH is inspired by a mainstream conception of the nature of science: a faith in the objective and normatively untainted status of the biomedical sciences coupled with an assumption about the relative reliability of data associated with interactive levels of disablement. Indeed, the philosophy of science implicit in the ICIDH and its successors has two methodological consequences of sufficient interest to us to spend a moment on.

First, as already noted, because of its commitment to the assumption of biomedical grounding, on its strong interpretation, the ICIDH is wedded to the view that each instance or occasion of disablement, however interactive, has a biomedical basis. Second, it is assumed without argument that all of the phenomena of disablement are susceptible to objective, normatively neutral scientific investigation, of one sort or another.

Both of these methodological assumptions I believe to be wrong. The strong interpretation of the assumption is mistaken because it misconstrues the range of handicapping; and the second assumption is mistaken because it implies that handicaps are observable consequences of disabilities and impairments. These are methodological errors because, as I will argue more fully below, the very act of identifying some social disadvantage as a 'handicap' is an act of normative judgment embodying general conceptions of political morality. Handicaps are themselves normative phenomena inasmuch as they necessarily embody judgments we make about what is fair or unfair, what people should or should not put up with, what is normal and what 'different.'

Now, though I think it is vital to distance disablement theory from these two theoretical prejudices, the bulk of the conceptual analysis set out in the ICIDH and the 1991 CSICIDH version remains relatively untouched by them. And since I believe that disablement policy would greatly benefit from implementing some version of the ICIDH analysis, I think it important to set out the three-way conceptual distinction with care. It will be obvious in what follows how the analysis can be modified to abandon the faulty methodological stance of the ICIDH.

Impairment

According to the ICIDH, the externalization of an abnormal physical state is captured by the concept of impairment defined as 'any loss or abnormality of psychological, physiological or anatomical structure or function.' (The recommended French equivalent term is *déficience*.)[9] Impairment is, so to speak, the first level of manifested abnormality, defect, or somatic anomaly. Included are structural anomalies, defects in, or losses of limbs, organs, tissues, or other structures, as well as functional disturbances at the level of organ or system. Although impairments cannot be latent, they can arise at any time, be temporary or permanent, serious or minor.

There is one feature of this otherwise straightforward definition that is potentially confusing, since it marks a clear deviation from our ordinary use of the term. Impairment is made somewhat problematic by the inclusion of functional limitations, thereby, it might be argued, obscuring the boundary between somatic states and somatic activities. Wood and Badley have a way of avoiding this, although they do not make their intentions very clear. Implicitly, they rely on a distinction between functions and activities. A function is something an organ, organ system, or other part of the human body does, while an activity is any integrated and complete bodily movement or behaviour. Activities are attributed to whole people, functions only to parts of people.

Thus, the scope of disfunctioning, in the sense of impairment, should not be extended beyond the conceptual boundaries of the notion. A disease of the eye, for example, may bring about a defect or limitation in the normal functioning of that sense organ. This condition is an ocular impairment or a disorder of visual function, and the ICIDH classifies it as such. Despite our temptation to say otherwise, however, the impairment here should not be thought as an 'inability to see.' Seeing is a behaviour, an integrated activity expected of people, not eyes. (To anticipate, an inability to see is a disability that may or may not arise from an ocular impairment.)

Our ordinary notion of impairment may not be limited in this fashion, though given the vagaries of ordinary language, it is difficult to be sure. By ensuring this restriction by stipulation we can put a plausible label on a concept that denotes all deviations from biomedical norms, including those functional or structural deviations linked to disease conditions. Impairments, then, constitute the relatively unproblematic biomedical dimension of disablement.

Thus, the notion of impairment denotes the broadest collection of health conditions that, as it were, are but one removed from the physical states, themselves.[10] Conceptually speaking impairments are physical abnormalities exteriorized. Specifically, there are four properties of the notion that serve to set it apart from the other two dimensions of disablement, disability, and handicap. These properties need to be explored briefly, since they will help us to characterize the biomedical model of disablement in the next chapter.

Normative Deviation

An impairment constitutes a deviation from a set of biomedical norms – those norms of structure and function that together produce a sort of composite ideal of the totally healthy human being. The ICIDH makes no attempt to specify in any detail what this ideal biomedical status is, suggesting instead that the 'definition of its constituents is undertaken primarily by those qualified to judge physical and mental functioning according to generally accepted standards.'

Several, potentially controversial, questions are glossed over by deferring to those qualified to judge according to 'generally accepted standards.' Historians of the biological sciences have made it clear that the criteria of biological normality have not been static over the centuries, or untouched by social and cultural forces.[11] We will return to more specific worries about normality below when we consider the policy role of the American Medical Association's highly influential *Guides to the Evaluation of Permanent Impairment*. But the ICIDH skirts this issue, and probably for good reason. It is important to make the concept impairment as inclusive as possible and to avoid controversies about the sources of our biomedical norms.

Naturally enough, in practice health professionals will focus almost exclusively on serious, non-transitory, or otherwise clinically remarkable deviations from the norm. Yet the usefulness of the notion of impairment would be undermined if it catered to a wholly clinical focus. It is important, for example, to be able to include as impairments symptomless pathological conditions, or subclinical diseases that might only be manifested through a screening program that detects the onset of the body's reaction to a developing, pathological process. Asymptomatic HIV seropositivity is the most dramatic instance of this sort of impairment, but there are many others.

It is also important not to limit the class of impairments to those conditions that are statistically abnormal or unusual. For though the arthritic changes concomitant with ageing processes probably constitute a statistically common event, arthritis none the less produces obvious skeletal impairments. The biomedical norms that underwrite impairments are idealizations that do not purport to reflect the natural course of events. Though it is probably inevitable that the statistical status of a physical condition will influence the biomedical decision about what is and what is not a norm deviation, we would justifiably lose confidence in our biomedical scientists if statistical normality became a sufficient condition for biomedical normality. No competent physician would deny a patient treatment because arthritic conditions are the 'natural' product of ageing.

Nor, more generally, would it be appropriate to make any correlation at all between impairments and what is 'natural.' Since the term is ambiguous, one might argue with equal plausibility that every impairment is 'natural' or that none are. We would not be tempted to say, though, that pain, discomfort, and nausea have no disabling consequences when they are symptoms of 'natural' conditions such as pregnancy. Moreover, tagging people with disabilities with the label 'unnatural' would only burden them with the stigmatizing connotations that that word has had for many centuries.

Because severity, duration, normality, and naturalness criteria are, for good reasons, not built into the definition, *any* manifested deviation from a biomedical norm, however minor, transitory, or common, and regardless of the further consequences it may have, should count as an impairment. The concept of impairment is thus highly inclusive and underdeterminative, and properly so.

Deviational Neutrality

As manifested instances of biomedical norm deviations, impairments are consequences of diseases, disorders, abnormalities, and other conditions we would normally think of as misfortunes or 'problems.' Yet the notion itself is neutral with respect to what might be called the evaluative reception of the norm deviation. That is, instances of being slightly over the norm for height for males, or prematurely grey, or (the ICIDH's example) being born with a fingernail missing, are all impairments, even though they may be inconsequential or, as in the case of abnormal height, potentially even beneficial.

Deviational neutrality is an essential feature of this dimension of disablement. For the distinction between impairments and disabilities can only be made if care is taken to ensure that the former are neutral with respect to further disabling and handicapping ramifications. That is, impairment cannot, without circularity, be conceptually dependent upon a prior understanding of disability. If it were, then the social and psychological considerations that go to the nature of disabilities would also determine which physical abnormalities counted as impairments. Such a result would undermine the assumption of biomedical grounding in both its strong and weak interpretations.

Suppose, for example, that one characterized impairments as physical conditions that limit the range of physical activities and behaviours which, in the social environment in which one lives, are commonplace. This would mean, as a conceptual matter, that socially contingent factors, such as prevalent attitudes and expectations about human activities, would determine the character of impairments of organic functions. Since there are no independent restrictions on which attitudes and expectations these are, it would be in theory possible for some, or none, of them to accord with our current biomedical understanding of the correlation between physical anomaly or disease condition and degree of somatic disfunctioning. This would mean that the biomedical dimension (which focuses on somatic functioning) would not be intrinsic to the concept of disablement, or, put more bluntly, impairments would be social constructions. To avoid this conflation of impairments and disabilities the ICIDH characterizes impairments as, so to speak, mere physical abnormalities – neither desirable nor undesirable, good nor bad, advantageous nor disadvantageous. The judgment, however, natural and immediate, that a particular impairment is bad, undesirable, or disadvantageous takes one from exteriorization to objectification or socialization, that is, from the realm of disablement associated with impairments to that associated with disabilities and handicaps.

Admittedly, a not insubstantial price is paid for this manoeuvre. The ICIDH definition attempts to defuse the negative connotations of the ordinary sense of 'impairment' in the hope of producing a more general and neutral term. But this may be impossible: no context is so controlled or 'professional' as to prevent those who use the term 'impairment' from inferring some form of inadequacy, some intrinsic failure or lack. This fact, of course, further complicates the attempt to make a sharp distinction between impairments and disabilities.

Still, we should not make too much of this complaint because at issue here is the appropriateness of a concept, not whether 'impairment' is the best word for the job. There is, it might be argued, a place for the concept of physical difference (or if that term is not neutral enough, then perhaps physical specificity might do), a concept that does not, even implicitly, refer to advantageous or disadvantageous consequences flowing from the physical condition. A physical difference (or specificity) is an evaluatively neutral, utterly non-stigmatizing biomedical norm deviation. It is, of course, a nice question whether such a difference is conceivable for human beings.

As it happens, there has recently been a minor movement among some writers in the human rights area to use the term 'difference' in this way, as a wholly neutral designator of what, as a matter of fact, sets some people apart from others. Thus, race, religion, sex, and mental and physical disablement are said to be instances of difference.[12] This is a helpful device, and I will resort to it from time to time. Unfortunately, the notion of (physical) difference may be so broad as to be utterly removed from the language of disablement. In any event, impairment will do service for us.

Universality of Deviation

It is clear that, according to this definition, no human being is not impaired in some manner. Inasmuch as there are many different dimensions of structural and functional abnormality, it would be quite extraordinary if a real human being were within the range of normal throughout. Such a person would be, by definition, ideal. We might even wish to say, tempting paradox, that possessing an impairment is itself the norm among humans.

This feature of the notion of impairment was of little concern to Wood and Badley. Minor or inconsequential deviations from the biomedical ideal are usually ignored and have little effect on the health care system. Still, the universality of impairment is not a trivial matter. It entails that at some level – although admittedly perhaps too abstract a level to be of practical significance – disablement itself is a universal human condition. More precisely, disablement is universal, but only because one dimension of it, impairment, is universal.

Etiological Neutrality

Finally, since impairments are first-level consequences of physical abnormalities, broadly construed, they are neutral with respect to etiology or causal history. A condition will count as an impairment however it arose or developed, whether it was the result of a genetic abnormality or a road traffic accident, a disease, a trauma, or intentionally self-injurious behaviour. The functional consequences of the lack of an arm are identical, whether the arm was missing at birth, severed during an accident, or amputated because it was diseased.

Impairments are therefore not particularly interesting as causal entities. They do not denote processes or other ongoing conditions; instead they describe manifested abnormalities and offer a synchronic or dynamic rather than a diachronic or static perspective on the health experience, an obvious advantage for epidemiological study.

Etiological neutrality is itself a result of the attempt to devise a broad and neutral notion, midway between intrinsic states and disabilities. Inasmuch as disabilities and handicaps are further along as consequences, and so yet further removed from the 'intrinsic situation,' there is no question but that they too are etiologically neutral.

Since many impairments can be directly linked to disease conditions, information of the sort provided by the ICD is essential for clinical management. None the less, diseases form only a relatively small subset of impairments. An impairment need not be associated with any underlying disease condition, let alone an acute condition, nor will someone with an impairment, even a highly visible one, be necessarily taken to be sick. Some impairments have no further consequences at all; they are simply physical anomalies that are unremarkable, ignorable, and socially 'invisible.' But those impairments that do interfere with one's life, by curtailing or limiting activities, shift conceptual categories and become disabilities.

Disability

When the overt behaviour of an individual, viewed as an integrated whole rather than a collection of parts, is restricted because of the presence of one or more impairments, the health experience has become objectified. This signals the presence of a disability, defined in the ICIDH as 'any restriction or lack (resulting from an impairment) of ability to perform an activity in the manner or within the range considered normal for a human being.' (The recommended French term is *incapacité*.) Disability involves a limitation upon one (or more) integrated activity, ability, or behaviour generally accepted as a component of everyday living or else part of a repertoire of skills and other specialized abilities associated with a specific talent, profession, job, or other social role. Disabilities may be temporary or permanent, reversible or irreversible, progressive or regressive, serious or minor; and, like impairments, they can be the product of the normal and natural, but none the less debilitating processes of ageing.

It is important to notice that the notion is open-ended and can be operationalized in various ways, depending on what repertoire of activities, abilities, behaviour, skills, and so on is 'normally expected.' As is obvious from the definition, the notion of disability is an inherently relational concept: there is no such thing as disability as such. Before the notion can be meaningfully employed one has to specify a repertoire, social role, or other standardizing context that sets out what is expected. There have been attempts to establish an across-the-board, non-specialized, or basic repertoire of activities, general enough for most assessments of disability. This is the so-called activities of daily living (ADL) functional assessment standard. Several such instruments are currently in use, and the ICIDH also provides one. As a matter of administrative practice, though, the most commonly used standard involves repertoires of productive capacity with respect to the employment market. This last is called 'work disability' or 'employability.'

However it is operationalized, disability is a concept of positive rather than negative freedom. This traditional philosophical distinction points to the difference between the freedom to do or become what one wishes without permission of or hindrance from others (one's negative freedom), and the actual *capability* to do or become what one wishes (one's positive freedom).[13]

Rules, regulations, laws, and other forms of coercion, manipulation, and threat are all limitations upon one's negative freedom – some justified, some not. These are familiar restrictions. Lack of training, accommodation of needs, or realistic opportunities are also restrictions; they are limitations upon one's positive freedom, one's capacity to exercise one's freedom to do or become what one wishes. Both kinds of freedom open the door to options and choices, but only positive freedom captures the actual capability to achieve or bring about what one chooses. Since the importance of negative freedom presumes one's abilities to do or become something, if one so chooses, the value of negative freedom must be derivative from positive freedom.

Thus, we can say that a disability is one kind of limitation upon our positive freedom, one reason why we are not capable of doing or becoming what we wish. It is for this reason – and this reason alone – that disabilities are negatively valued.

The conceptual transition from impairment to disability, from exteriorization to objectification, may seem subtle, but it is real enough. Impairments restrict organic functioning; disabilities restrict the repertoire of abilities and behaviours normally expected of people, in one context or another. This is a difference of impact. An impairment, even if visible, may make no difference to how an individual behaves or is viewed by others; but a disability alters an individual's behaviour in an overt fashion, if not immediately and directly (a mobility disability, say), then eventually (a memory disability).[14] Disabilities affect capabilities, what people actually can do or become. As the ICIDH puts this point, it is through the process of objectification that 'a functional limitation expresses itself as a reality in everyday life ... In other words, disability takes form as the individual becomes aware of a change in his identity.'

In the case of an amputation or other gross anatomical loss it does seems artificial to separate impairment and disability. How is the disfunctioning manifested by the absence of an arm different from the restriction in the ability to perform normal arm activities? The answer is simply that in some instances the distinction is indeed artificial, but that a measure of artificiality and abstraction is necessary to preserve the integrity of the conceptual distinction. And it should be remarked, it is impairment not disability that is the abstraction. For impairment provides the essential conceptual bridge linking physical conditions and disabilities. The notion of disability, however, is concerned with the everyday, practical world of seeing, communicating, dressing, and getting around – the world of capabilities.

It should be clear that there can be no one-to-one correlation between impairments and disabilities. An impairment that does not restrict activities is not a disability (although it might become a handicap). Nor is the degree of restriction of activity a direct function of the severity of the impairment, since the extent of the limitation upon one's positive freedom a disability represents depends on the context in which the disability arises. Moreover, even if the background impairment is relatively severe, the actual disability may be minimal if it is accommodated, if, that is, aids and assistive devices make it possible for the individual to accomplish most or all expected activities.

Sometimes the beliefs and attitudes we have about our impairments, rather than the impairments themselves, can restrict our normal activities and so become disabilities. Differences in the degree of fear, apprehension, or other psychological response may produce very different disabilities in individuals with identical impairments.[15] Even the less extreme and more common reactions we have to the expectations others form of us as 'sick' people may produce disabilities not directly associated with the impairment – a phenomenon sometimes called 'illness behaviour.' Finally, certain psychologically induced disabilities may engender further impairments, which in turn may produce other kinds of disabilities. Thus, individuals with the same impairment may possess different kinds of disabilities, while individuals experiencing the same disability may have different impairments.

The lack of a determinative or causal relationship between impairments and disabilities is a direct result of the conceptual character of disability. As we shall see in more detail below, the notion is intrinsically interactive: it identifies limitations on capability produced by an impairment in a context, either everyday or work-specific. An impairment leads to disability when that kind or degree of functional abnormality 'matters' to the individual in a social environment, and his or her expectations and life plans, whether mundane or specialized. Change the expectations and the social environment and in some contexts the disability may cease to exist, leaving the impairment behind.

This does not mean that disability is an ephemeral, meaningless, or arbitrary classification. Quite the contrary, the category has a very rich and significant social meaning, and it is not a matter of chance which incapacities or behavioural limitations it is applied to. What is important about the category, though, is that what counts as a disability will be contingent on a variety of social, cultural, and social-psychological factors. Moreover, the concept of disability is inherently unstable, drifting sometimes towards the biomedical arena and sometimes towards the sociological, political, or moral arenas. This instability is particularly evident when one explores the sense in which a disability is a normative deviation.

Normative Deviation

Although impairments are not identifiable by their etiology, they remain biomedical entities. Thus, impairments are properly seen as inherent disorders or abnormalities which, though perhaps caused by the outside environment, none the less inhere in a particular body and can be described independently of the environment. The orientation of disabilities, however is not biomedical but rehabilitative, and this is emblematic of the difference between the two notions.

The rehabilitative orientation of disability has ensured that our primary social response to disability has been a matter of remedying or ameliorating physical incapability and providing the skills needed to cope with restrictions on everyday and productive activities. Thus, what counts as a disability depends on what is perceived to be the normal or expected range of activities for a particular individual, given – as the 1991 CSICIDH versions adds – that individual's biological characteristics.

This in turn implies that disabilities are not intrinsic states of people but rather deviations that implicate standards arising from a relationship between an impairment and the social environment in which the individual with the impairment happens to be situated.

Disabilities are deviations from what might be called norms of capability, norms that set out the abilities and behaviours customarily expected of people. Since what is customarily expected of each of us shows the influence of a wide and complex range of social, cultural, and economic factors, these norms are very different from biomedical norms.

The ICIDH is very clear in rejecting a reduction of capability norms to functional restatements of biomedical norms. Though related to the potential performance capacities of normal anatomical structures and somatic functions, capability norms are not theoretical or abstract standards derivable from a biomedical understanding of the human body. They are, rather, practical and commonsensical standards of human capability, the reasonable scope of positive freedom in one context or another. The activities that are customarily expected of people do not lie at either extreme – the upper limits of peak performance or the absolute minimum of sustainable life. What is customarily expected is the average, the unremarkable. It is for this reason that the ICIDH wisely suggests that capability norms are a matter not of the presence or absence of something, but of 'excess or deficiency' – too much or too little of what is usual, expected, and unremarkable.

Must we defer to experts for a precise specification of these capability norms? True, we might expect those trained in rehabilitative therapy to have a better working understanding of the normal range of human activity than the rest of us. But this is a different sort of expertise than goes into the description of purely biomedical norms: it is an expertise of the practical not the ideal. The vocational or occupation therapist relies on patterns of movement, ability, skill, and so on that people actually require to make their way through the world. And this is appropriate for the nature of disabilities, since they are restrictions on what people actually do and what they try to become.

It should be kept in mind, however, that though rehabilitation enhances an individual's positive freedom by increasing his or her range of functional abilities, the same goal can be furthered in other ways. Because disabilities are the consequences of impairments in specific social contexts, an individual's positive freedom can also be enhanced by making changes to the social environment. This is why the goal of accommodation, though it obviously includes rehabilitation, is not restricted to it. A ramp or an elevator can increase the positive freedom of someone with a mobility disability as much as, and usually more than, rehabilitative therapy could ever hope to achieve.

But does a fully accommodated disability cease to be a disability; or would it be more accurate to say that it remains, but its ontological character has changed from actual to potential? It is probably not crucial which style of speaking we adopt, as long as we keep in mind that an impairment-induced disability could reappear if accommodations are removed.

In any event, though biomedical norms provide the reference point for descriptions of the range of customarily expected activities and behaviours, capability norms retain a social and social-psychological dimension. This dimension suffuses the logic of disability – what we can and cannot say about disabilities and people with disabilities. This is apparent in the next feature of the concept.

Normative Relativity

It is inevitable that the spectre of cultural or social relativity arises with the notion of disability. The mere fact that the ICIDH characterizes the activities that disabilities limit as 'tasks, skills, and behaviours' suggests the need to seek out the social or cultural context in which a collection of bodily movements is transformed into a 'task' or a 'skill.' Because of this unavoidable reference to the background social context there is a sense in which disabilities are culturally relative social constructs. It is vital to understand what that sense is and what it entails about disablement.

Consider how the ICIDH deals with the relativity of capability norms in its disability classification scheme, or D Code. This instrument is, as mentioned, an ADL scheme and posits seven broad and uncontroversial categories of disabilities – behaviour, communication, personal care, locomotion, body disposition, dexterity, and a miscellanous category called 'situational.' These categories (increased to ten in the CSICIDH version) flow from a purely physiological characterization of what the normal human body is capable of. It would be very implausible, that is, to suggest that these are contingent on social variation. Subsumed under these categories, however, are successively more specific, and more culturally contingent, subcategories.

For example, under the category of disabilities of body disposition one finds the subcategory of 'domestic disabilities,' which includes any activity associated with the individual's day-to-day life at home. Under this we find disabilities of subsistence, which at the lowest level of particularity listed includes the ability to open cans of food. The D Code stops at this level of specificity, but, if there was some point in doing so, we could go on to list yet more specific skills or tasks, ones which might presuppose a very concrete time, place, and culture.

The virtue of this hierarchical arrangement is that it utterly defuses worries about cultural relativity. We may confidently assume that being unable to walk will always count as a disability, for everyone, everywhere. But, being unable to perform all normal, locomotive behaviours *except* that of negotiating a zigzag path between highly trained and agile players while kicking a football may not be a disability at all, or if it is, it is a non-ADL disability for a very few people in special circumstances.

In other words, the degree of controversy over whether some condition is or is not a disability is a direct function of the level of specificity of the capability norm. Capability norms are always a matter of socially created expectations; but in some cases the scope of the norm is such that disputes over what society actually expects simply cannot be entertained. What we need is precisely what the ICIDH and similar classifications provide: a highly inclusive notion of disability that allows for a measure of transcultural generality but is flexible enough to accommodate a fair degree of social variation about the range and scope of activities people are customarily expected to be able to undertake. It is in this, harmless, sense that the norms of disability are socially relative.

Situational Contingency

There is, though, a further dimension of leeway provided by the ICIDH characterization of disabilities. As defined, the notion is contingent on the particular situation or context in which an individual finds him or herself. Even within the same society and culture, customary expectations with respect to the range of activities performed, and especially with respect to the manner in which they are performed, are almost always contingent on where and under what circumstances these activities take place. What is 'normal' locomotive ability for a member of a college track team is very different from that for a college professor. Moreover, reference to finely grained attributes of activities seems unavoidable when one considers the customarily expected hand movements of a concert pianist or, for that matter, the physical requirements of almost any skill. Thus, the same individual in different roles or in different jobs will likely have different ranges of activities that are customarily expected of him or her. That is as it should be.

If the concept of disability is to be sensitive to this variation, provision must be made to capture the effects on customary expectations of the various situations or contexts in which people normally find themselves. But the increased individualization this requires, although it poses no conceptual problem, creates extraordinary complications in the identification and measurement of disabilities.

Plainly, even the best disability classification instrument cannot be adequate for all purposes – vocational rehabilitation, workers' compensation, school or housing placement, identification of specific vulnerabilities of classes of people with disabilities, and so on. Consider job placement. For this purpose, it would be an absolutely salient fact about, for example, a hand-gripping disability that it will be far less restrictive for an accountant than for an olympic gymnast. Determining someone's employability requires a precise characterization of the range of skills, tasks, and other activities affected by a disability, and no single assessment instrument may have this flexibility.

We should, then, be deeply suspicious of any proposed 'scientifically objective,' or purpose-neutral demographic profile of people with disabilities. What counts as a disability depends on how one characterizes the background capability norms, and that will depend in part on how finely one contextualizes the relevant expectations. The population of those who have a disability will, accordingly, expand or contract as one adjusts the norms. If very finely gauged capabilities are deemed 'customary,' one should expect everyone to have one or another disability; if only very general capability norms are used, however, far fewer people will be so classified. In short, as not infrequently occurs in social policy, the nature and seriousness of the social problem of disablement is subject to representational manipulation.[16]

Still, it is a theoretical point worth making that situational relativity is highly paradoxical unless it is limited in some fashion.

For suppose one insisted that the more individualized and concrete a disability classification scheme is, the more accurate it is. One would then be committed to the pursuit of more and more finely gauged, contextual characterizations of capability norms. But we could not follow this mandate for very long before it would be obvious that our norms needed to be subjective. That is, a truly individualized disability is one that restricts the activities of one particular individual, understood with respect to 'norms' of capability that only apply to that individual. But a 'norm' which in principle only applies to one case is not a norm at all.

The problem here has a very practical dimension. Social policy designed to meet the genuine needs of people with disabilities must accurately and concretely characterize those needs. But social policy cannot be completely individualized. At some point, and typically very soon, generalizations of one sort or another must be made about the usual or typical activity restrictions associated with a disability. Even though in a perfectly understandable sense every disability is a unique experience, still social policy cannot treat disability in that way. Generalization and abstraction are integral features of meaningful social policy. And, as we shall see, this is precisely why the economic model of disablement, which focuses on work-related capabilities, has dominated disablement policy.

Two more features of the concept of disability should be noted. Both follow more or less immediately from the basic normative structure of the concept but are interesting in their own right.

Deviational Non-neutrality

Evaluative neutrality at the level of impairment is a key claim of the ICIDH. Partly to ensure a role for the assumption of biomedical grounding, Wood and Badley thought it vital to characterize impairments as neutral deviations from biomedical norms. Handicaps, as we shall see, are disadvantages that arise solely because of the social valuation attached to deviations from biomedical or capability norms. Thus, handicaps are most assuredly not evaluatively neutral. What of disabilities?

Intuitively, and for the most part, we believe that disabilities are bad things. After all, a disability is a failure of ability to perform expected human activities. Failures of ability (as opposed to abnormalities) are always regrettable. They are deviations that matter to us, not because successful performance is statistically predictable, but because it is customarily expected and desirable; they are limitations on our positive freedom. Disabilities are conditions we as a society want to prevent or avoid, conditions the effects of which we expend social resources to reverse, ameliorate, or accommodate. It would be somewhat nonsensical, in light of this, to deny that disabilities are negatively valued.

One important qualification to this claim should be quickly made, though. Philosophers distinguish between intrinsic and instrumental values. These are not so much different kinds of values as different grounds for evaluating. To value something intrinsically means to find value inherent in the thing itself; to value something instrumentally is to find value arising from the consequences or effects of the thing. These two evaluative grounds are independent. Thus, something that is painful may be instrumentally valuable – a visit to the dentist, for example; while something that is inherently good may lead to bad consequences – the truth sometimes hurts. Logically speaking, anything can be instrumentally valuable, though not everything that is valuable can be instrumentally valuable alone.

Now, the basis for the negative evaluation of physical disability is intrinsic rather than instrumental. Instrumentally speaking, a disability may, in not unimportant ways, count as a positive thing: having a disability qualifies one for a pension or other form of financial support and may relieve one of certain onerous responsibilities. Yet, its potential instrumental value notwithstanding, a disability remains intrinsically bad inasmuch as it is a limitation on our positive freedom, something it would be better not to have, all things considered.

It is important to insist on this philosophical point, because a conflation of intrinsic and instrumental evaluation often sustains the highly misleading claim that it is indeterminate whether a disability is a good or a bad thing, even within a single social context. Scepticism about whether or not a disability is undesirable may add unnecessary confusion to disablement policy analysis.

Universality of Disability

Finally, if everyone has at least one impairment, does everyone have a disability? Given the character of biomedical norms and their evaluative neutrality, an individual without an impairment would be a statistical fiction, an anatomically, physiologically, and psychologically ideal human being. Capability norms, however, are not evaluatively neutral, nor can they be adequately expressed in biomedical terms. Should we conclude, then, that disability is not universal?

We cannot, because the identification of disabilities is contingent on the degree of specification of the background capability norms, and that is further contingent on what repertoire of abilities, skills, tasks, and behaviours is, in a particular culture or context, customarily expected. One cannot say a priori whether the condition of total absence of disability is realizable. If the level of performance under a particular category is set high enough then everyone will have a disability; set low enough, very few will.

Of course, it might be objected that a standard of performance that no one, or very few, can satisfy hardly qualifies as a standard that is 'customarily expected.' More concretely, an economist pondering the cost-effectiveness of vocational rehabilitation programs would find unreachable capability norms wholly fanciful, and supremely impractical, since they set eligibility criteria for these programs so low that anyone would qualify as disabled.

Still, in terms of social policy there may be legitimate purposes served by positing unreachable capability norms. A system of universal health care might require for administrative and policy reasons a very broad characterization of disability, since a very narrow one might skew allocative decisions away from prevention and rehabilitation toward extraordinary, expensive, and technology-intensive medicine.

This certainly does not mean that only in very contrived or artificial circumstances would universality of disability prevail. It is perfectly possible that some fairly circumscribed disability *is* universal, in every social and cultural setting. Disability in seeing may be such a case. It is safe to say that the vast majority of people are not – or at some point during their lifetime will not be – able to carry out all reasonable human visual tasks, without visual aid of any sort.

The realistic possibility of a near-universal disability points to an intriguing feature of disablement. If everyone possessed a particular disability it would be extremely unlikely that anyone would be socially disadvantaged because of it. This is not to make the conceptual point that, if a disability is universal, after a while it might cease to be one. It is rather to reinforce the sociological observation that social institutions respond to the actual capacities and states of health of the people that make them up, so that a truly universal disability would be so unremarkable as to be socially 'invisible.'

Suppose, for example, that in some society nearly everyone, for whatever reason, had ocular impairments which, at best, brought them into the category of having moderately low vision. We would expect in this society that considerable social resources would be automatically set aside for the ongoing task of reducing the effects of this universal disability. Research into the development of visual aids would be generously funded and environmental accommodations – audio-enhanced traffic signals, large-print newspapers, raised marks on knobs, dials, and others control gear, and so on – would either be legislatively required or brought about by consumer demand. We would expect that social, economic, and political institutions would take visual disability into account as a fact of life (like cold weather in northern climates) and accommodate the restrictions on activity that result from this universal phenomenon.

As well, in such a society visual disability would be socially unremarkable and would have no effect on participation in social activities, or the degree of respect everyone enjoyed. Stigma, stereotypical responses, and prejudices would be rare; indeed, they would be unintelligible. Discrimination in employment or in the provision of services on the basis of visual ability would be anomalous. 'Normal' vision could hardly be for them a qualification for employment, or anything else. The society, in short, would adjust itself so that the adverse consequences of the disability, both biomedical and social, were minimalized or eliminated. The goal of accommodation with respect to this disability would be realized.

What this fictional but not unrealistic case suggests is that being socially disadvantaged because of a disability is a separate, and by no means inevitable, consequence of the disability. Having an impairment or a disability, in short, is not the same as being handicapped.

Handicap

According to the ICIDH the socialization of an individual's experience of somatic abnormality, functional limitation, or activity restriction may involve interpersonal or social responses that are disadvantageous to the individual. The social reception of impairment and disability is, in the first instance, primarily attitudinal. Often these responses quickly evolve beyond attitude to overt behaviour, ending ultimately in the legal, bureaucratic, or political responses of social institutions. The institutional, administrative, or policy response, which is implicit in the structure of the very programs designed to assist people with disabilities, typically reinforces and legitimatizes the original attitudes. When all or most of these social responses are adverse to the interests of the individual, which is usually the case, the result is the socialization of impairment and disability and the creation of the experience of being handicapped.

In the original ICIDH, a handicap is defined as 'a disadvantage for a given individual, resulting from an impairment or a disability, that limits or prevents the fulfilment of a role that is normal (depending on age, sex, and social and cultural factors) for that individual.' (The recommended French term is *handicap*, although some have argued that *désavantage* would better capture the stipulative meaning.)[17] Handicaps are thus socially created disadvantages that arise from the social reception of impairments and disabilities. The explicit focus of this dimension of disablement is social valuations of physical states (or perceived physical states); there is no question here of normative neutrality. Moreover, nearly every aspect of the conceptual structure of the notion is shaped by and so relative to social and cultural forces.

The ICIDH characterization of handicap is the weakest part of that document. The definition's wording is misleading because it suggests that handicaps, insofar as they 'result from' impairments and disabilities, are socially disadvantageous physical conditions. But this belies the expressed theory of the ICIDH that handicaps are social-psychological events, socially created limitations upon positive freedom. The drafters of the ICIDH were, it seems, misled by the everyday connotations of the word 'handicap' which strongly imply that handicaps are physical things – namely, impairments and disabilities. And several critics of the ICIDH who argued that the category of handicap was redundant seem to have been similarly confused.[18]

The 1991 CSICIDH version goes a long way to eliminating this confusion. The CSICIDH defines, not 'handicap,' but a 'handicap situation' as 'a disruption in the accomplishments of a person's life habits, taking into account age, sex and socio-cultural identity, resulting, on the one hand, from impairments or disabilities and, on the other, from obstacles caused by environmental factors.' A handicap, in other words, is the situational result of an interactive process between two, obviously very different, sets of causes: the characteristics of a person's impairments and disabilities and the characteristics of the environment that create social or environmental obstacles in a given situation.

Thus, as already remarked, the CSICIDH sets out a fourth dimension of disablement, that of obstacles. An obstacle is a social, cultural, institutional, or natural (for example, geographical or climatic) factor that determines the organization and structure of the social context in which people with impairments and disabilities live and work. Obstacles are always potentially handicapping, but create handicap situations once, together with impairments and disabilities, they bring about a disruption in the behaviours, activities, and social roles that ensure the survival and development of a person in society.

Although this is an improvement, the CSICIDH version suffers from a major difficulty, created by its implicit adherence to the strong version of the assumption of biomedical grounding. The CSICIDH requires that one actually have an impairment or disability in order to claim validly that one has a handicap. But this is simply false: it is perfectly possible for someone to be discriminated against in accommodation or employment (a handicapping event) because people believe, falsely, that one has a contagious disease. Handicaps are socially created disadvantages that arise from the social reception of the characteristics of impairments and disabilities. And a social reception can be just as effective in creating handicap situations if it is groundless.

Once we drop the requirement that a handicap situation must be caused by an impairment or disability, then the distinction between handicap and obstacle becomes tenuous.[19] It is more appropriate to say that handicaps are the situational result of the interaction between the social reception of impairments and disabilities (beliefs that may be true or false) and the social environment. But, since the social reception of impairments and disabilities is often itself disadvantageous, and so would qualify as an obstacle, the distinction the CSICIDH wants to draw collapses.

What I am insisting on, in short, is that handicap be a dimension of disablement that is wholly socially constructed and causally detached from physical states and conditions. Impairments do not cause handicaps; at most they contribute to the creation of disabilities. Disabilities are limitations upon our positive freedom that are causally linked to impairments. But handicaps are socially constructed limitations upon our positive freedom that are causally linked to social perceptions about impairments and disabilities.

A related point underscores the importance of being careful about the language used to define the concept of handicap. In ICIDH the classification scheme for handicaps distinguishes categories of handicapping in terms of the degree to which an individual 'with reduced competence' will be disadvantaged in relation to his or her peers. And the definition of handicap in the CSICIDH version identifies a handicap situation as a disruption in the 'accomplishments of a person's life habits.' Both formulations are problematic because they imply that handicaps are, or are the result of, failures attributable to the individual. But this is quite incorrect: the 'failure' here can only be attributed to the social reception of the impairment or disability or the background social environment.

With all this in mind, the rough contours of the notion of handicap come into focus. First, the normative force of the notion is unambiguous. A handicap is a socially constructed limitation on our negative freedom to do or become what we choose. As such, handicaps and potential handicap situations are always intrinsic misfortunes, states of affairs to be prevented, avoided, or overcome whenever possible. Unlike disabilities, which are also intrinsic misfortunes, it is unlikely that a plausible case for the instrumental value of handicaps could be made.

Second, handicaps are never latent phenomena. People with handicaps will always be all too aware of the fact that they are being treated differently and adversely because of a handicap situation. Even in ordinary usage it would be very odd to say that someone was suffering from a 'hidden' handicap, if that meant the individual was totally unaware of the social reception to an impairment or disability. If a handicap is truly and completely hidden, it is probably not a handicap at all.

Still, there is no reason to think that people who are handicapped are aware of the full range of adverse social consequences they could encounter. Like other forms of discriminatory treatment, being handicapped is a conditional obstacle, in the sense that if one never ventures into a particular social setting (never applies for a job, for example) one might never encounter the obstacles to full participation that exist.

Third, handicap situations will be subject to all forms of social, cultural, and situational contingencies. This variability raises the spectre of relativism again, and in particular the question whether there are any predictable relationships between handicaps and handicap situations. On the evidence we have, there is no clear answer to this question. It might be argued that the social reception of impairments and disabilities is quite unpredictable, since it depends on expectations and standards that are variable across cultures, across social classes within a single culture, across professions and so on. It might also be argued that some transcultural trends and regularities are reasonably reliable.

This is not a particularly worrisome controversy, however, since there is no reason to think that socially produced phenomena such as handicaps are wholly arbitrary and beyond the scope of serious investigation by social scientists. Indeed, as a rule, stereotypical and discriminatory practices always exhibit a kind of perverse rationality that appears to fully justify them. A stereotype about disability that was wholly arbitrary or which did not attach itself to some observable aspect of the physical condition of an individual would likely not be believable.

Finally, what of the property of universality? The point has already been made that if everyone had the same disability we could be fairly sure it would not result in handicap situations, let alone handicaps. But could everyone be handicapped to some extent? Though conceivable, this is not a plausible social situation, since the dynamics of discrimination and marginalization seem to preclude a social environment in which *everyone* was discriminated against by someone. Even if this state of affairs could exist for a time, one would expect that soon alliances would be formed and specific subgroups would be marginalized and subjected to a more pronounced and debilitating degree of handicapping.

In sum, unlike the concepts impairment and disability, which point to features of the individual who is affected by a somatic deviation or dysfunction, handicap is a dimension of disablement that clearly and unambiguously points outward to the attitudes, behaviours, and practices of others. All of the conceptual properties of this complex notion arise in one way or another from its social and social-psychological character. But before we look at these properties, we need to consider an aspect of the conceptual distinction between handicap and the other two dimensions that has the most profound effect on disablement theory.

Conceptual Independence

Handicaps belong to a very different ontological category than impairments and disabilities. An impairment is experienced as a physical state, an attribute of a particular individual. Though disabilities are created by social processes that give significance to dysfunctional states, they too denote ascribable physical attributes of people. With handicaps, by contrast, what is experienced is a condition of social disadvantage, manifested in a variety of ways – from feelings of worthlessness or embarrassment, to being socially cast out and experiencing problems sustaining personal relationships, to the loss of employment and the destruction of life plans, to segregation, institutional dependency, and other forms of discrimination, stigmatization, and marginalization. These adverse handicapping conditions are not attributes of the people with disabilities; they are conditions imposed on them.

Since handicaps are constituted by adverse consequences that are the product of social forces – attitudinal, behavioural, and institutional – their existence is wholly contingent on those forces. Handicaps are thus social constructions. This makes them ontologically different from both impairments and disabilities.

The practical significance of this ontological difference should be obvious. A disability that can be corrected by external aids and other accommodations, and which does not attract stigmatization, may not be socially disadvantageous. But where there are no socially created disadvantages there is no handicap. Thus, although it would be hopelessly utopian to strive for the elimination of impairments and disabilities, it would be a perfectly appropriate social aim to eliminate handicaps entirely.

This ontological difference also underscores the independence of the three dimensions of disablement. Since the sequence from intrinsic physical condition through to impairment, disability and handicap is neither linear nor causal, there are no regular or predictable correlations between disabilities and handicaps. Two, quite different disabilities may yield the same sort of social disadvan-

tage and two individuals, in different environments or social circumstances, may experience different handicaps as the result of the
same restriction in their activities. As well, there is no consonance in
degrees of disability and handicap, so that two individuals with the
same degree of disability may be handicapped to different degrees
and the same extent of handicapping may result from disabilities of
differing degrees of seriousness.

By the same token, the development from impairment to disability
to handicap is neither causal nor unidirectional. Disabilities in one
area (hearing, say) can contribute to impairments in another area
(dysphasia). And it is possible for a handicapped individual, wholly
resigned to and living out the consequences of a socially imposed
'sick roles,' to develop additional and new disabilities, perhaps even
further impairments, as the result of this firmly held self-perception.

In a word, since handicaps arise from perceptions of and attitudes
about impairments and disabilities, the social processes of handicapping may be influenced by features of impairments and disabilities that are, from both an etiological and clinical point of view,
quite unimportant, or totally without scientific basis.

Thus it is that public and visible impairments – missing limbs,
short stature, or disfigurements – are much more likely to have
adverse social consequences than ones that can be successfully
concealed. Individual prejudices and systemic discriminatory
practices are only possible where there are observable differences that
allow differentiation between 'normals' and 'abnormals.' Similarly,
embarrassing disabilities – incontinence, say, or the inability to talk
clearly or move one's limbs smoothly – will often cause more adverse
reaction than less obtrusive, or more socially acceptable, disabilities.
Someone with an acute memory impairment, however, may suffer
less social disadvantage because that condition is invisible and in
casual encounters may go wholly unnoticed. Needless to say,
visibility and degree of embarrassment are poor indicators of the
medical seriousness of a physical impairment.

Another aspect of conceptual independence is that a handicap may
result from an impairment directly, without the mediation of a state
of disability. A highly visible impairment, a facial disfigurement for
example, might be socially disadvantageous, either by being a
persistent source of debilitating embarrassment or, more seriously, by
interfering with relationships and employment prospects. This would
be true even if the individual's repertoire of customarily expected

capabilities was not restricted in any significant way. Alternatively, a disability that can be corrected or accommodated by an external aid may be effectively eliminated, although the impairment will persist. At the same time, though, the individual may be profoundly disadvantaged – handicapped – by discrimination arising from a stigma of inferiority, dependence, and frailty.

Finally, and the ICIDH and CSICIDH notwithstanding, it is perfectly possible for there to be *groundless* handicaps, that is, handicaps without background impairments or disabilities. For example, if someone suffered from a highly contagious disease but is now completely cured, it is not unlikely that he or she may continue to suffer adverse social consequences of what is now a non-existent physical condition. Moreover, precisely the same stigma and discrimination may be experienced by someone who was never contagious if there is a persistent, generally held but incorrect belief to the contrary.[20]

Normative Deviation

Returning to the properties of the concept of handicap, we need first to identify the background norms to which handicaps refer. Since handicaps arise from the social reception of biomedical and capability norms, they constitute deviations from social standards about what accomplishments of one's life habits (to use the CSICIDH terminology) are expected of individuals, given the social roles normal for them. A handicap is a complex social evaluation of an impairment or disability as well as all the adverse attitudinal, behavioural, and institutional consequences that flow from it. It follows then that the standards upon which these social judgments are based must constitute the norms with respect to which handicaps are deviations. For convenience, we might call these standards capability evaluations.

Capability evaluations are social or cultural imperatives, paradigms of what one can do and be. They are not so much discrete judgments as commonplace standards that everyone knows, and implicitly accepts. They represent what we, as a culture, normally expect of people and from people, the scope of our positive freedom as it concerns our social existence. It might be helpful to compare these with what philosophers have in mind when they speak of 'forms of life,' that is, complex, not easily describable, but empirically verifiable, patterns of factual and normative belief about the world, ways of speaking and behaving, social customs and practices.

Just as an example, consider the various, ever-shifting paradigms of physical beauty found in our culture. Somatopsychologists are beginning now to unravel the complexities of our psychological responses to these paradigms, our implicit or explicit judgments about the value of beauty and the importance of being beautiful in the way mandated by the paradigms, and the myriad activities we daily engage in in pursuit of physical beauty. All of these things constitute a way of being in and of a part of our social world, a form of life. This is a competence evaluation. To express it as 'being physically beautiful is important' is not adequate, although that is the crux of it.

Since capability evaluations subtend complex social phenomena, the existence of a handicap is dependent on the persistence of an adverse social evaluation of an impairment or disability, real or perceived. And since they are ubiquitous forms of life, to say that someone is handicapped is in effect to reinforce the social assessment that the individual is physically incompetent, a failure in one or another respect. Both the assessment and the social consequences that flow from it are patently disadvantageous to the individual, as a member of the society or group that incorporates the capability evaluation.

Whatever else might be said about this assessment, it is hardly a normatively neutral description of an individual's impairment or disability. Handicaps are often permanent attachments to an individual's social persona. They also alter the individual's social status. Where once we had an individual – citizen, father, employee, friend – who happens to have an impairment or a disability, we now have a 'handicapped person,' someone whose social identity is a function of membership in a devalued category.

Describing how capability evaluations arise, the forms they take, and the effects they have on our social representations of disablement are ongoing social-psychological projects. As we shall see these data form part of the social-psychological foundations of the social-political model of disablement, the model that focuses on handicaps and handicapping in its analysis of disablement. But there is more to handicaps than this from the perspective of policy analysis. The quality of the handicapping experience itself depends on the dimensions of disadvantage.

Dimensions of Disadvantage

In any society we should expect a wide variety of disadvantageous consequences, of different degrees of severity, to be associated with different impairments and disabilities. This is in part because there is no direct correlation between impairment or disability and social disadvantage. As well, individuals respond in different ways to obstacles, including the social reception of their physical condition, depending on the resources they can command, the coping strategies they can employ, and the support they receive from others.

Valuable research into the experience of handicap situations is now becoming more common, and this research suggests that there may be two basic kinds of social disadvantage.[21] The first is material disadvantage, including relative economic position, access to social resources and services, and other indicators of material circumstances. The other, and more subtle, is social-psychological disadvantage. This typically involves social isolation manifested by a panoply of difficulties in social interaction, including the making and keeping of personal relationships.

Important as the empirical research is, there remain some prior conceptual questions that need to be addressed if the key notion of social disadvantage is to have a role to play in policy analysis. In particular, we need to decide whether the logical boundaries of this notion should be left as flexible as possible or whether clear criteria about what is and what is not socially disadvantageous should be applied.

This is a much more difficult question than it might at first appear. For the notion of social disadvantage, like the analogous notion of need, is resistant to the sort of operationalization demanded by policy analysis. There are at least three dimensions of the notion of disadvantage that are responsible for many of the confusions in disablement policy.

First, since disadvantage is a matter of degree we need to know whether there is a threshold of disadvantage, whether in other words there is a degree of deviation from a capability evaluation that is so slight or negligible that it simply does not qualify as a handicap. Suppose the only adverse social consequence of wearing eyeglasses for reading is the possibility that some people with normal vision might, on the odd occasion, be less than patient with you if you have to find them before you can read. Suppose it never goes beyond this mild reaction. There is no discrimination, overt or otherwise, no penalty paid or privilege sacrificed; no further social consequence at all. Granting that there is an impairment here, perhaps even a mild disability, is this really a physical handicap?

A second, closely related problem is raised by the observation that the task of identifying handicaps depends on our capacity to record the actual experiences of people with impairments or disabilities. But can we always be confident that the perspective of the handicapped individual is the proper one to adopt? This is not a worry about malingering or outright fraud. It is rather a concern about the adequacy of the first-person experiential perspective on matters that are social rather than personal.

As remarked earlier, there is no reason to think that people with disabilities have a complete and accurate knowledge of all the social disadvantages and handicap situations they could face. There may also be a danger that disadvantages that have been overcome by extraordinary effort on the part of an exceptionally motivated individual will, because of this isolated success, lead to a misrepresentation of the typical level of disadvantage that non-exceptional individuals experience. Finally, sociologists argue that the processes of stigmatizing often have the effect of convincing the 'deviant' individual that adverse social responses, far from being unjustifiable, are deserved or inevitable. Given all of this, perhaps a close relative, companion, direct care worker, or service provider would be better able to identify disadvantages than the individual.

Finally, are all adverse consequences social disadvantages? Could not some social responses be justifiable, in the sense of being medically warranted, for example? A person who is blind is, by virtue of indisputable biomedical facts, unable to drive a car safely. But if as a matter of social policy we take steps to prevent blind people from driving cars, would this be an instance of the sort of discrimination about which policy analysts should be concerned? Is this social practice a handicap at all?

Now the point of raising these three problems is not to make any attempt to solve them but rather to underscore a feature of handicaps totally obscured by the methodological presumptions of the ICIDH and the CSICIDH version. These are not conceptual puzzles that can be solved a priori, let alone questions awaiting empirical investigation; they are rather issues about the extent of our social obligation to people with disabilities. Setting the threshold of disadvantage, adopting a perspective for identifying disadvantage, and drawing a line between warranted and unwarranted social disadvantages are all social policy decisions and, however they are made, will embody general conceptions of political morality that determine the range and scope of our social obligation to people with disabilities.

This means that the concept of social disadvantage, and so the notion of handicap itself, is intrinsically normative. One cannot explore the internal logic of these notions for very long before realizing that what they say about our social existence is contingent on moral and political judgments about what is fair and unfair, what society does and does not owe its citizens, what political equality entails, and the like. Answers to these questions presume what I am calling the normative basis of disablement theory, namely the moral and political foundation of social policy with respect to the rights and entitlements of people with disabilities. This basis is a permanent feature of the concept of disablement and cannot be prised off without creating conceptual confusions of a practically dangerous sort.

Disablement and the ICIDH

By far the most significant contribution of the ICIDH and its successors is the insistence that there must be a clear, conceptual distinction drawn between impairments and disabilities, on the one hand, and handicaps, on the other. To be sure, these documents are flawed, principally because of their ideological commitment to two dubious methodological assumptions. None the less the recognition that there are three conceptually independent dimensions of disablement qualifies as a turning-point in the history of disablement theory.

The view that disablement is fundamentally a biomedical phenomenon was an article of faith for many years. The early pioneers of rehabilitation in the postwar United States, Doctors Howard Rusk and Henry Kessler, challenged this assumption in part in order to wrest control of vocational rehabilitation from the medical establishment. Kessler subsequently argued that while it is true that the basis of disability is some physical defect or impairment, the phenomenon of disability also comprehends the social and economic status of the affected individual, a status that results from the 'inability to meet certain standards of physical, social, occupational, and economic competence.'[22] And one of the most highly respected and influential contributors to the debate over definition, Saad Z. Nagi, has long argued that the medical and social aspects of disablement must be distinguished.[23]

Yet, significantly, neither Kessler nor Nagi saw the need for an explicit, conceptual, and practical distinction between the concepts of disability and handicap. And both thought it appropriate to correlate handicaps with functional inabilities or incompetences. Thus, although Kessler argues at length that physicians are not qualified to determine the true character or extent of a disability (in part because medical determinations are often affected by prejudices about the incapacities of people with disabilities), he never asks whether some of the debilitating consequences of a disability might be the result of a non-accommodating social environment. For his part, up until recently, Nagi has defined disability as 'a form of inability or limitation in performing roles and tasks expected of an individual within a social environment,' leaving it ambiguous whether the locus of disablement lies with an 'inability or limitation,' with the nature of the 'roles and tasks' expected, or with with the non-accommodating 'social environment.'[24]

Although Kessler, Nagi, and others saw the social dimension of disablement, they were content to make the point that social, cultural, and economic factors are influential and must be taken into account in the determination and assessment of disablement. They did not see the need to insist on a theoretical distinction. Although Wood and Badley were certainly not the first to do so, their ICIDH brought the conceptual distinction into the forefront, where, as evidenced by the CSICIDH version, it remains.

Clarifying the three dimensions of disablement is the first step toward any serious theory of disablement. Impairment, disability, and handicap are all inherent elements of our complex discourse of disablement and supplement each other in a host of ways. Yet, they remain conceptually discrete, non-reducible facets of a single, complex notion – disablement.

Like an extremely rich archeological site, the concept of disablement has many layers, each of which offers a partial picture of a dimension of the notion, but none of which represents the furthest development, or completed evolution of all that disablement is.

Disablement *is* impairment, disability, and handicap, and none of these is fundamental or prior.

The immediate consequences for disablement policy, and its impasse, are obvious enough. Since disablement is composed of three dimensions, it would seem that policy ambiguities and anomalies can be avoided, or at least their diagnosis clarified, by dividing disablement policy into components associated with each dimension. Medical diagnosis and treatment components are impairment issues; adaptation and rehabilitation components are disability issues; and discrimination and access issues come under the rubric of handicap.

This clarification has already been taken up, and in a sense institutionalized, in Quebec, where the Office des personnes handicappés organizes its activities and policy thinking in accordance with the conceptual framework provided by the CSICIDH. In the Office's far-reaching and innovative 1984 report, *On Equal Terms*, the four-part, conceptual distinction is employed to characterize categories of service programming.[25]

Still, the history of disablement policy suggests a more complicated and dynamic situation than can be captured by this approach. What one sees is not merely a confusion between dimensions of disablement but a contest between conceptual orientations that arise when one dimension is posited to be the model of what disablement really is. There have been three such models of disablement that have influenced policy analysis – the biomedical, the economic, and the social-political. Each takes one dimension of disablement to be fundamental and builds a theory of disablement upon it. Each in different ways has left its mark on our disablement policy. And adherents of each have claimed that it represents the essence of disablement.

In the next three chapters these three models will be considered in detail. In each case, the aim first of all will be to situate the model by showing its intellectual roots and the social and historical forces that brought it about. Then, the strengths and the weaknesses of each model will be explored in the context of a review of the effects each model has had on disablement policy. Finally, I shall try to show how each model has suggested one or more fundamental normative accounts, or normative bases, which provide the grounding for the entitlements or rights vested in, or accruing to, people with disabilities.

3 The Biomedical Model of Disablement

Characteristics of the Model

The most commonly held belief about disablement is that it involves a defect, deficiency, dysfunction, abnormality, failing, or medical 'problem' that is located in an individual. We think it is so obvious as to be beyond serious dispute that disablement is a characteristic of a *defective person*, someone who is functionally limited or anatomically abnormal, diseased, or pathoanatomical, someone who is neither whole nor healthy, fit nor flourishing, someone who is biologically inferior or subnormal. The essence of disablement, in this view, is that there are things *wrong* with people with disabilities. This is the intuition that sustains the biomedical model of disablement. This model attempts to capture disablement as a whole in terms of *impairment*. And this has two immediate, theoretical consequences.

The first, and most obvious, is that the other two dimensions of disablement, disability and handicap, and more particularly the social phenomena they denote, are either wholly ignored by the model or, more problematically, reformulated as versions of impairment. Ultimately it is this move that makes the model both distortive and incomplete, as we shall see.

But second, in the course of transforming impairment into a model of disablement as a whole, the notion sheds its (always flimsy) mantle of normative neutrality. For, in this model disablement is not mere physical difference or specificity, it is a 'defect' inherent in the individual. And more to the point, people with disabilities are represented in this model, not as physically different but as defective, subnormal, biologically inferior. The biomedical model, in short, embodies an evaluative ranking.

This does not mean that the model necessarily implies moral fault, culpability, or any other failing for which individuals could be held responsible. The implicit ranking is normative, but not moral. Being commonly perceived to be 'biologically inferior' need not mean that one is viewed as having a defective moral character. It is important to make this point because, historically, one of the primary achievements of the biomedical model was to replace moral innuendos about people with disabilities – that they were tainted and ill-fated sinners, being punished by vengeful gods for unknown sins[1] – with the (putatively) value-free and objective discourse of science. Of course, at the same time, the scientific approach has not been without its moral message. We need only think of the Malthusian response to disablement, with its clear eugenic messages.[2]

Moreover, far from being a manifestation of xenophobia or ill will, the biomedical model reflects some of our most benevolent impulses. It is quite natural to think that since people with disabilities are defective and infirm, because they suffer or cannot do what normal people can, they are victims of a personal misfortune and need our help, our sympathy, and our charity. These well-meaning and benevolent attitudes underwrite the representation of people with disabilities that the model fosters, namely, victims with special needs.

To be sure, we are only just beginning to unravel the sociopsychological complexities of our responses to those who are physically different from ourselves. Somatopsychologists have investigated the intriguing interrelations between our attitudes toward and beliefs about people with visible impairments.[3] Social historians have explored the events and forces that may have shaped our representations of those who are physically, or mentally, different.[4] And experts in a wide range of other disciplines – biological, anthropological, sociological, political, historical, and literary – have offered explanations of why we respond as we do to physical difference, be it sex, race, colour, or deviation from the normal.

The character of our responses to physical difference has doubtless changed over the centuries. An optimist might even detect an evolutionary improvement in our attitudes, at least towards those with physical defects. The primitive xenophobia that characterized some of the darkest moments in our history seems to have given way to attitudes founded on feelings of sympathy, pity, and charity. As our knowledge about human biology, physiology, and psychology has increased, this charitable response has been supplemented with a general faith in our ability to prevent, cure, or overcome impairment.

But running through this history is a commonsensical intuition that has not changed much over the centuries, namely, that disablement is, at bottom, a physical attribute of people. Even though it is obvious that the difficulties confronting a person who is blind are the product of a non-accommodating social environment, we will continue to believe that the 'real problem' is not social: there is something *wrong* with a blind person; he or she cannot see.

The model also gains credibility from the prestige and social influence of medicine, the allied biomedical sciences, and the medical institutions. Many areas of disablement policy have been thoroughly, and perhaps permanently, 'medicalized,' and several policy objectives have been set by bioscientists.

It is important to remember, though, that it has only been relatively recently that medicine itself came 'out of the dark ages of sciolism and traditional superstition into the light of science.[5] Medicine now is an adjunct of the biological sciences with their apparatus of controlled experimentation, standardized and calibrated measurements, and epidemiological-statistical methods. The biomedical sciences have incorporated into the practice of medicine the ideal of the scientific enterprise, namely, the production of objective, transcultural, and evaluatively neutral knowledge. So too, biomedicine has come to adopt the optimism of technology, the belief that it is a realistic goal of biomedical understanding to modify the onset, development, or consequences of pathological conditions by technological means.

Thus, something akin to a mythology has accompanied the increased social prominence of biomedicine, an optimism founded on an unwavering faith in technological or invasive solutions to infirmities and other mortal 'failings.' The dominant theme of this mythology is that of control and mastery, with stories of dramatic surgical procedures and scientific 'breakthroughs' bolstering the imagery of medical heroes who, by knowledge and endurance, can successfully confront and overwhelm the evils of disease, injury, and other threats to human life and happiness.

In short, modern biomedicine has become the pre-eminent scientific and technological enterprise for understanding, explaining, and repairing biologically defective human beings. Along the way, of course, the biomedical professions have become powerful social forces in their own right, constructing representations of disablement and people with disabilities, and shaping our disablement policy.

The characteristics of the biomedical model of disablement are merely immediate, theoretical products of medicalization: the establishment of a definitive discourse of medical expertise; the ontological location of disablement in the body of an individual; and the resulting representation of that individual as a patient, a sufferer, a person with a medical problem and special needs.

Sociologically speaking, medicalization was bound to have profound effects on disablement policy. Any organized scientific enterprise can legitimately make a claim to objective truth, thereby benefiting from the authority and social power such a claim brings with it. This is part of our cultural understanding of science, and it is deeply rooted. Thus, physicians and other health professionals, relying on the great explanatory power of the biological sciences, are credited with a wide-ranging expertise on nearly any matter within the general purview of the health professions. The representations of disablement as impairment and people with disabilities as patients are thus socially authorized by experts who are credited with having knowledge of such things.

Medicalization is not without its critics, of course. Many writers have warned of the dangers involved in turning social problems into medical problems[6] Perhaps the most dramatic example of this comes from critics of psychiatry who argue that the notion of a mental disease is nothing but a label used to stigmatize non-conforming individuals.[7] In their view, whenever health professionals treat homosexuality, criminality, or some other complex human behaviour as a medical problem, the behaviour is transformed into a disease-like condition – through a process of emphasizing only those causal factors that are congenial to the theories and technologies of biomedicine. More often than not, though, this transformation is highly distortive, since it fixes upon a 'problem' with the individual and ignores the social environment, thus establishing expectations that can have disastrous personal and social consequences.

In the case of physical disablement in general, medicalization seems far less of a concern, since we assume that people with disabilities always have medical problems that call for medical solutions. This assumption is so strong that we tend to believe that only by adopting the biomedical perspective will the true needs of people with disabilities be met. Because of this, the model identifies the goal of accommodation – in the restricted sense of meeting special health needs – as prior to and more important than the goals of respect and participation. By representing the person with a disability as a patient the most appropriate personal and institutional response seems to be the accommodation provided by caring, comforting, and curing.

But what precisely is involved in medicalizing disablement, or, to ask the same question in a different way, what are the theoretical foundations of the biomedical model?

At the theoretical centre of the model is a philosophical assumption that is characteristic of most scientific enterprises. That assumption might be called biomedical realism, the view that the entities described in a biomedical explanation have a real, substantial, and objective existence wholly independent of any social environment. In the words of a recent text, 'diseases are items that form the furniture of the world ... [they] have a real existence, and that existence is as historically, socially, and culturally invariant as is the existence of Victoria Falls.'[8] Though realism posits the independent existence of diseases, it says nothing about whether our current biomedical theories about diseases are true or not. Realism does suggest, however, that as a general strategic matter, our current, tested, and confirmed biomedical theories, even if time should prove them wrong, are probably the best guide to the truth we have.

Biomedical realism is truly the rock-bottom foundation of the biomedical model. Sociologically speaking, it bolsters the status of the expertise of biomedicine by entrenching and legitimating the medicalization of disablement. Moreover, realism is the philosophical basis for what I have labelled the assumption of biomedical founding, on its strong interpretation.

Because it is so fundamental, biomedical realism is not often a matter of controversy, even among theoreticians. What is controversial, however, is a specific application of the doctrine that has left its mark on the theory and practice of medicine. The medical model of disease, as it is usually called, defines the subject-matter and the methodology of biomedicine.

Though called a 'model of disease,' strictly speaking it is a model of scientifically adequate theories about diseases, since it purports to lay out the essential components and ground rules of disease explanations. The model analyses a disease into three sequentially arranged components: the antecedent causal history or etiology of the condition; the somatic changes, or pathology, that result; and the manifestations of those changes in subjective symptoms or intersubjective signs. The model also sets out two methological theses about disease explanations: (1) that every disease can and should be defined entirely in relation to measurable deviations from biological or somatic norms,[9] and (2) the 'doctrine of specific etiology,'[10] that for every disease there is, in principle, a unique causal explanation that specifies all the antecedent biological causes jointly sufficient for its occurrence.

The medical model of disease and biomedical realism have mutually reinforced each other, and it is commonly assumed they come as an inseparable package. Yet, though the model is incompatible with antirealism or nominalism (the theory that something is a disease just when it is so deemed by a recognized authority), it is still a matter of some dispute what methodological and ontological propositions the model presupposes. Philosophers of science agree that the model admits of at least two interpretations, a strong and a weak version.

Those who advocate the strong version insist that the model necessarily entails definitional essentialism, the claim that for every disease there must be a definition that, exhaustively, lists characteristics and properties individually necessary and jointly sufficient for the existence of a disease.[11] Other advocates have insisted that, as well, the model entails the theory of universal nosology (sometimes called the theory of generic disease) – roughly, the view that there is only one classification of diseases that is valid for all times and for all social environments.[12]

By contrast, the weaker version rejects both these claims and in their place offers a methodological hypothesis about the limited, though decisive role of social and culture forces at the conceptual level. This hypothesis suggests that socially and culturally contingent beliefs about the levels of performance expected of people determine what forms of impairment will be treated as diseases.[13] Although these criteria are fairly stable, there is some discernible variation across time, place, and culture; moreover, they are evaluative criteria since they tell us what forms of physical difference are undesirable and warrant our concern and assistance. On the weaker version of the medical model, in short, there is a non-biological dimension to the concept of disease.

Despite appearances, the weaker version is not at odds with biomedical realism. For it does not deny that diseases have a real, objective existence. It claims instead that although the mechanism by which conditions come to be identified as diseases is socially and culturally contingent, once a condition is so regarded any explanatory theory of it must be firmly grounded in the biosciences.

The debate between advocates of the strong and the weak versions of the medical model of disease is not over. The result is a parallel controversy about the nature of medicine. The strong version sees medicine as a univocal, objective, wholly neutral practice grounded in the biological sciences. The weak version, while acknowledging the ultimate power and authority of biomedical explanations, holds that a variety of social and cultural forces influence the theory and practice of medicine.

As it happens, this controversy is part of a far larger debate about the concepts of disease and health. At issue here is whether medicine ought to focus on pathology defined in purely biological terms (say, as 'species atypical functioning,' as one influential writer has suggested)[14] or whether instead medicine should adopt a broader, less theoretical and more clinical conception of health as its basis.[15]

It is important to at least gesture toward some of these arcane controversies because they show that it is not all that clear what medicalization actually implies. On the strong reading of the medical model, for example, to medicalize disablement, or anything else, would probably entail a refusal to consider any non-biological event to be relevant to a theory of disablement. This would mean, in our terms, that disability and handicap would be utterly rejected as dimensions of disablement. But the weaker reading, coupled with a more clinical, health-based understanding of medicine, would not have that consequence.

The ferment over the foundations and essential nature of medicine has not yet altered the received view of what medicine is or what medicalization entails. As a result the main consequence of the medicalization of disablement is that a disease-centred methodology is imposed on social policy and attention is directed to the 'patient' and his or her special needs and away from the social environment.

The representational consequences of this are fairly obvious. Medicalizing disablement highlights impairments, thereby locating the 'problem' of disablement within the body of an individual. Disablement is a biomedical concern that can only be discussed or treated in biomedical terms, so that disablement is brought within the expertise of physicians. The experience of people with disabilities is thus interpreted as data that only biomedical experts can properly decipher.

Many advocates for people with disabilities have complained that this medicalized representation is one of the major obstacles they face in the achievement of full participation in society. They argue that being represented as a victim or as a patient with special needs is a form of handicapping. This is a powerful objection to the model, but before we can evaluate it fairly we need to consider how what is valuable and valid about the biomedical perspective has been employed in disablement programming.

The Political Uses of Biomedicine

There is obviously much of value in the biomedical perspective on disablement. Because of the complexity of disablement there is a persistent need for a workable characterization of the targeted population. This the biomedical approach can provide.

More specifically, at nearly every stage of policy development there is a need for statistical data about disablement – the need to count the population, to classify forms of disablement, to quantify degrees of incapacitation, and so on. This information has an impact on policy development, but the demand for it can only be met if there are reliable standards for measuring disablement, as well as a technology for putting these standards into practice and a background theory for interpreting the results. For the standards, technology, and theory the biomedical sciences are the obvious source.

The biomedical sciences also supply a theoretical premise without which disablement policy would flounder, namely, the assumption of biomedical grounding. This premise links the complex and internally conflicting discourse of disablement with physical phenomena. With it there is a dimension of disablement that is not a social construction, even if our understanding of it is contingent on social and cultural factors.

Although the strong interpretation of the assumption of biomedical grounding is part of an ideological package that ought to be seriously questioned, one must take great care in what it is one is rejecting. For nothing at all is gained by swinging over to the other extreme and denying that the biomedical dimension has any authority over what is and what is not a form of disablement.

There are many hidden dangers in the provocative claim that disablement itself is a social construction. Though a not uncommon rallying cry for those who adhere to the social-political model of disablement, it is very worrisome. For without some conceptual link to biomedical phenomena the overall discourse of disablement is vulnerable to political manipulation, not all of which could in any sense be viewed as beneficial to the plight of people with disabilities.

Suppose we were charged with the task of designing an employment equity program to benefit individuals who, because of their disabilities, have not found a place in a particular sector of the labour market. Given this objective, scepticism about which impairments are severe enough to qualify could fatally undermine the program. As we saw, every human being has impairments; but only certain of these are, in normal circumstances, biomedically severe enough to produce disabilities. If as policy analysts we have no firm standard for identifying, let alone assessing, impairments, then the eligibility requirements for disablement programming will be seriously compromised.[16]

Moreover, the conceptual grounding secured by the biomedical model also gives content to the goal of accommodation. To bring about accommodation we must have an idea of which needs or benefits are relevant and which are not. Biomedicine can identify a class of relevant needs with precision and, more important, can provide a clear measure of the degree to which they are satisfied. Though it is undoubtedly true that the medical needs of people with disabilities are not always central to their lives, it is helpful for policy analysts to have a determinative way of assessing them.

These virtues of the biomedical model account for its plausibility as a way of coming to terms with disablement. It is understandable that members of the health professions should cling to the view that medical accommodation is the primary goal of disablement policy, in that if a person with disabilities can be 'fixed' that will be the end of the matter.

Still, the popularity and influence of the biomedical model cannot be accounted for entirely in terms of its theoretical virtues. Although it is inconceivable that disablement policy could be indifferent to biomedical facts, the situation is often the reverse, with the model dominating or pre-empting policy decisions. Plainly, biomedicine has served political purposes as well as scientific ones in disablement policy.

Part of the historical explanation for the political use of biomedicine is suggested by Deborah Stone, who, in her 1984 book *The Disabled State*, has traced the role played by biomedicine, medical practitioners, and professional organizations in the development of disablement programs in the United States.[17] Stone has looked particularly at the two disability compensation programs administered by the federal Social Security Administration – the Social Security Disability Insurance (SSDI) program and the Supplemental Security Income (SSI) program – as well as the various state-run workers' compensation programs. Although her story is very much an American one, it has broader ramifications which have been supported by other historians of disablement.[18]

As an administrative category used to identify a group of people entitled to social aid, disablement was not always medicalized. In earlier eras people could receive forms of assistance from private or social sources on the basis of disabling conditions like blindness or lameness without any prior determination, official or otherwise, about their state of physical health. It was far more significant that they were in need, or else deserving because of the military service they had performed: we have evidence of pensions being awarded to soldiers injured in war as far back as classical Greek times.[19] That disablement is connected to biomedicine in contemporary society, Stone suggests, is merely a contingent artefact of history.

Stone set out to explore the political justification for non-merit-based distribution systems in market societies – which is to say, the rationale for the welfare state. From this perspective it is significant that disablement as a social category considerably antedates the blossoming of the biological sciences in the eighteenth and nineteenth centuries, since this suggests that the distributional category was medicalized for social and political, rather than scientific, reasons.

At first blush, it might not seem obvious why, from an administrative point of view, the biomedical language of impairment should have been relied on for eligibility requirements for various forms of social assistance, disability pensions, and workers' compensation programs. For whereas biomedicine is continuously refining and updating its causal explanations of impairments, administrative categories are by their nature rigid, dichotomous, and insensitive to individual differences. Moreover, biomedical classification represents – or so is the hope – biological fact, whereas administrative categories are wholly artificial products of political compromise.

More to the point, the administrative category appropriate to these social programs is not impairment at all, but disability. Even discounting linguistic variation, for as long as they have been in place both American and Canadian workers' compensation, social assistance, and other income security programs have been explicit that the social problem being addressed was a reduction in productive capacity, loss of wage-earning ability, employability, or some other *disability*-related phenomenon.

Despite all this, it is a universal North American practice in legislation governing these programs to define 'disability' as an impairment of a certain duration and severity. Ontario's Family Benefits Act is paradigmatic; there a 'disabled person' is defined as 'a person who has a major physical or mental impairment that is likely to continue for a prolonged period of time and who, as a result thereof, is severely limited in activities pertaining to normal living, as verified by objective medical findings accepted by the medical advisory board.'[20] Thus, although an individual is said to be entitled by virtue of a 'disability,' what is actually being compensated is an ADL (activities of daily living) disability occasioned by one or more medically determinable physical or mental impairments. The effect of this statutory language has been to create biomedical eligibility requirements, thereby medicalizing the administrative category of disablement. But the question that interests Stone is: why has this happened?

Her explanation is this. If one scrutinizes the history of disability-related programming the recurring theme is a concern about fraud and deception. While the two other ancient categories of social welfare policy, old age and childhood, were more or less automatically taken to represent authentic conditions of incapacity and genuine need, that assumption could not be made about disability since many disabling conditions could be feigned, or at least that was the perception.

And this perception has a long history. In what may be the first administrative definition of disability in the Code of Justinian, a distinction is drawn between the true or worthy poor and the 'sturdy beggars' who have been 'reduced to this state through idleness, and not by disease.'[21]

Later in the fourteenth century when the first 'poor law' was passed in England, a similar categorical distinction was drawn between unemployed vagrants who, despite appearances, were able-bodied and could be made to work and the genuinely disabled who could be allowed to beg. At bottom this distinction between the 'worthy' and the 'unworthy poor' is best explained, as Stone clearly demonstrates, in economic terms. In any event, the move to medicalize disablement followed upon the perceived social need for certainty in the assessment of genuine disabling conditions.

One significant social consequence of this process, more obvious in this century than earlier, was that health professionals, primarily physicians, found themselves in the role of guardians over the integrity of redistributive and compensatory disablement programming. Biomedical assessments of impairment were viewed, both in and out of the health professions, as politically – neutral and objective eligibility tests for entitlement to social assistance – one of the surest safeguards against fraudulent claims.

Thus, writing before the release of the *Marsh Report* in 1943 about the prospects for a national program of social security in Canada, Harry Cassidy, while wholeheartedly approving of Sir William Beveridge's plan for Britain, bluntly noted that the problem of administering disability benefits would not be easy, since 'certification of sickness by physicians to prevent malingering by claimants poses many awkward technical problems.'[22] And later, in 1948, when the United States Advisory Council on Social Security released its seminal report on disablement programming, it made it clear that a biomedically based legal definition of disability was crucial: 'The definition of "disability" used in a disability program will in large part determine the feasibility of administration and the costs of the program. The proposed definition is designed to establish a test of disability which will act as a safeguard against unjustified claims.'[23]

Since deception was thought to be a major problem, symptoms and other self-reports of disability were thought to be inherently suspect for administrative purposes. Thus, we find that legal definitions of disability were always framed in terms of 'reliable and objective medical findings,' or in the American idiom, 'medically determinable impairments ... verified by the use of clinical and laboratory techniques.'[24]

Although biomedical or impairment-based legal definitions of disability began to dominate the legislation – where one can find them still – for planning purposes government agencies relied on other techniques for determining the presence and extent of disability. In particular, statistical and epidemiological studies of disability – such as Statistics Canada's Health and Activity Limitation Survey (HALS) – operationalize and measure disability, not in 'objective' biomedical terms, but primarily as a matter of self-definition in disability terms. As a result these instruments ask questions intended to elicit self-perceptions of functional limitations in everyday and work contexts.

Still, as a rule, program administrators favour the 'pure' biomedical approach to definition as this leaves the impression that questions of eligibility are determined in a politically neutral and scientific fashion. For their part, individual physicians are reluctant to take on the onerous and often impressionistic task of determining when someone qualifies for disability benefits, although especially in the United States it has always been in the interests of the medical profession as a whole to occupy the powerful position of gatekeeper to multi-billion-dollar disablement programming.

According to Stone then, the gradual process of medicalizing disablement – the process whereby the biomedical model gained credibility and authority in matters of public policy – involved at least two ideological moves. The first brought about the legitimation of disablement as a ground for non-merit-based social redistribution. This was ensured by representing disablement in terms of incapacitating impairments, and people with disabilities as innocent victims of misfortune with legitimate needs. The second move concerned the accreditation and validation of disablement by means of a scientific – and so objective and politically neutral – discourse, namely, that provided by the biomedical sciences.

Implicitly too, medicalization determined how the needs of people with disabilities would be characterized: since disablement is a medical problem, the social response, in whatever form it takes, must realistically address these medical needs. Even the apparently modest expansion of legitimate needs to include vocational rehabilitation was fiercely resisted by the medical establishment until the biomedical model loosened its grip on the concept of *disablement*.[25]

Effects of the Model on Policy

Though the effects of the biomedical model suffuse disablement policy, they are not always noticeable. Sometimes one has to look behind the scenes – to, for example, presumptions about which ministries or departments should have jurisdiction over disablement issues – to appreciate how profound an influence the model has had and how it reflects the two ideological moves Stone and others have tracked.

To give concrete form to this influence we can turn to what Stone sees as the distinctive imprint of medicalization on programming: disability evaluation. In the role of gatekeeper to social benefits, the medical profession was called upon to develop ways of assessing and measuring disability, typically understood as a limitation of one's repertoire of work-related activities, that is, employability. The resulting technical solution to this administrative problem – now firmly in place – in effect collapses disability into impairment.

In most North American jurisdictions, and certainly throughout Canada, the biomedical instrument most commonly used to assess work disability for workers' compensation, disability benefits, and related programs is called a medical rating schedule. In its crudest form, this is nothing more than a list of obvious function-limiting impairments – missing fingers and limbs, partial or complete loss of hearing and eyesight, and so on – with each impairment assigned a numerical value, commonly a percentage, that is taken to represent the degree to which an individual *as a whole* is functionally impaired.

Given the demands of administrative simplicity and certainty, reliance on medical rating schedules is the most influential practical consequence of the medicalization of disablement. There are those, and Stone is among them, who think that this is a serious problem, since the effect of these schedules is to transform a potentially complex evaluation of work disability into a crude, falsely precise, assessment of impairment.

The ancestor of modern medical rating schedules seems to have been the anatomical chart used by commercial insurers and European mutual-aid societies to assess compensation for industrial accidents. Though certainly schematic and incomplete – since they listed only those impairments normally expected to result from industrial injuries – these charts were a sensible solution to a relatively straightforward problem of compensation, and it seemed reasonable to continue to use them when workers' compensation and other programs came on the scene.

Impairment schedules were immediately popular with program administrators and legislators because their rationale was straightforward and intuitive: if each function-limiting impairment can be characterized as a measurable degree of loss of normal functioning, and surely medical science has come far enough to do that, then that loss should be able to be represented as a percentage of a postulated state of anatomical and functional 'wholeness.' Since each impairment contributes to a discrete measurable loss, the sum of these percentages, it would seem, must represent the total level or degree of dysfunction of the individual. And this must be a measure of disablement.

Though no one, least of all physicians, thought that this attempt at quantification was particularly reliable, the process appeared far more dependable than other alternatives. A true socioeconomic assessment of work disability, for example, based on a complex, multidisciplinary judgment about how an impairment affects the individual's employment prospects, in light of a host of non-medical factors, struck legislators, policy analysts, and administrators alike to be a dangerously indeterminate standard. Better to leave the matter of certifying degree of work disability to the biomedical professionals. Even if their judgments are somewhat inaccurate and impressionistic, better that than to be politically contentious.

It was clear to all, though, that some of the schedules were much too crude to be useful. As a result, in many jurisdictions workers' compensation programs turned to two techniques for measuring impairments. One approach produced a fixed-sum award calculated on the basis of a 'scheduled injury' crudely associated with one or another of the rough categories of a 'meat chart' that listed, quite literally, missing parts. For 'unscheduled' injuries, an attempt was made to determine the actual degree to which the injury had decreased the claimant's wage-earning capacity, employability, or some other employment-centred understanding of disability. Plainly, this second approach required more sophisticated, or at least more subtle forms of disability evaluation and measurement, and it posed the administrative problems which legislators and policy-makers hoped the medical professionals would solve.

In her book, Stone clearly shows that in the United States the medical professionals, as represented by the well-organized and powerful American Medical Association, were at first not entirely comfortable with their role as guardians of the integrity of disability programming. The AMA realized that disability evaluation and certification would never constitute an especially lucrative medical sideline, and it might cause more trouble for the ordinary practitioner than it would be worth. At the same time they were anxious to ensure that the profession remained independent from the government and were fearful of the prospect of more and more physicians working directly for the government as disability evaluators.

General practitioners did not like the idea of being caught in the middle, mediating between the interests of the government and their patients. And many had had experience certifying health complaints for commercial insurance, veterans benefits, and civil service programs and were extremely sceptical of impairment-based, statutory definitions of work disability.

But by 1956 in the United States it was clear that the Social Security

Disability Insurance Program would be based on an impairment conception of 'work disability'; nothing else was politically possible. The AMA decided that the prospect of government control over the profession was the greater threat, so, beginning in 1958, its Committee on Medical Rating of Physical Impairments produced and published a series of guides for evaluating permanent impairment. These were designed to ground disability evaluation in scientifically respectable, quantitative biomedical terms.

Originally each guide was to provide a list of function-limiting impairments, understood as biomedically identifiable conditions within an individual's anatomical, physiological, or psychological make-up, that were purely 'health problems' and as such independent of the social environment. The separate guides were collected together into one volume in 1971. Thoroughly revised in the 1980s, the third and most recent edition appeared in 1988.[26]

As it happened, the AMA guides did not become the sole basis for disability evaluation as the committee had hoped. The American Social Security Administration produced its own 'Listing of Impairments' that contained more than 100 medical conditions.[27] And in other jurisdictions a variety of evaluating techniques and instruments were soon devised. None the less, as Ellen Smith Pryor has recently remarked, the AMA guides have come to play a dominant role in compensation programs throughout North America.[28] They have formed the basis for several of the schedules used by the Social Security Administration in the United States and are extensively used by physicians in many public and private compensation contexts, including tort damages; they have made inroads in Canada as well.

Setting the details aside and looking at the stated theory of the original AMA guides, one would be hard-pressed to find any indication of a conflation of the notions of impairment and disability. Quite the contrary, from the outset the expressed aim of the AMA guides was to ensure that biomedical phenomena were *not* confused with socioeconomic phenomena. The AMA committee was well aware of the need to make this distinction since one of its members was Dr Henry Kessler, who, as already remarked, was the author of the first widely used disability evaluation system that explicitly distinguished the medical and non-medical criteria involved in a determination of disability.[29]

In the most recent edition of the AMA guides the editor tries to explain where the boundaries of biomedical expertise lie by giving the example of a workers' compensation program that statutorily requires that each partial disability rating include an assessment of what percentage of the 'employable use' of an individual's functional capacities has been impaired. Patently, the editor informs us, such an assessment requires more than a biomedical determination of an individual's physical condition; we need also to know the nature of the job, the individual's experience and training, alternative employment prospects, and many other factors that are completely outside of the physician's sphere of expertise. There is therefore no formula for combining medical and non-medical factors, although if the statutory criteria are to be given effect, someone must be responsible for making an overall evaluation that brings these incommensurable factors together. None the less:

It is evident that the *Guides* do not offer a solution for this problem, nor is it the intention that it do so. Each administrative or legal system that uses permanent impairment as a basis for disability rating needs to define its own process for translating knowledge of a medical condition into an estimate of the degree to which the individual's capacity to meet personal, social, or occupational demands, or to meet statutory or regulatory requirements, is limited by the impairment. We encourage each system not to make a 'one-to-one' translation of impairment to disability, in essence creating a use of the *Guides* which is not intended.[30]

Despite its editorial disclaimers, one does not have to go far into the details of the *Guides* to notice that the judgment the evaluating physician is directed to make is not simply a judgment about impairments. In every case, the judgment is about disabilities. It is true that the commentary *says* that the job of the evaluating physician is to explain the health status of the claimant and the nature of his or her impairment to claims examiners, so that they, not the physician, can understand the impairment and relate it to 'industrial loss of use,' employability, or whatever the jurisdiction's standard is. But in every case it is the physician who is making, certifying, and legitimating the connection between impairment and disability. This fact is effectively disguised by the simple expedient of relabelling disability as 'impairment of the whole person.'

Indeed, some of the AMA guides' protocols calibrate degree of impairment in terms of an implicit ranking of handicaps. Neither the ranking nor the correlation is justified or explained, although the impression is given that they reflect a consensus among practitioners.

In the case of 'facial disfigurement,' for example, the guide notes that since the face plays an important role in an individual's physical, psychological, and emotional make-up, 'facial disfigurement can affect all these components and can result in social and vocational handicap.' Thus, 'unilateral total facial paralysis' counts as roughly twice the impairment of the 'loss or deformity of the outer ear' because the former is far more visible, and so socially prejudicial, than the latter.[31]

These problems aside, as medical rating instruments go the AMA guides are widely regarded to be superior, and for good reason. By comparison Ontario's *Permanent Disability Rating Schedule*, still in use in some cases, is extremely schematic and lacks important detail.[32] In effect, Ontario's schedule merely lists 'missing parts' and gross dysfunction and assigns them percentage values. Even the vastly improved 'Guidelines for the Evaluation of Permanent Impairment,' proposed in 1985 by the Medical Services Division of the Ontario Workers' Compensation Board, is far less comprehensive than the AMA guides. Thus, the recent move to adopt the AMA guides represents a considerable step forward.

Ontario's system of impairment rating is mandated by section 45 of the Workers' Compensation Act,[33] the relevant subsections of which read:

45(1) Where permanent disability results from the injury, the impairment of earning capacity of the worker shall be estimated from the nature and degree of the injury ...
45(3) The Board may compile a rating schedule of percentages of impairment of earning capacity for specified injuries or mutilations that may be used as a guide in determining the compensation payable in permanent disability cases.

Like any workers' compensation scheme, Ontario's requires that a compensable 'impairment of earning capacity' (that is, work disability) arise from a work-related or workplace accident. For this reason a distinction has to be drawn, however artificially, between disabilities that can be linked to the workplace and those that cannot. From the wording of section 45 it appears that the legislature intended that this be accomplished by using a rating schedule as a tool for assessing 'impairment of earning capacity' *directly in terms* of 'the nature and degree of the injury' (that is, the impairment).

There is a plausible rationale for proceeding in this way. Workers' compensation is a scheme for compensating workers for injuries sustained during the course of employment; it is not comprehensive disability insurance of the sort recommended by Ontario's Social Assistance Review Commission in its 1988 report, *Transitions*.[34] Thus, when the Workers' Compensation Board (WCB) assesses compensation in a particular instance it looks at the nature and degree of injury and ignores particular circumstances that may affect the actual impact of the injury on an individual's earning capacity. In this way the administration of the act can ensure that as far as possible every worker who suffers an identical injury will receive an identical permanent pension. The concert pianist who loses a finger should receive the same pension as a piano mover who has suffered the same injury.

This rationale argues for a consistent application of some sort of assessment instrument to all individuals, regardless of their particular circumstances (although, as we shall see, it also undermines the claim that these schemes are genuinely governed by the normative principle of compensatory justice). But consistency aside, there is also the question of *validity*. What is the basis for the percentages found in a rating schedule? Why, for example, is hip disarticulation 'worth' 65 per cent, whereas immobility of the knee only rates 25 per cent? What do these numbers represent and what is the scientific basis for them?

These worries have been addressed, though only indirectly and inadequately, in Decision No. 915 of the Workers' Compensation Appeals Tribunal, decided in May 1987. The tribunal was asked to consider whether Ontario's rating schedule complies with the requirements of section 45(3) of the act.[35] The tribunal had to resolve an apparent conflict between the stated purpose of the rating schedule and how it was understood by physicians in the Medical Services Branch of the WCB, the physicians who perform all of the disability assessments in the province. In its decision, the tribunal noted that whereas the *Claims Services Division Manual* describes the purpose of the schedule as showing in percentage terms 'the approximate impairment of earnings capacity in an average unskilled worker,' the head of the WCB's staff of medical examiners had testified that the schedule, as far as they were concerned, provided a 'clinical rating' indicating the impact of the injury on activities of daily living, with no consideration given to any occupational implications.

The tribunal held that 'there is no scientific basis' for the selection of the percentage values found in the schedule. No scientific attempt has ever been made in Ontario or elsewhere to develop empirical data on the actual effect of particular injuries on the earning capacities of the average unskilled worker. And, in the tribunal's opinion, the scope and complexity of this research makes it unlikely that any such project could ever be undertaken. Thus, the schedule is not, and likely will never become, a biomedically valid instrument.

What, then, do the percentage values in the rating schedule represent? The tribunal stated that these values, though in no sense scientific facts, have become rough conventional guides: 'They reflect serious efforts by medical practitioners, intimately familiar with the nature of various disabilities and their effects on patients, to conceptualize in percentage terms the relative seriousness of various disabilities compared one against the other ... [Although] originally surrogates for a reality perceived to be beyond reach of scientific analysis, through long usage they have in effect come to be accepted as that reality.'

But then, what of the claim that, in practice, WCB physicians who are charged with the task of assessing 'impairment of earning capacity' rely on the rating schedule as a guide for a clinical judgment of disability? To this the tribunal responded that this use of the schedule is consistent with its true status as a source of, as they put it, 'conventional benchmarks' for approximating lifelong work disability. There is a fundamental difference, in short, between designing a rating schedule and applying it. As a matter of design, the schedule is not a scientific tool at all but a set of ad hoc conventional benchmarks that roughly correlate injury with work disability. But, when the WCB physician applies the schedule, he or she is not assessing disability in some sort of absolute and biomedically sound manner: on the question of 'impairment of earning capacity' the physician is not an examiner at all but an estimator.

By way of a conclusion, the tribunal argued that there is no conflict between Ontario's WCB policy and practice because, whether they are aware of it or not, medical examiners are in fact – given that the rating schedule is merely a conventional, non-scientific guide in any event – making plausible estimates of 'impairment of earning capacity' as required by the act. The rating schedule itself satisfies the requirements of the act because it a bona fide attempt to standardize the impact of injuries on the earning capacity of average unskilled workers. Though it is not a scientifically valid instrument, the tribunal argued, 'under all the circumstances and having regard to the possible alternatives, it cannot be said to be insubstantial or inherently unreasonable.'

In essence then, the tribunal in Decision 915 suggested that the policy objectives of workers' compensation are such that the primary concern must be consistency, not validity. As long as we can assure the good faith of designers of rating schedules, and as long as these are reasonable, there is nothing to worry about.

But this is hardly an adequate result. Why should physicians be involved at all? The answer seems to be that although medical rating schedules are not scientifically valid, this should not be a concern because WCB physicians are, as a matter of fact, basing their decisions on biomedically sound assessments. Having defused the scientific pretensions of the rating schedule, in other words, the tribunal then invokes medicalization at a different stage in the assessment process to legitimate it. Implicit in this line of reasoning – which one sees in other areas of disablement policy as well – is the principal distorting effect of the biomedical model, namely, that disablement falls wholly within the domain of the biomedical sciences. We need now to turn to this aspect of the model.

Why the Model Is Distortive and Incomplete

There is no doubt that the initial plausibility of the biomedical model seduces us into believing that a major part of what is 'wrong' with people with disabilities is that they have ongoing medical troubles that require them to make extensive use of medical resources and services. This is one of the assumptions that exerts a powerful influence on disablement policy. Since it is certainly true in some cases that the medical needs of people with disabilities loom large, it seems both commonsensical and harmless to assume that disablement, jurisdiction- ally so to speak, is a concern of medical institutions.

Yet, I have already remarked that some have insisted that this is not a harmless assumption and that it is responsible for many forms of handicapping attitudes and practices that regularly hinder the legitimate goals of people with disabilities. The gist of this critique is that the model forces people with disabilities into a social role that is inappropriate and stigmatizing.[36]

This is the so-called sick role, a role which in Talcott Parsons's classical formulation[37] is based on socially visible, physical differences that would usually constitute a form of social deviance, but that instead create a legitimating role exempting people from blame and normal role obligations. This exemption, however, is conditional: to benefit from the role the sick individual must be a 'good patient' and actively seek to recover. The sick role is a temporary exemption, a form of social indulgence accorded to people who, through no fault of their own, are innocent victims of disease processes or trauma.

The sick role, in other words, is premised on reversibility. In the paradigm case, the patient suffers from an acute disease condition or trauma and is expected, with suitable medical treatment, to recover. With a tolerance born of the value neutrality of medical explanations of 'deviance,' those occupying the temporary role of the sick are relieved of responsibility, blame, and stigma.

But the person with a disability may be suffering from a condition that is neither acute nor curable. Because of this the person is permanently sick, a fact which creates tension in the social role. The temporary exemption from blame will, in time, either be lifted – in which case the individual is held responsible for not trying hard enough to recover – or be transformed into a permanent exemption from all normal role obligations. In the first case, non-recovery may be attributed to lack of motivation or some other personality trait, an inference reminiscent of the phenomenon of blaming the victim.'[38] And in either case the precondition of the role – that the patient cooperate with the source of help – becomes, for those who are permanently sick, a denial of autonomy. If one does not recover one is like a child who never grows up or an apprentice who never learns the trade. People with disabilities face a stigma of double incompetence: they are not only sick, they cannot even fulfil the minimal obligations of the good patient.

Moreover, this incompetence is blameworthy. In our highly competitive culture sickness is more than a condition of physical difference. It is also a symbol of vulnerability, fallibility, and weakness – conditions of dependency that, we believe, people ought to strive to avoid.[39] Medicine is seen as our principal ally in this struggle. But, given our conviction that science and technology can always meet the challenge posed by a threat to human life and health, people with disabilities – especially those who are chronically ill or dying – come to represent the failure of biomedicine's mastery over the human body.

As the mythological images of medicine are both ennobling and professionally self-serving, failures must be explained away, and their embodiments hidden. One all too familiar way of doing both of these things is to attribute the failure to the victim and to blame, fear, and eventually physically isolate the victim. As one woman with disabilities writes: 'We are the failures of modern medicine ... 'we testify against the omnipotence of medical science and represent a frightening truth. We are feared and hated and viewed as hopeless patients.[40]

We should also be wary of the effects on people with disabilities of the inflation in the importance of health as an end in itself. Like the compulsive pursuit of cosmetic beauty, this can only devalue the lives of those who will never be completely healthy, whole, or vigorous.

In general, then, the autonomy of people with disabilities is prejudiced by the sick role. The role demands that the individual surrender to professional direction in order to satisfy the condition of being a good patient, and devote his or her energies to the (possibly futile) goal of cure or recovery. Though much has been written about the overbearing 'Aesculepian authority' and paternalism of the medical professions,[41] it is not always appreciated that the effects of these professional attitudes are more deeply felt by people who, but for the cooperation of physicians, might be denied eligibility to disability benefits. It was doubtless for this reason that the radical disablement advocacy group, the independent living movement, insisted that, wherever possible, self-care should replace forced reliance upon the medical health system.[42]

Why must we assume that people with disabilities are 'sick' in any sense? Although they may have permanent impairments, and can profit from rehabilitation, assistive aids, and other accommodations, many people with disabilities make no more use of medical services than anyone else. An amputee on crutches or a person who is blind or hearing-impaired may have no additional health problem or special medical need whatsoever. Even for those who do require extensive assistance in everyday activities, it is becoming increasingly obvious from the point of view of cost alone that long-term care should be provided by attendant care outside of medical institutions.

There is another, somewhat more abstract way of putting all of these objections to the biomedical model. And that is that disablement is not a pathology explicable by the etiologically focused medical model of disease. Even when the disabling impairment *is* a disease condition, there are other important dimensions of disablement that should not be ignored. The lives of people with disabilities are not adequately captured in biomedical terms.

This last point was dramatically emphasized in a submission before the Royal Commission on New Reproductive Technologies by Pat Israel of Disabled Women's Network, Canada. Ms Israel expressed the concern about the growing use of prenatal screening techniques such as amniocentesis to identify possible genetic problems that could lead to a child with disabilities. She remarked that 'Doctors constantly use very negative terminology to describe a fetus with a disability ... words such as defective, abnormal and anomaly ... I've heard of one doctor telling a pregnant woman "you have a monster inside of you."'[43] She went on to explain that impairment-language distorts the decision whether to terminate a pregnancy because it ignores what the life of a person with such a medical condition is like.

A different kind of objection to the biomedical model has been suggested by, among others, the American political scientist Harlan Hahn.[44] Hahn argues that viewing disablement as 'an organ defect or deficiency that is located exclusively within the individual'[45] is directly responsible for the present unsatisfactory state of disablement policy. As Hahn sees it, disablement policy can be primarily characterized as an expression of sympathy and concern coupled with a persistent inactivity and failure of political will. But this is precisely what we should expect when the biomedical model dominates, since the model reinforces our culture's inability to imagine the need to change the physical and social environment in which people with disabilities live. The biomedical model, in other words, is itself responsible for the fact that changing the individual is widely regarded as the exclusive solution to the problem of handicapping.[46]

The theoretical source of these policy consequences, Hahn goes on, is just the methodological presumptions of the medical model of disease: 'medical etiology,' he argues 'treats disabilities as separate diagnostic categories rather than focusing on the universal problems of disabled people and ... stresses the causal relationship between the origins and the outcomes of various types of disabilities, even though there often is not a close correspondence between the two phenomena.'[47] Thus, the etiological focus of biomedicine turns our attention away from the social dimension of disablement and links diagnostic categories directly to programs for improving the individual's functional capacities. And since existing data on disablement rely on biomedical methodology, the connection between impairments and handicaps is ignored or obscured.

The biomedical preoccupation with etiological classification does more than distort the social character of disablement, according to Hahn. The etiological focus is also directly contrary to the political interests of people with disabilities, since it has 'fragmented the disability community by stressing the functional traits that divided them rather than the external obstacles that they faced as a common problem.' Groups representing the rights of people with disabilities are invariably organized around diagnostic categories and must compete among themselves for social attention. As a result, few attempts are made 'to form alliances or coalitions that might facilitate the emergence of a broad social and political movement of citizens with various types of disabilities.'[48]

The thrust of this and the earlier critique is that the biomedical model, because of the representations of disablement and people with disabilities it creates, fosters handicap situations – that is, the model itself is a handicap-creating obstacle. Hahn in particular argues that the model, by depoliticizing disablement, is a second-order or *metahandicap* in that it interferes with attempts to eliminate the social disadvantages associated with impairments. The biomedical model deludes us by directing our attention away from the real problem of handicapping.

Since these criticisms deal primarily with the social consequences of representations, general perceptions, and ways of understanding disablement, they often seem to be impressionistic and difficult to substantiate. From the evidence of the experience of people with disabilities, though, these objections to medicalization ring true, and this is a very important piece of the data that must not be ignored.

It is also important to recognize that these objections are directed to the biomedical model of disablement, not, more generally, to biomedicine. That is, the model is a metahandicap because it implies that the biomedical dimension of disablement is all there is to disablement.

This critique of the model offers us a new perspective on medical rating schedules. For in these we can discern the transformation of a complex, multivariable, and social dimension of disablement – disability – into the more tractable biomedical dimension of impairment.

In her discussion of the AMA guides mentioned in the last section, Deborah Stone argues that it is vital for policy-makers and legislators to question seriously the administrative reliance on any sort of biomedically founded rating schedule.[49] She argues that the assessment procedure in the *Guides* is 'full of errors of reification and false precision.' In particular, the procedure 'assumes a direct correspondence between physiological processes and functional abilities. It conceives of functional ability as a single but composite entity that can be measured on an integer scale. Finally, it assumes an equivalence between different anatomical or physiological systems, so that, for example, a loss of either 20 percent of normal respiratory capacity or 20 percent of normal musculoskeletal function yields a 20 percent impairment [of the whole person].'

At bottom Stone's complaint – and it is a general one applicable to any medical rating schedule – is that the quantitative machinery of the *Guides* is inherently deceptive in that it puts a scientific gloss on a judgment that is based on inferences from clinical data about 'physiological processes' to functional abilities. Or, as she put this at another point,[50] although it is indisputable that clinical tests and protocols measure *something*, it is not an objective, scientific fact that they measure 'whole-person impairment' or inability to work. Even if we assume that clinical testing and measurement can be free from error – which she also doubts – still 'someone has to *decide* what level of any measurement is indicative of inability to function and how the information from different tests ought to be combined.' In other words, behind all the quantitative machinery, the charts, tables, and graphs, one will inevitably find 'a process of consensus that [is] no more objective than the informal molding of a group opinion.'

Why should we think this troubling? Suppose that Stone is right and the entire inferential network of the *Guides* is built upon nothing more solid than a consensus among physicians. Does this mean that the AMA guides are unreliable, biased, arbitrary? Would it be better to make the process more democratic and allow everyone to *vote* on the relationship between impairment and 'whole person' disability?[51] Or, as the Ontario's WCB Appeals Tribunal argued, if it is unlikely that we will ever have the empirical basis for a scientifically valid schedule, why not be content with the considered judgments of biomedical experts? Stone's response is that these judgments are made by physicians and disguised as 'purely' scientific. This is, she suggests, deception on a grand scale.

This last point has been taken up and expanded by Ellen Smith Pryor in her wide-ranging discussion of legal and administrative determination of compensable loss.[52] Like Stone, Pryor concludes that medical rating schedules are inherently deceptive tools for assessing work disability, since they do not, and could not, provide legislators, administrators, and the legal community with what they purport to offer. She departs from Stone only in the strength of her conviction that any sort of biomedical assessment tool is flawed insofar as it is held out as providing 'objective, accurate, fair, and reproducible evaluations of individuals with medical impairments.' She concludes that 'policy-makers should appreciate that the search for an "objective," "accurate," or purely "medical" system is and always will be fruitless. And they must resist the seductive but false hope that use of a scientifically or medically authored ratings system can bypass the need to make the hard choices necessary for any loss assessment system.'[53]

At the level of detailed analysis, Pryor has no difficulty making her case that there are countless normative judgments, great and small, implicit in the protocols and procedures of the AMA guides. Nor does she have any trouble showing that many of these judgments are anything but uncontroversial. She notes, for example, the extraordinary degree of gender-bias implicit in the assessment standards: lack of sensation in the penis is assessed as a 5 to 10 per cent whole-person impairment whereas lack of sensation in the vulva or vagina constitutes no impairment at all, since sexual intercourse is 'possible.' And from the many illustrative case studies we learn that housecleaning of various sorts constitutes ordinary daily activities for women, whereas golf, tennis, hiking, and other sports are ordinary activities for men.

Pryor also correctly notes that the AMA guides rarely give any explanation of how the normative judgments required to warrant 'whole-person' calculations have been arrived at. And because the underlying criteria for these judgments are nowhere set out, let alone justified, she concludes that it is not possible to make any judgment about the *Guides'* validity or reproducibility (consistency of results among different evaluators). She admits that that is less true for inferences based on impairment ratings that can be, and usually are, based entirely on the highly reproducible results of recognized instruments like the goniometer or inclinometer. But, if anything, these assessments are the exception rather than the rule in the AMA guides.

After making these telling points though, Pryor unfortunately goes on to undermine her otherwise very helpful critique of the AMA guides, and by implication the biomedical model, by opting for the extreme position that true disability evaluation is impossible because there are no objective and uncontroversial normative criteria to which appeal can be made, by anyone. As she explains it, any attempt to measure functional loss must specify the functions it is measuring and, whether these are 'organ-level' functions or 'whole-person' activities, decisions have to be made about which function to assess and what standards of normality to use. But, 'the need for these decisions dooms the *Guides* claims that its impairment evaluation scheme is objective and purely medical.'[54] This is because no consensus exists with respect to which human activities are important or 'everyday.' In addition, she insists that 'disagreement over the relevant norms is possible even for organ-level impairments.'[55]

But if 'objectivity' about normative questions is impossible, surely that would undermine Pryor's positive thesis that policy-makers should set aside medical assessment schedules and not shirk their duty to 'make the hard choices necessary for any loss assessment system.' If normative judgment-making about functional loss is immune to objective determination, why should we trust *anyone* to make these decisions?

Be this as it may, it is clear why the AMA guides, and the administrative context in which such instruments are relied upon, have provoked Stone, Pryor, and others to insist that they distort disablement policy. These instruments transform an extremely complex, multifactorial, and holistic judgment about the relationship between an individual and his or her environment into a simplistic, (pseudo-)quantitative assessment of something else entirely. This is disturbing for two reasons.

First, medical evaluations of disablement are inherently ill-informed and stereotypical. It is intrinsic to the enterprise of medical rating that 'whole-person' assessments are produced primarily, and often exclusively, on the basis of findings about impairments. Yet, even when they are thoroughly grounded in information about impairments, such evaluations are not properly grounded in relevant information about the individual's environment. The AMA guides are exceptional in their attempt to, somewhat surreptitiously, introduce ADL judgments and individualized, environmental information into the process. But this input is minimal and inadequate, and in any event is overshadowed by clinical findings about impairments.

Moreover, in lieu of actual data about the individual's environment, medical rating instruments make implicit reference to stereotypical assumptions about 'normal' activities and performance levels. For example, as Pryor notes, 'normal sexual function and participating in usual sexual activity' is listed as an activity of daily living, but since no specification of 'normal' and 'usual' is provided that vacuum will almost certainly be filled with stereotypical sexual patterns and social and cultural prejudices. More important though, throughout the *Guides* reference is made to more specific 'ordinary' activities which, without background information, merely reinforce stereotypical assumptions about what individuals ought or ought not to be able to do.

Like all stereotypes, these assumptions seem perfectly commonsensical and commonplace, precisely because they reinforce the ill-informed beliefs about people and their proper roles that suffuse our culture – hence the glaring gender-bias that Pryor draws attention to. Furthermore, like all stereotypes, the assumptions found in the AMA guides tend to sustain the discrimination in attitude and behaviour that is characteristic of handicapping.

The second reason why the medicalization of disablement manifested by the AMA guides adversely affects policy is that, for administrative and political reasons of the sort Stone has described, this approach to disability evaluation is self-legitimating and pre-emptive. The prestige and social authority of the institutions of biomedicine – hard-won and coveted by generations of physicians and manipulated by policy-makers and administrators for their own purposes – has legitimated this approach to disability assessment. Having automatically acquired the mantle of legitimacy, the process of medical determination of disability will tend to pre-empt other bases for assessing the range and extent of disability and handicap.

For these two reasons the administrative reliance on medical rating instruments engenders distortions in disablement policy. Without any factual basis for an assessment of how an impairment actually interferes with individuals in their social environments, the evaluating physician will of necessity be drawn back, either to the security of 'hard' data about impairments, or to quick, stereotypical judgments about the predictable consequences of impairments on standardized activities of daily living. Although the socially interactive nature of disabilities and handicaps is fully acknowledged in the expressed theory of the AMA guides, it is ignored in practice. Since the end result of the application of this assessment tool is a judgment about the 'whole person,' the state of disablement becomes firmly rooted in the individual. Disclaimers notwithstanding, in other words, the point of the AMA guides is to assess quantitatively the extent to which a person, from the biomedical perspective alone, is a *disabled person*.

The Biomedical Model and Disablement Theory

Because of its emphasis on the impairment dimension of disablement, the biomedical model leads one almost inevitably to underestimate, or simply ignore, the social features of disablement. Purely as a conceptual matter, that is, the model makes little room for the handicap dimension of disablement and tends, even in the face of determined efforts to prevent this, to seek ways of operationalizing disability so as to make it conceptually indistinguishable from impairment.

Since the model does not represent the social environment as being part of the 'problem' of disablement, it both fosters and authorizes the assumption that obstacles are given and cannot, or need not, be altered in order to accommodate people with disabilities. Since disablement is a biomedical problem inherent in the individual patient, and calling for the expertise of the biomedical scientist, the only consistent social strategy for disablement policy is that of meeting the 'special' and individualized medical needs of the 'patient.'

Since impairment is indeed a dimension of disablement, and people with disabilities usually do have impairments that create a range of medical needs, and finally, since biomedicine is the appropriate expertise to call upon to identify and respond to these needs, the biomedical model is highly plausible. Because it is, the model generates an equally plausible interpretation of the fundamental social goals of disablement policy. The theoretical strengths of the model – the firmly grounded standards of deviance and normality it offers and the powerful explanatory theory of impairments it employs – make it inevitable that the goal of accommodation will be interpreted medically, and so will focus on ways in which the individual can be changed. The model's capacity to identify, and quantify, the needs of people with disabilities ensures that accommodation will assume a position of priority in matters of policy. And this has three consequences for disablement policy analysis.

First, if accommodation is the primary social goal, and if it is given a biomedical gloss, then disablement policy must highlight the ways in which people with disabilities are *different* from others. That is, while the goals of respect and participation have a distinctly egalitarian and integrative cast to them, accommodation, on almost any reading, is a goal that stresses needs and differences. When understood biomedically the needs that are to be accommodated are precisely the needs that set people with disabilities apart from others.[56]

Second, if accommodation is prioritized, in normal circumstances where not all that could ideally be done through social policy will be done, the goals of respect and participation will be sacrificed when doing so helps to secure accommodation. In policy terms this means that, roughly speaking, egalitarian and integrative objectives will rank below medical needs-based objectives.

Taken together, these consequences have the effect of requiring people with disabilities who wish to influence policy to represent themselves in terms of their differences, their needs, and their deficiencies. If the 'problem' of disablement is that created by impairment alone, then it is the impairment, and the special medical needs it creates, that must animate and motivate disablement policy. Respect and participation cannot be, on this view, directly relevant to the true 'problem' of disablement.

Finally, then, the prioritization of the medically interpreted goal of acommodation entails a needs-based approach to disablement policy. But not just any needs-based approach. The needs here are those which one philosopher has termed 'course-of-life needs,' that is, needs which if not met would create a persistent and serious deficiency in one's life, needs anyone (whatever his or her preferences) would want met.[57]

Now the needs recognized by the biomedical model would normally be taken to be a subset of all basic needs since, presumably, not all vital needs call upon medical resources. Inasmuch as the model entails a conceptual reduction of disablement to impairment, so too it entails a reduction of 'disablement needs' to medically recognizable needs.

But restricting the scope of the 'special needs' of people with disabilities in this way creates several anomalies when applied to the actual conditions under which people with disabilities live. In particular, this interpretation of accommodation seriously limits the potential scope of legitimate disablement policy. Even if the level of need is great, so that no one could seriously doubt that someone with an impairment had unmet basic needs, pointing this out does not itself answer the question of how this claim compares with the countless other claims that are made on society's resources. It is this difficult macroallocative issue that is often the crucial one for disablement policy, since the needs of people with disabilities compete with powerful entitlements issuing from other policy sectors. Yet there is nothing in the biomedical model that could provide policy analysts with the tools for addressing this issue.

None the less, by providing us with a precise characterization of (at least some of) the needs of people with disabilities, and thus an equally precise description of the resources and services required to meet these needs, the biomedical model creates a normative basis for disablement theory. The model gives us a clear picture of the ways in which a group of citizens would be unambiguously benefited by social programming and allocation of resources and thus a well-grounded reason for thinking that it would be a good thing if social policy were so arranged.

Historically, the most significant contribution of the practice of medicine to the *normative* component of disablement theory was its clinical insistence upon etiological neutrality. Although etiology is a central element of the scientific explanation of impairments and thus the basis for determining medical needs, still, from a clinical point of view, it is not particularly relevant *how* a patient developed the impairment. A patient is a patient, whether the impairments are self-caused or the result of an accident, an epidemic, or the intentional actions of others. The principal effect of this clinical focus on needs, as opposed to responsibilities, is to undermine a belief about impairment that reaches far into the past, the belief that impairments, and the suffering they cause, are deserved punishments for prior sins.

This shift obviously recentred the normative basis of disablement theory. The person with disabilities is, on the biomedical model, in need, and it is good and proper that this need be met. Pain, suffering, and incapacitation are bad things that should be avoided if possible; and those who help to make this happen are providing an important and valuable service.

These very basic normative intuitions – so obvious, so invisible, that we can easily fall into the trap of thinking that medicine is 'value neutral' – possess a logic that more or less dictates the character of the normative basis of disablement theory.

What intuitions entail is that it is essential that the entitlements associated with disablement are positive in nature, entitlements that aim to satisfy real medical needs. Medical care, the paradigm vehicle for the satisfaction of these needs – and so the manifestation of accommodation on this model – is aimed at the active provision of care and cure, when this is possible, or palliation when not. What we have here, then, is a model of entitlement that mirrors the incipient model of care in clinical medicine. On its own, therefore, the biomedical model tends to suggest a charity or needs-based normative basis for disablement theory.

The biomedical perspective, and the model of disablement it creates, focus our attention on impairments. Since impairment is a genuine and intrinsic dimension of disablement, the biomedical approach provides a perfectly valid perspective on disablement. This is why the biomedical model strikes us as intuitively obvious, at least at first glance. Closer inspection indicates, though, that the model produces a distortion of disablement that has had its effects on the nuts and bolts of disablement policy. The biomedical model, in a word, has contributed to the general impasse in disablement policy.

4 The Economic Model of Disablement

Characteristics of the Model

The economic model of disablement, conceptually grounded in the disability dimension of disablement, is the dominant model for disablement policy throughout the world. It might be more accurate to call this the 'policy model' of disablement. Still, I label this model 'economic' because, despite its complex history, it has retained an ideological commitment to the priority of economic analysis in the social response to disablement. I show more precisely below how economic rationality has left its imprint on specific disablement programs. First, though we need to explore the ways in which the ideological commitments of the model have been responsible for both its many virtues and its many drawbacks.

The economic model is the product of this century, and its emergence as the dominant perspective on disablement policy parallels, not coincidentally, the emergence in Europe and North America of what is usually called the welfare state. The history of the evolution of this model is far too complex to set out here; it has, however, been thoroughly researched by social historians and we can profit from their work.

At the outset it should be remarked that the history of the model is controversial, since it is not clear which of the easily identifiable ideological, social, institutional, and professional components of the model were the causal antecedents and which the consequences. There is even some controversy about the original impetus for the social recognition of disablement as a socioeconomic problem.

One plausible account of the rise of the economic model is suggested by Deborah Stone,[1] who argues that modern liberal societies have two distributive mechanisms, one based on work and the other on need. The coexistence of these systems poses a problem for social policy, since needs can only be satisfied if there is a surplus to redistribute and people may be unwilling to produce this surplus, although perfectly willing to rely on the benefits of the need system when they are themselves in need. This is an instance of the 'free-rider' problem well known to political theorists.[2] What is required to deal with this issue, Stone argues, is an administrative categorization of those groups in society who deserve the benefits of the need system – the truly needy, one might say. Disability is such a category. Disability, then, is a socially constructed category made necessary by inescapable features of collective action and founded upon an individual's incapacity to participate as a worker in the distribution mechanism founded on merit.[3]

As already mentioned, injured veterans unable to participate in society's work-based distribution system have long been beneficiaries of the category. That the needs of veterans were 'deserving' could not be denied, and so we see disablement programming flourish after wars.[4] The early versions of social insurance programming in Bismark's Germany in the 1880s explicitly tied the 'invalidity' of veterans to earning capacity. And in the United States in particular, disability as a category for entitlement to both private and public insurance schemes at the turn of this century was assessed in terms of the ability of the applicant to pursue 'gainful occupation.' American social security legislation, when it came on the scene in the 1930s and 1940s, retained this vocational conception of disability.

Stone argues, and other researchers have documented, that the confusions and anomalies found in disablement policy in the United States and elsewhere are in part the result of the difficulty of reconciling a vocational and economic conception of disability with a biomedical conception of impairment. As we have seen, the biomedical understanding of disablement was favoured by policy analysts and administrators in order to protect programming against the threat of fraud and malingering. Stone analyses the tension between economic and biomedical conceptions as nothing more than the inevitable result of attempting a political reconciliation of the conceptually irreconcilable.

Yet Stone tends to underestimate the significance of what amounted to a conceptual revolution with the emergence of the economic model. For in various contexts, theoretical and practical, the model developed because of a radically altered understanding of disablement itself. The model underscores the need to understand disablement as something other than a medical problem. In a word, the recognition of disability as a distinct dimension of disablement, not reducible to impairment, was a scientific and intellectual achievement of considerable significance. The model, in a very real sense, created the social problem of disablement.

The important distinction between a biomedical condition of functional impairment and limitations an individual may experience in performing normally expected activities (what we might call his or her capability limitations) was hinted at by the English physician R. Fortescue Fox in his discussion of remedies for disabled veterans after World War I.[5] To recall, the distinction was first clearly set out by Henry Kessler in 1935,[6] and in the 1960s Saad Z. Nagi popularized this and other important conceptual distinctions.[7] In light of this and other research often done by sociologists,[8] Wood and Badley put together the ICIDH.

The impetus for all this work was the need for a realistic characterization of disablement as a social problem, amenable to social solutions. The reasoning of pioneers such as Lawrence D. Haber of the United States Social Security Administration[9] was that disablement is primarily a matter of the behavioural consequences of impairments. These consequences are a function not just of biomedical indicators of disease but of sociological indicators of the individual with the impairments. Impairments, Haber argued, do not necessarily represent limitations in required or reasonably desired activities; rather, capability limitation is an integrative phenomenon. To understand it we need to know both the nature of the pathological condition or functional abnormality and the behavioural consequences within a social context.

Thus, the social problems brought about by returning veterans and the underclass of unemployed people with disabilities were seen as problems arising from the impact of impairments on the social environment. Researchers came to the conclusion that purely biomedical determinants of impairment are not predictive for policy purposes. To get a handle on the nature and extent of the social problems posed by disablement, policy advisers realized that they needed basic demographic information about the population needing assistance, as well as information about employment conditions, prospects in different parts of the country, cost and availability of retraining programs, availability and cost of accommodation, and the like.

Taken together, the epidemiological requirements for a category of disability and the policy-analytic requirements for realistic social planning made it essential that biomedically describable functional limitations be distinguished from capability limitations. No one proposed abandoning the biomedical perspective entirely, for that information was stable, objective, and useful. The idea was to supplement it, or rather to situate it within a concrete social setting. What was required was an assessment of the individual's capabilities with respect to those activities that are required of a member of a specified sector of the labour market.

The scholars who tried to provide this information immediately saw that the relationship between the two dimensions of disablement was extremely complex – if for no other reason than that levels of disability are manifestly a function of the individual's personal characteristics (for example, age, education, experience) as well as general labour-market conditions.[10] Even the difference between a 'temporary' and a 'permanent' disability, perhaps the most important administrative distinction of all, depends on considerations that go far beyond medical prognosis.

More or less contemporaneously with the realization that the social problem of disablement needed to be more precisely identified was the emergence of vocational rehabilitation as a distinct, and respectable, adjunct to medicine. As it seems in retrospect, the growth in interest in the restoration of capability as an appropriate social response to disablement parallels, at the level of professional institutions, the recentring of disablement from impairment to disability. As rehabilitation therapists argued – in part to legitimate their special expertise – their task was to respond to the *true needs* of people with disabilities,[11] needs that went far beyond the limited scope of biomedicine.

In 1947 the American Medical Association, after much lobbying, was moved to approve 'physical medicine and rehabilitation' as a medical speciality. Led by energetic proponents like Henry Kessler and Howard Rusk, this 'third phase of medicine' was identified, somewhat grandly, with the aim of restoring the individual to 'maximum physical, emotional, mental, social, vocational and economic usefulness.'[12] The legitimation of the 'physiatrists' had a profound effect on the character of disablement programming for all people with disabilities, not merely veterans. Gradually, the focus of this programming, and the legislation governing it in North America, incorporated the aims, the aspirations, and the optimism of vocational rehabilitation. Though originally an adjunct of clinical medicine, physical rehabilitation slowly transformed itself into a broad and multidisciplinary approach to disablement. Two basic, and very intimately connected structural changes characterized this important evolution.

First, it was perhaps inevitable that those who envisaged their profession in terms of client-oriented restoration of *actual* capacity would find the medical model of disease to be irrelevant to the kinds of therapies they offered. The therapist attended to the incapacitating consequences of chronic impairments, not the impairments themselves (which, if they involved still-active pathologies were the proper sphere of medical treatment). If the aim of rehabilitation was to increase an individual's repertoire of capabilities by expanding the range of abilities needed for adequate functioning in the individual's specific situation, then the therapist would do well to expand the model of care far beyond the medical. Soon the widening ideological gap between models of care was manifested by a proliferation of free-standing rehabilitation clinics.

Over the years rehabilitation literature has come to express this transformation as a debate between the 'clinical' approach to rehabilitation and the, variously described, 'human,' 'humane,' 'social-scientific,' or 'ecological' approach.[13] What is emphasized, at least by those who wish to distance themselves from medical professionals, is that the rehabilitative approach must seek to respond to the whole or social person in an integrative fashion. Rehabilitation is both restorative and educative, a service made available to 'clients' (rather than 'patients') on a more contractual (rather than paternalistic) footing. The services provided go beyond the narrowly therapeutic to include mental and physical assessment, life skills and prevocational training, counselling and job placement services, as well as a wide range of habilitation services to foster independent living.

Out of this ideological controversy has come a transformation of the superstructure of rehabilitation science. Recent texts have adopted management models of service provision, in terms of which optimal care flows, not from a single rehabilitation practitioner, but from a team composed of professionals representing a wide range of services – medical, rehabilitative, social welfare, and vocational. It is felt that management models help to integrate and coordinate these expertises to better serve the client.[14] Needless to say, a management approach lends itself to, and may even be a manifestation of, economic analysis.

The second structural transformation concerns the broad aims of the discipline, but in more concrete terms. Since rehabilitation's earliest days at the turn of this century its practitioners have pondered how to identify disabilities and, once identified, how to show how the rehabilitative services provided actually respond to the needs created by disability.

These concerns point to two operational processes: an assessment of needs and an assessment of needs met. At bottom both of these are problematic because disability is an inherently interactive concept and there is no such thing as disability as such. That is, disability can only be identified when the notion is operationalized in terms of some specific repertoire of capabilities that are 'normally expected' or one; only then is assessment and outcome evaluation meaningful.

Prior to the publication of the ICIDH – which was designed to put the assessment question on a more secure footing – there were three approaches to assessment, which yielded three kinds of functional assessment instrument. The PULSE instrument, developed in the United States in 1957, represents the first approach. It is a 'whole person' or 'global' functional assessment built on six basic physical functions and using relative degree of 'independence' as the primary rating measure.[15] Attempts to limit the scope and improve the validity of 'global' instruments led to the second approach, this time relying on activities of daily living or ADL scales. These instruments, of which there are many, emphasize self-care and mobility, the two primary capabilities of interest when the focus of rehabilitation is that of enabling the patient to leave the institutional setting. Finally, serving more specialized concerns, several 'categorical' instruments have been designed to give functional profiles for specific impairments.

As research tools, and as ways of providing a practical basis for evaluation of rehabilitation outcome, all of these instruments have at one time or another been criticized for what are essentially measurement problems: standardization, scalability, reliability, and validity.[16] And some researchers have argued that a critical examination of these instruments presupposes agreement about that on which there is no agreement, namely the concept of health.[17]

Since 1980 and the publication of the ICIDH, however, attention has been drawn to a very different kind of criticism, namely, that these instruments are purporting to assess not one, but three separate phenomena. This criticism had several consequences for the professional understanding of rehabilitation. First and foremost, the primary lesson of the ICIDH has been that functional assessment is not a purely technical (let alone biomedical) problem that can be left to experts. Therefore, the search for a single ideal instrument for 'global' disablement is chimerical and the therapist is well advised to keep data about impairments, disabilities, and handicaps distinct.[18] Second, what is needed is a collection of assessment devices, some precise and quantitative, others less so, for identifying different dimensions of disablement.

Coupled with the recognition that functional assessment tools must be clear about the distinction between impairments and disabilities is the concern that therapists need to be more precise in their characterization of disability. The literature throughout the 1970s and 1980s reflects a surge of interest in assessment tools that serve the specific aims of vocational rehabilitation. Instruments used to characterize 'fitness for work' and 'employability' began to incorporate task identifiers, skill levels, career aptitudes, and work behaviours as indicators of work-specific physical, intellectual, and motivational capabilities.[19]

These changes in assessment methodology have dramatically transformed the process of rehabilitation outcome analysis and evaluation as well. These days advocates of comprehensive vocational rehabilitation do not envisage one set of evaluators, but several, each serving the various professions involved in the process of providing the interlocking services of medical rehabilitation, psychosocial rehabilitation, and independent living or habilitation services.[20] Separate outcome analyses are required for each service component, with some sort of overall program management evaluation providing the comprehensive picture.

The development of a broadly based conception of rehabilitation has had many consequences for the profession and for the provision of services to people with disabilities. However, it has not been welcomed by social-policy analysts, since it greatly complicates the basic parameters of disablement policy, namely, the nature of disability and the character of the needs of people with disabilities. Just as legislators and policy analysts were attracted to the biomedical representation of disablement for program-eligibility requirements, they have also been attracted to operationalizations of disability that are easy to work with and motivate. There has as a result been a strong motivation at the level of policy-making not to follow the lead of rehabilitation theorists and broaden the focus of disablement programming but rather to retain the operationalization already in use, namely, work disability.

Motivating work disability as paradigmatic of the concept has never posed a problem. Given the nature of policy analysis, economic considerations are always dominant, and it is plausible to argue that working is so central to one's social being that, if disablement policy is to have a single focus, it should be employment. As a recent Canadian government report put the point: '[Employment] is a fundamental form of social participation and source of personal satisfaction. It is also a prerequisite for access to the cornucopia of goods, services, opportunities and experiences that are available in an affluent society, to those who have the money.'[21] Since people with disabilities have one of the highest unemployment rates of any identifiable group in society, it seems obvious that the goal of participation demands that ways be found to allow people with disabilities to enter, and succeed in, the labour market.

At a deeper ideological level, as several writers have pointed out, focusing on employability, or 'helping people so that they can help themselves,' has an undeniable resonance with the version of individualism that is prevalent in North America. Even those ideologues who insist that the state should not tamper with the workings of the labour market usually do not object very strongly to policies that raise the level of employability of those who are unemployed. This puts disablement policy in the same politically acceptable category as education and job training.

Although it is one thing to be aware of the economic ramifications of disablement and something else again to conceptualize disablement as an economic problem, the shift from the first to the second was immediate and imperceptible. In their influential 1976 study, Monroe Berkowitz, William G. Johnson, and Edward H. Murphy make this transition with ease. The objective in their study was 'to determine the relationship between the health of adult males who are experienced labor force workers and the supply of labor: in other words, to estimate the relationship between impairment, socioeconomic influences, and labor supply that in some cases produces *the limitation in labor force activity conventionally described as "disability"* [22] And a more recent treatment argues that while the economic perspective is not the only way of operationalizing disability, only with the economic approach is it possible to see clearly the role of disability policy, and to discern what options are available to society in fulfilling this role.[23] In other words, impairment only matters from the perspective of social policy because the presence of an impairment represents a cost that must be borne by someone. Hence, the rationale of disablement policy is to deal with these costs.

Thus, by means of a few short steps the 'problem' of disablement has become the problem of the costs of disablement. What costs are these? They are the losses of economic welfare experienced by both the person with the disability and all of those affected by the impairment. The costs to the individual include medical costs, loss of earnings, costs of special aids and accommodations, and, more subjectively, loss of social and psychological well-being. The costs to others include both lost labour opportunities and the external or spillover cost of 'collective compassion.' The rationale of disablement policy must thus be to distribute, and in the process reduce, these costs. Since the only feasible measure of cost is economic, it follows that disablement policy is nothing more than an application of economic policy to disablement.

In the economic model the only intelligible rationale for disablement policy is the distribution and reduction of the costs imposed by disability. The major cost, and from the economic perspective the cost most amenable to social-policy response, is that arising from limited productivity. When disability adversely affects productivity – by limiting a potential worker's repertoire of productive capabilities – then the focus of policy should be to counteract the limitation. This might involve reducing the effects of an impairment and providing skills and training (that is, creating new productive capabilities), or it might involve altering the employment milieu itself by job creation, job adaptation, or work-site accommodation.

Yet the shape disablement policy will take – what programs and initiatives are selected, who is eligible for them, and how they are financed – will depend entirely on economic analysis. Since everything about the economic model flows from this way of thinking about social problems we should characterize it more precisely.

Cost-benefit analysis (to use its more common name) is both reductivistic and aggregative, in the sense that it distils social problems like disability down to questions of costs and then assesses social-policy options in those terms. The economic standard by which policy options are evaluated is that of efficiency. Economic efficiency concerns the best use of limited resources, given demand. An efficient distribution of benefits, in the simplest case, is that in which the benefit accrued on the marginal unit of allocated resource equals its marginal social cost, so that it is impossible to get more benefit more cheaply.

Applied to the general strategic goal of increasing productivity, efficiency demands that the monetary costs realized by increasing the level of overall productivity in the labour force (the supply side of the labour market, as it is called) do not exceed the costs expended in social and other programming to realize those benefits. Therefore, since disability is a cost, and the aim of policy is to reduce overall cost, efficient disablement policy should aim for that equilibrium point where the next policy dollar expended will reduce the overall disability cost less than a dollar. This will of course entail, in realistic circumstances, that there will still be unmet impairment needs – specifically, those that are too expensive to satisfy.

Disablement policy has one other economic objective besides reduction in disability costs. This policy must also determine, and then implement, mechanisms to achieve the appropriate sharing of impairment costs. Although standard economic analysis allows that this objective has an 'equity' dimension – so that some ways of allocating costs will strike us as unfair, discriminatory, or even cruel – insofar as the efficiency standard governs policy a restraint is imposed on how expensive our equity-sensitive programming can be allowed to be. In circumstances of scarcity equity will be superseded by efficiency when any attempt to be fair will be too costly.

In its general outline economic thinking is familiar and need not detain us longer. But before I turn to specific aspects of the economic approach to disablement, it is important to see why the economic model manages to produce a consistent and coherent picture of disablement for the purposes of policy and manages to do so in a straightforward, easily understandable fashion.

In the first place, the model provides policy analysts with an expertise in terms of which every aspect of disablement can, at least potentially, be analysed. We are all too familiar with the economic interpretation of most aspects of social existence and are comfortable with the view that everything has a cost and that that cost is ultimately monetary (or at least fungible). In practice, it goes without saying, economic expertise is always recognized as relevant and will be deferred to.

The economic model also builds upon a very sophisticated understanding of what, metaphorically, can be called the 'location' of the problem of disablement. Since disabilities are contingent on social, cultural, and economic expectations and arise out of the interaction of impairments and social environment, it makes no sense to locate them within an individual's body (for precisely the same reason it would be nonsensical to locate unemployability *in* the worker's body). By the same token, a disability (like a social cost) is not located entirely in the social environment either. As Saad Nagi has insisted for years, disabilities are not things at all but relations: 'Disability is determined by the interaction of limitations in function ... with factors of a situational and environmental nature.'[24] Thus, in the economic model the problem of disablement is also relational, a matter of assessing costs of disabilities as these are embedded in particular social contexts.

Finally, the economic model represents disablement as an economic problem approachable, if not solvable, by economically informed social policy. That is, disablement is represented in this model as an intrinsically social problem standing in need of a policy response. In turn, the model represents people with disabilities as people with an economic problem, those who by virtue of the social reception of an impairment experience a limitation upon their repertoire of productive capacity. Significantly, as we shall see, both of these representations are responsible for the uses and the misuses of the economic approach to disablement policy.

Virtues of Economic Analysis

While the biomedical model provides the essential grounding for disablement, and makes it possible to accumulate hard and reliable data about people with disabilities and their medical needs, the economic model provides the foundation for disablement policy as social policy. Because of its focus on impairments, the biomedical model cannot integrate disablement into social policy. In particular, the biomedical perspective does not address the macroallocative issues that are at the heart of policy analysis, issues concerning how the claims of people with disabilities are to be weighed against the other claims made upon society's finite resources. But these are precisely the issues that the economic model addresses. The economic model creates disablement policy. Conceptually, the model achieves this by focusing upon the disability dimension of disablement. As a limit upon an individual's positive freedom to do or become something, a disability constitutes what – at least in the first instance – is socially important about impairments, namely, their impact on the lives of people in society.

The inherent flexibility of disability, the result of cultural and situational contingency, makes the notion very useful to the policy analyst. Intuitively, we have no trouble accepting that different repertoires of capabilities are expected of people at different times and places. This suits the needs of policy analysis admirably, since it gives the analyst the freedom to experiment with repertoires of capabilities to find those that are valuable, not merely to the individual, but to society at large. This is the proper sphere of social-policy analysis. But as we have seen, although ADL or some other 'global' set of capabilities may have epidemiological importance, the policy analyst will be drawn to one or another operationalization of 'work disability.'

Work disability represents a key domain of social planning, one which can easily be linked to a range of related social problems, such as poverty, unemployment, and unmet medical needs. The economic understanding of disablement does not supplant the biomedical dimension; the two are perfectly compatible, once the conceptual distinction between impairment and disability is institutionalized. Indeed, by concentrating attention on work disability the economic model integrates biomedical expertise into social policy while rejecting the biomedical model itself. Diagnosis, prognosis, and therapy become means, not to some abstract conception of health, but to a very concrete social good, that of restoring, or creating, productive capability in individuals with disabilities.

Employment tends to be a sufficient condition for economic integration; people who are employed are both producers and consumers, they participate in the economy. Since the advantages of economic integration are obvious, for both the individual and the society, it is appropriate to represent disablement as an economic problem concerning employment, or more specifically, the supply side of the labour market.

The economic model also makes it possible to translate disablement and related social problems into a common language so that one can compare the costs of providing unmet medical needs with the benefits of reducing poverty, or compare the benefits of job creation with the costs of reducing the availability of income support programs, and so on. This common language, always necessary as a tool for comparing the impact of proposed policy solutions, may also be used to express policy objectives, even policy goals.

The emergence of rehabilitation, to be sure, must be credited as having reoriented our social understanding of disablement by addressing a collection of needs, caused by impairments, that are not adequately served by purely medical procedures. The insight of rehabilitation was that impairments are not merely medical conditions but create limitations on repertoires of capability preventing individuals from obtaining their realistic aspirations. The true needs of people with disabilities, in other words, concern limitations upon the scope of their positive freedom, in actual day-to-day situations.

But it was the economic model that refined this insight by providing a social context for the identification of those capabilities that really count, namely, those required in the workplace. Thus, the model offers a standard of disability assessment as well as a basis for outcome evaluation. Vocational rehabilitation adopted these standards so as to offer a realistic solution to disability, namely, a measurable increase in employability or wage-earning potential. And, once it became common to understand disability as the interaction of impairment and supply-side labour-market conditions, the economic model effectively absorbed the theoretical contribution of rehabilitation by correlating the social costs of rehabilitative services with the social benefits in increased productivity. This in turn created a determinant measure of the effectiveness and efficiency of the social response to disablement.

The economic model has also left its stamp on the familiar configuration of social welfare programming in Canada – from contributory social insurance programs like workers' compensation and unemployment insurance, to non-contributory social assistance programs like the Canadian Assistance Plan and Family Allowance. As we shall see, assistance programming for people with disabilities is often motivated by a net social benefit rationale rather than a pure charity or beneficence rationale, making it possible for the social planner to point to across-the-board economic advantages to the programs. Other social initiatives are given a 'market-mimicking' structure. Both rationales are economic in spirit.

Interpreting problems of disablement policy wholly in economic terms has two obvious advantages. First, when the point of a program or government initiative is expressed in economic language, its success or failure can be evaluated by generally accepted economic criteria. Putting disability within an economic framework, it has been argued, makes it possible for social planners to discern the options available to society in fulfilling the ultimate goals of disablement policy.[25]

In particular, the economic framework avoids the problem of competing perspectives. An initiative to, for example, hire people with disabilities can be assessed by comparing the benefits that result to the people hired (salary, self-respect) with the costs (loss of public assistance, higher taxes). But the program can also be assessed by comparing the benefits and costs to the employer (value added to productive output, on the benefit side – salary and costs of accommodation, on the cost side). In terms of economics these perspectives are commensurable. Program evaluation is economy-wide and incorporates these (and other) comparisons to determine the overall social cost and benefit ratio.

Second, economic program evaluations, and all the information on which they are based, are fully commensurable with evaluations and data found in all the other areas of social policy. The economic model provides, quite literally, the common coin in terms of which to assess the diverse forms of social responses to perceived social ills. Not only can policy analysts compare the costs and benefits of two different disablement programs – say, vocational rehabilitation and employment equity. They can also compare the costs and benefits of disablement programming with ways of responding to other calls on social resources.

Economists are quick to point out, though, that by providing a science and a discourse that make across-the-board policy evaluation possible, economic analysis does not purport to solve macroallocative questions, since these ultimately depend on priorities this analysis cannot provide. And it is true that the value of economic efficiency –

getting the most benefit for the least cost – cannot itself by a social goal. This is so not because economic efficiency is unimportant, but because it is entirely dependent on normative judgments – about what counts as a 'benefit' or a 'cost' – that cannot, without circularity, be made in economic terms.

This normative gap is perhaps best seen in the case of 'tragic choices,' especially those that pit the very lives of a few against the economic prosperity of everyone.[26] When desperate candidates for scarce and costly life-saving resources compete, both among themselves and with other groups with other expensive needs, no single allocative system can avoid tragic results for someone, or for that matter, pre-empt our moral concern. The best economics can offer is a common discourse in which to compare the costs and benefits of possible allocations.

This last point suggests another virtue of the economic model. It is not enough to be able to integrate disablement policy with social policy by translating the problems of disablement into a discourse common to other policy areas. For, if the salient goals of people with disabilities are *incommensurable* with the goals in other areas, then the commonality of discourse can only frustrate the legitimate needs of everyone. But, it might be argued, this problem only arises when the economic model is not consistently applied, for on the face of it the economic interpretation of the goals of participation, accommodation, and respect enhances rather than hinders the realistic prospects of disablement policy. This is because the model is committed to the priority of participation, understood as economic integration.

The principal objective of the economic strategy towards disablement has always been to reduce the social costs of disability by increasing the level of employability among people with disabilities. In addition, it is an article of faith among economists that by expending social resources to help people integrate into the labour market, the overall long-term social costs of disablement will be reduced. And reducing costs is often held out to be the strongest justification for state intervention in the economy.[27] For example, this reasoning was certainly the prime motivation for the development of vocational rehabilitation programming for veterans after the First World War.[28]

Because the model clearly assigns priority to the goal of participation, the goals of accommodation and respect occupy a somewhat secondary or derivative position. But unlike the biomedical model, which by giving priority to a medical interpretation of accommodation has little room for the other two goals, the economic model *can* plausibly integrate all three. One need only argue that participation (understood as economic integration) presumes accommodation when that goal is interpreted to include the satisfaction of medical needs and whatever is required to expand repertoires of productive capability. Thus, accommodation is instrumental to participation on the model.

As for the goal of respect, the economic model can plausibly interpret it as the inevitable psychological benefit of economic integration. A failure to be respected, or to respect oneself, the argument would go, is surely in part a manifestation of exclusion from the normal activities of social living. Unemployment and poverty, needless to say, undermine self-esteem. One need not aim directly at respect to achieve it; indeed aiming at respect alone, and ignoring the goal of economic integration, is arguably unrealistic or self-defeating.

Giving priority to the goal of participation – and providing a way of incorporating accommodation and respect into that goal – may be the principal virtue of the economic model. In any event, the model does offer a discourse for making realistic social decisions about social problems, and thus it appears to be our best bet for resolving the impasse in disablement policy. Certainly it has captured the creative imaginations of policy analysts, and it is not difficult to see how disablement policy has been shaped by this model.

Effects of the Model on Policy

In this century the economic model of disablement has strongly influenced, when it has not wholly determined, the focus, the regulatory structure, and the rationale of the social security components of disablement policy, that is, workers' compensation, social insurance, and social assistance schemes.

The emphasis on disability, operationalized as employability or wage-earning capacity, has shaped the eligibility criteria for these programs. Structural rules regarding rates and periods of benefits, liquid asset exemptions, 'taxed-back' earning deductions, calculation of contributory earnings, and the other familiar features of modern social security programming all display the influence of economic analysis. Finally, and most significantly, the rationale of these programs, and thus the implicit standards and measures of success and failure, flows from social objectives aimed at the central goal of participation, interpreted as economic integration.

This is obviously not the place for an exhaustive review of the core disablement programming in this country. Disparities between provinces, lack of coordination between programs within each province, disincentives, and inequities are well-known problems. They have been investigated by several commissions and have provoked calls for a comprehensive reform of the entire income security and social assistance system, of which disablement programming forms a part.[29] Still, though a complete review is impossible, and unnecessary, three basic components of our social security response to disablement need to be reviewed with care (using Ontario's legislative schemes as examples). My aim here is not to rehearse details but to describe in broad terms the legacy of the economic model in social programming.

Workers' Compensation

Ontario's Workmen's Compensation Act of 1914 was Canada's first piece of social insurance legislation providing non-charitable, state-regulated, and compulsory income protection against a prevalent risk, namely, work-related injury or death.[30] Ontario's act, modelled on Britain's 1897 legislation, was based on the then-revolutionary doctrine that money should be paid for injury or death without a prior finding of fault. Widely viewed as a superb example of social legislation, the act spawned similar acts in other provinces.

From the beginning, the animating rationale of workers' compensation was economic efficiency. By the turn of the century and with the growth of large-scale, and far more dangerous industries, work-related accidents resulting in permanent or temporary impairment had increased dramatically. Common law negligence actions, the only avenue for compensation, were of limited help, since it was difficult to prove liability and the employer would normally be shielded by one or more legal defences. But as the accidents increased, juries began to hear these actions, and legislation limited the effectiveness of the defences of 'common employment' and 'voluntary assumption of risk,' the tide turned and injured workers began to win legal battles. This was a concern to large corporations and their insurers, both of whom began to lobby for a more predictable and cost-spreading solution to the problem of industrial accidents.

Some sort of universal insurance scheme was the obvious answer. The risks created by an increasing reliance on bigger and more dangerous machines were risks attendant upon a socioeconomic development, not the negligence of employers. Having the costs of industrialization fall on a few victims of circumstances was offensive to equity; more important, the efficiencies of compulsory insurance were extremely attractive. Employers as a group were willing to make small and regular payments to a fund if that freed them from the risk of enormous and unpredictable jury awards. The insurance approach was attractive to workers and their unions who wanted protection without having to rely on the vagaries of the courtroom.[31]

Because the ultimate rationale of workers' compensation is economic, the operationalization of disability it presumes is congenial to economic analysis. Therefore, compensation for non-pecuniary losses – pain and suffering – and other consequential disabilities not reducible to wage-earning capacity was excluded from the scheme. Workers' compensation, both historically and conceptually, is an alternative to tort-based compensation, which is by its nature more open ended in its understanding of consequential damages. For instance, there is in principle no reason why a tortfeasor could not be found liable for damages associated with handicapping.[32] In exchange for the uncertainty of tort law, workers' compensation drastically restricts the range of compensable disability.

Although the only object of compensation consistent with a no-fault, compulsory, and universal insurance scheme for industrial accidents is work disability, the biomedical model, as we have seen, also has had an influence here, so that the most common way of estimating loss of productive capacity is directly in terms of 'the nature and degree of the injury.'[33] Thus it is that employability is assessed, not as an economic phenomenon, but as a medical impairment. This is, of course, one of the many policy anomalies traceable to the conceptual confusion about disablement.

As is well known and often remarked on, this approach perversely guarantees both under- and overcompensation, inasmuch as there is no predictable relationship between type or degree of impairment and actual or potential loss of earning capacity. This built-in anomaly probably makes little difference for temporary benefits which are paid for relatively short periods immediately following the accident. But the financial consequences of it for the assessment of permanent partial or permanent total disability are potentially considerable (although extremely difficult to calculate).

There is, as we have seen, an equity argument that is sometimes cited at this point: as long as awards are made consistently on the basis of biomedically ascertainable grounds, relatively immune from political manipulation, the question of whether earning capacity is actually, or accurately, being measured is not really important. Unfortunately, the argument from economic efficiency goes in precisely the opposite direction. From that perspective, the only plausible rationale for workers' compensation is defeated if the measurement of compensation bears no relationship to actual economic costs.

To make matters worse, reformers – both incrementalists and radicals alike – view the operation and rationale of workers' compensation (and other industrial accident insurance programs) to be fundamentally arbitrary. Their point is simply that, from a broader compensatory point of view, no principled distinction can possibly be made between economic and non-economic losses resulting from industrial accident. For example, some reformers have argued for a scheme directed to permanent partial disability that compensates for both of the harms that can arise from workplace injury: limitations upon the injured worker's capacity to enjoy normal, everyday life, and limitations upon the worker's capacity to earn what he or she would have normally expected to earn from working.[34] Schemes that adopt this two-stage approach are already in place in Saskatchewan, Flor-ida, and elsewhere.

Other, more radical, reformers insist on taking the obvious next step. Why should we distinguish between work-related accidents and all of the other accidents that occur in daily living, when the impairments that may result are indistinguishable, especially when the range of disabling consequences is identical.[35] In the 1988 report *Transitions*, this argument is forcefully made, although the comprehensive scheme it offers retains the employment focus.[36] But the background issue here is the simple one I have labelled etiological neutrality: the character of a disability as a limit of positive freedom is not affected by the manner in which it was brought about.

There are many factors motivating these and other suggested reforms of workers' compensation. There are disputes within economic policy analysis over long-term effects of programming, from both an efficiency and an equity point of view. Other reforms are motivated by the desire to loosen the hold of economic rationality on social policy, or to substitute one implicit normative rationale for disablement entitlements for another. As we shall see later, though, some of the tensions inherent in workers' compensation programming are irresolvable, since they put pressure on the very notion of compensation that is supposed to provide the ultimate normative basis for this form of social insurance. Indeed, it is this residue of compensation that set workers' compensation apart from other, more straightforward, social insurance programs.

Social Insurance Programming

The structure and much of the rationale of all social insurance programming in North America can be traced to the German insurance schemes for health, industrial accidents and pensions that became law under Chancellor Otto von Bismarck in the 1880s. Much of Canada's programming, especially unemployment insurance and pension plans, was also influenced by the Beveridge Report of 1942 which laid out Britain's grand plan for the elimination of want.[37] Leonard Marsh's 1943 *Report on Social Security for Canada*, which distilled a mass of research and writing in Canada, the United States, and Britain, advocated a greatly expanded role for social insurance.[38]

Although social insurance was doctrinally controversial, initially the concern was how best to, so to speak, socialize the basic insurance principle of risk-pooling. At no stage was the background economic rationale of the insurance model questioned; indeed for both Beveridge and Marsh the efficiencies of the insurance approach to unemployment and other social ills were its primary virtues.

Social insurance programs are not designed to be financed out of general revenue but entirely, or largely, from contributions of those who can benefit from them. But unlike private insurance schemes, the profit motive is absent and coverage is compulsory by law. These schemes are 'social' in the sense that, in Marsh's words, they are 'underwritten by the community at large.' From the outset, and continuing to this day, the arguments for and against the advisability of the state entering into the realm of insurance in this manner have been carried on entirely in the discourse of economics. And properly so, since these programs are all designed with the same objective in mind – economic security.

In the case of private disability insurance the economic rationale is straightforward: because there is no certainty about disablement (at least during one's 'prime' working years), whatever variation in their degree of risk aversion, everyone will be willing to buy the certainty of some measure of financial security should disablement occur. Thus, on the supply side, it is possible with some accuracy to calculate the actuarial premium for various kinds of disablement. This, plus administrative costs, is the no-profit price an insurance company must charge to cover what it will have to pay out. Profit is then added on, as competition allows. Thus, an unrestricted, unregulated private insurance market will allocate risks and resources efficiently.

There are, of course, several problems associated with the insurance market as a whole that challenge this simplistic demand/supply argument. The most relevant of these for disablement theory is the so-called moral hazard anomaly. Moral hazard is the name given to a psychological regularity (assumed rather than verified) that undermines the operating assumption of the private insurance argument. This is the assumption that both the probability of an injury and the amount of the insured loss are exogenous to the individual, that is, not subject to manipulation by the insured party without the insurer's knowledge. Though it is not thought to be a serious worry that people will injure themselves simply to collect insurance, especially when the disability created is serious, there is a concern that the degree of incapacitation consequential upon an unforeseen injury will be exaggerated. To counter this, private insurance carriers often seek multiple medical assessments, or demand deductions or coinsurance from frequent claimants.

Like their private counterparts, social insurance arrangements are structured to respond to the same sort of economic analysis. To ensure a basic floor of coverage and regulate the demand side of the market, social insurance programs are almost always compulsory for the population that is to benefit. Thus, the two basic social insurance schemes in this country, the Canada/Quebec Pension Plans and Unemployment Insurance, base eligibility on a set period of employee contribution, matched by compulsory employer contribution.

As a response to supply-side problems, including moral hazard, social insurance programs characteristically provide universal flat-rate benefits. This sacrifices individual equity – which, our intuitions suggest, would require benefit rates to be a function of contribution rates: the more insurance 'bought' the higher the benefits received. Instead, social insurance seeks social adequacy by guaranteeing that everyone receives a basic minimum from the scheme. In turn, this entails that social insurance has a, unusually very limited, income redistributive effect, since some claimants are bound to receive benefits that exceed the value of their contribution. This effect may be offset by additional provisions, such as those found in the Canada Pension Plan, which supplement the flat-rate amount received with some proportion of the retirement pension to which the worker would have been eligible, but for the disability.

The point here is that since social insurance programs like the Canada/Quebec Pension Plan are fashioned from more or less the same economic premises as private insurance, they are predictably inadequate for the financial needs of many people with disabilities. This is not the result of administrative failures; it is intrinsic to the plan. Insurance is governed by considerations of compensation or, more broadly, corrective justice, rather than needs-satisfaction.

Thus, for example, the characterization of disability for the purposes of a Canada Pension Plan disability pension requires medical evidence of a 'severe and prolonged' impairment, understood, in disability terms, as a condition that renders the individual incapable of pursuing a gainful occupation for an indefinite period.[39] Yet, in order to be eligible for this pension the person with the disability must have contributed to the plan for at last five of the last ten years, or two of the last three.

It is natural to object that many individuals with 'severe and prolonged' disabilities do not have the required employment history, or if they do it is at such a low level of pay that the pension benefits will have to be supplemented.[40] But, in its own terms and in accordance with the plan's structure, this is not a relevant criticism: whether or not a person has contributed to the plan has nothing to do with the degree of disability, but it has everything to do with the economics of pensions.

By the same token, Canada's disability tax benefits (an indirect form of social insurance) are of limited value, if judged in terms of needs met. People with disabilities can claim (or non-spousal relatives can claim on their behalf) both a disability benefit and a fairly broadly described medical expense benefit. Yet, since 1988 these 'benefits' have taken the form of non-refundable tax credits which, although not so obviously regressive as the disability deductions they replaced, still do not respond well to the actual expenses of people with disabilities. And since the credit is non-refundable it provides no benefit whatsoever for those who are too poor to pay tax.

In sum, in this broad area of disablement programming the principal effect of the economic model has been to incorporate into programming an image of disablement as limited, localized, and temporary loss of productive capability. The point of this image is that this is the sort of disability that can plausibly be dealt with, at the social level, by mechanisms that mirror the market solution – that is, private insurance.

The economic characterization of disablement applies to some people with disabilities, but certainly not to all. People born with disabilities, or people who have become impaired very early in their lives, have not in the appropriate sense *become* less productive since there is no prior state of capacity which can be used as a benchmark for measuring what has been 'lost.' Thus, as a general matter, social insurance programming, like the economic model itself, is insensitive to those states of permanent disablement that cannot be transformed into risks that a prudent, risk-aversive individual would insure against.

Social Assistance Programming

Although social insurance schemes, especially unemployment insurance, have always attracted the complaint that they have distortive effects on the market, proponents could defuse this objection by insisting that they were intended to mirror market solutions and the state was merely making it possible for the insurance approach to be more efficient. Social assistance, or welfare, however, could not be characterized in this fashion and so needed a very different, but economically acceptable, justification. Social historians agree that, from the earliest days of social assistance, the legitimating rationale was an appeal neither to compassion nor to charity, but to economic efficiency. Historically, whether in inchoate or sophisticated forms, justification has taken the form of what is called the net benefit or national efficiency argument for state intervention.[41]

The national efficiency argument can take several forms, depending on the macroeconomic assumptions one makes and the specific kind of program one has in mind – be it public health, education, poor relief, or disablement relief. But the thrust of the argument is simple enough: state intervention into the economy is justified because the resulting non-market distribution of goods, resources, or money will, in one way or another, invigorate the overall economy. Or to put it more bluntly, the overall economic benefits of social assistance programming outweigh the overall economic costs.

The variations on this theme are many, but common to most is the assumption that poverty is a social ill and the cause of all other socially expensive ills. The author of a recent American text on social security – using, consciously or not, language than can be found in late-nineteenth-century social tracts – states that 'poverty causes economic insecurity not only for the poor, but for the entire economy, since the undesirable by-products of poverty include disease, crime, delinquency, and immorality ... [Moreover] poverty results in lost production because of the waste of human resources.'[42]

Because of the important justificatory role that the national efficiency argument plays in the case of social assistance, the priority the argument gives to poverty has been carried over to programming. Yet there has always been a need to retain the categorization of causes of poverty so that the subclass of the 'deserving poor' could be identified. Although poverty is said to be the result of disease, crime, and delinquency, only the first of these has been thought to qualify the individual as deserving of relief; the 'sturdy beggar' can be made to work.

The national efficiency argument has frequently shared the spotlight with another, more altruistic consideration, namely, the unqualified obligation of the state to respond to unmet needs. A close reading of the influential Beveridge Report, for example, reveals a reluctance to wholeheartedly adopt the national efficiency rationale in its baldest form. Although the most consistent theme in this document is the claim that full employment is the surest road to a healthy economy, at various points Beveridge suggests that a purely motivated 'attack upon want' must be the guiding principle of social security legislation.[43] It is never made clear, though, how that 'principle' is to provide guidance, and one is left with the strong impression that such remarks are purely rhetorical. The same can be said about pleas for compassion and the like.

More recently national efficiency arguments for social assistance programming have become less grand and more subtle. The general prediction of economy-wide benefit that will result from some form of social assistance is now bolstered by raising doubts about the value of unregulated competition in the face of evident market failures. Often social assistance programs are justified as second-best solutions required by extraordinary circumstances – usually recessions or depressions. But this line of justification would never suffice on its own, since social assistance is redistributive, and its survival in cultures committed to the free market will always be tenuous. It is thus understandable why a more straightforward economic rationale for these programs would be relied on whenever possible.

Undoubtedly because of the fragile support the national efficiency argument provides for social assistance, this programming is notoriously incoherent and inadequate. It is also always under threat of cut-back and restructuring. To make matters worse, recipients of 'welfare' are regularly stigmatized as failures or objects of the state's overgenerous charity. Surprisingly, this is even the case with social assistance programming for people with disabilities – who have long enjoyed the strongest claim to the status of the 'deserving poor.'

Social assistance in Canada (outside Quebec, which has its own arrangement) is provincially administered under a federal/provincial cost-sharing arrangement called the Canada Assistance Plan. Guidelines under the plan set out some general parameters that structure specific programs, but there is considerable leeway for interprovincial variation. For example, some provinces – Ontario, Alberta, British Columbia, and New Brunswick – have special income support programs for people with disabilities, while others do not.

Ontario's General Welfare Assistance Act[44] is administered municipally. Eligibility depends on whether the applicant qualifies as 'a person in need.' Although people with long-term disabilities usually qualify, and the GWAA has Supplementary Aid Provisions that make assistive devices and other accommodations available to them, the act is not particularly suitable for people with disabilities. The act is intended for emergency assistance only, and disablement is paradigmatically a matter of long-term incapacitation. Therefore, people with permanent or long-term disabilities, whether or not they take advantage of the GWAA, will eventually find themselves administered under the provisions of the Family Benefits Act.[45]

Under the Family Benefits Act persons with disabilities may be eligible for the Guaranteed Annual Income System for the Disabled (GAINS-D) benefits. Eligibility here is determined by two criteria: medical and financial. The relevant definition of people with disabilities is given in the regulations as 'those who have a major physical or mental impairment that is likely to continue for a prolonged period of time, and who, as a result thereof, are severely limited in activities pertaining to normal living as verified by objective medical findings.'[46]

Once again, even though the aims of the legislation concern ADL disability, the standards of biomedicine are at the very core of the definition: the grounds for determining when a physical or mental impairment is 'major' and what activity limitations are 'severe' are all biomedical, not socioeconomic. Even though social assistance programs are not intended to be contributory insurance schemes with a prior work requirement, reliance on biomedical determinations can best be explained as an attempt at drawing a line between 'voluntary' and 'involuntary' employability. In the United States an analogous initiative is the Supplemental Security Income Program, created in 1973 expressly to provide federal assistance to those categories of the needy who, never having worked, fail to qualify for the disability insurance scheme. Despite its focus, the SSI 'welfare' program uses a 'medically determinable ... inability to work' definition of disability. This suggests to one critic that there is a perceived need to be assured that an individual, so disabled that he or she has never been employed, none the less is legitimately part of the class of the 'deserving poor.'[47]

The second qualification for GAINS-D assistance is a two-pronged financial requirement. There is first an initial eligibility requirement that the person with a disability does not have cash, bonds, stocks, securities, or other liquid assets over a specified value, or any fixed assets (other than a primary place of residence). If the applicant passes this hurdle he or she must submit to a 'needs test' which compares basic living needs with available resources. If there is a budget deficit, the applicant is then eligible for assistance, at a rate determined by another complex calculation.

In the GAINS-D program, recipients who earn income from outside sources can keep only a portion of it, as determined by earning exemption guidelines. The monthly amount of the exemption is 'taxed back.' Recipients are guaranteed a flat-rate allowance that varies with family size and type of housing accommodation. Supplementary aid is available for special diets, medical supplies, and other extraordinary needs.

To round out the disablement assistance scheme, Ontario, like many other provinces, provides specifically work-related developmental and rehabilitative programming that is fully integrated into the Family Benefits Act. The Work Incentive Program provides a monetary allowance and health benefits to those who leave the Family Benefits regime in order to become employed (and to make it easier to return to the scheme if that is necessary). And, by means of the provisions of the Vocational Rehabilitation Services Act,[48] if the person is found incapable of pursuing 'substantially gainful occupation' a wide range of rehabilitative, counselling, training, and assessment services are made available.

Now people with disabilities constitute the largest group of recipients of social assistance in Ontario, nearly 50 per cent of all Family Benefits cases, according to one estimate.[49] What is of interest to us is not the adequacy of the various programs but the background assumptions, made explicit by the eligibility requirements. If we turn to these, there can be little doubt that the implicit rationale is to integrate assistance with the supply side of the labour market. Qualification for assistance is a function not of individual goals and aspirations, but of the needs of the labour market.

This was made abundantly clear in the 1978 Divisional Court case of *Re Mroszkowski and Director of the Vocational Rehabilitation Services Branch*.[50] The court in this case held that Vocational Rehabilitation Services was not obliged to support Mr Mroszkowski to the degree required for him to reach his potential, and personal goal, of becoming a lawyer. The court held that he 'ceased to be a disabled person when he was enabled by reason of acquiring a B.Sc. degree to obtain employment in a reasonable capacity within the labour market.'

From an economic perspective the case makes perfectly good sense. If one characterizes disability entirely in employment terms – rather than more generally as a limitation of positive freedom – then social assistance for people with disabilities becomes nothing more than a state expenditure designed to increase productivity. This cost must, on efficiency grounds, be offset by a benefit, and as an administrative matter one must ensure that the benefits that result are commensurate with the costs – that is, can be tracked economically. Thus, the economic model of disablement insists that the kinds of benefits a person with disabilities should receive as a result of disablement policy must be benefits that can translate directly into economic terms, since, ultimately, the normative basis upon which policy judgments are made is that which underlies economic rationality itself. It is, therefore, uneconomical to make it possible for Mr Mroszkowski to finish law school when he is sufficiently trained for *some* employment or other.

Why the Model Is Distortive and Incomplete

It is a common belief that social security programming in this and other countries is plagued by deep and persistent problems. One often hears of the 'crisis' of the welfare state, by which is usually meant the paradoxical combination of an enormous and ever-increasing economic burden from health, education, social security, housing, and other programs, and the apparently ever-diminishing improvement in actual conditions. In the United States, the last industrial state to introduce social insurance, the welfare state has always been viewed with suspicion, if not outright hostility, and as a result the rhetoric of 'crisis' has been heard the loudest there. Only recently has this rhetoric been challenged on the facts, and debunked as a subtle way of blaming the poor.[51]

Yet, crisis or not, every report of a commission of inquiry or independent agency looking into Canada's social security system has pointed to the same set of systemic problems: (1) the rules setting out eligibility, the determination of assets, and the calculation of benefits are overly complex and inconsistent; (2) the benefits, once received, are inadequate; (3) there are persistent inequities arising from a reliance on administrative discretion; and (4) there is lack of integration and coordination between programs, between levels of government, and between the private and the public sector. In addition it is generally agreed that people with disabilities experience these and other systemic problems more frequently, more directly, and with worse long-range consequences, than most other identifiable groups.[52]

Needless to say, these difficulties are not the product of the economic model of disablement alone. The complexity, disjointedness, and lack of coordination in Canada's social security programming are also the result of the constitutional division of powers in this country. Some programs are federal, some provincial, others, including the most important form of social assistance, are cost-shared by both levels of governments. Social insurance programs are for the most part federally administered and jointly financed from contributors. Programs geared particularly to people with disabilities, as well as private pension and sickness insurance arrangements, are not coordinated and require applicants to make their way through a confusing labyrinth of eligibility requirements and restrictions.

Jurisdictional confusions aside, social security programming in general and disablement programming in particular are uncoordinated and needlessly complex because each component originated as a response to some particular economic or social event, usually a depression or a war, which highlights the plight of people with disabilities. In the interim, there was little planning since the dramatic events had slipped by. Also, in Canada during the formative years immediately after World War II a debate raged between those who wished to align the country with Great Britain and follow the lead of the Beveridge Report of 1942 and those who were drawn to the United States with its inherent distrust of the 'initiative-destroying' actions of 'big government.'

Despite all of this there is a class of systemic problems affecting the operation of the core disablement programs that can be traced to the economic model itself. These often-criticized policy anomalies at one level of analysis concern the failure of existing programs to bring about economic integration, instead of creating and perpetuating a 'welfare culture.' But at a deeper and more informative level of analysis these anomalies point to a fundamental ambiguity of aim that is intrinsic to the economic model. It is this ambiguity I want to focus on.

In its starkest form, this ambiguity raises the question whether programming should strive to remove 'unemployables' from the labour market, or to bring them into it.[53] In Canada, as in most industrial nations, the greatest portion of funding allocated for disablement policy is devoted to programs that give people with disabilities a ticket *out* of the labour market. But a considerable portion of what is left over is spent trying to induce this same population to become employed. This anomaly is evident both at the level of specific regulations (for example, the 'tax-back' rates on outside earnings for social assistance) and at the level of the programming itself, in which there is a notorious lack of harmony between work incentive programs and general social assistance.

It is tempting to suggest, as the recent report *A Consensus for Action* does, that blunt disincentives of this sort in the system are the result of a lack of program coordination. But, while the piecemeal development of disablement programming is certainly responsible for disguising work disincentives and other policy anomalies, the cause of these contradictions lies elsewhere.

One cause is nothing more than the conceptual contradiction inherent in the economic model itself, namely, that of operationalizing disability for programming purposes as an economic condition that links physical impairment with unemployment. Locating disability in the intersection of a personal misfortune and a society-wide economic condition, while accurately capturing the contingency of the impact of impairment, has also created an ambiguity in the very goal of social security. From a purely economic point of view, the goal of participation may be satisfied if an individual becomes a member of the workforce, *or* if he or she chooses to opt out and, in effect, become permanently disabled. The choice to opt out constitutes a *form* of participation on the economic model simply because, as an optimizing choice, it represents the individual's best option as he or she sees it.

From this paradoxical situation it follows that social security benefits are not now, nor have they ever been, designed to eliminate poverty for people with disabilities. It would be economically inefficient if the benefits had this result, since then more people, who would otherwise opt for employment, would 'choose to be disabled' and that would potentially bankrupt the social security system. Or, to use the helpful language suggested by Deborah Stone, the true economic goal of disablement programming is to keep the merit-based and the needs-based distribution systems in equilibrium. To do so requires, in the normal case of relative scarcity of resources, that access to the needs-based distribution system be closely guarded so that the inevitable pressures to open the gates wide are minimized and only the truly desperate take advantage of the needs-based system.[54]

Because of the dominance of the economic model, in short, disability programs have become a major economic regulatory instrument in the modern welfare state. Depending on the general state of the economy, and in particular the dynamics of the labour market, disablement assistance and insurance schemes can either ease out of the labour market those workers who are older, slower, and less productive, or else make it easier to keep them in. For this economic fine-tuning, however, it is essential to have both social assistance and vocation rehabilitation programs in place. The first is needed to *restrict* the supply of potential workers by insuring that the less productive are either turned out of their jobs, not promoted, or not hired in the first place; in this way the more productive workers can find suitable jobs. The second is needed when the supply of workers is tighter and it is vital to *increase* the productivity of those whose labour capacity is required.

That most industrialized nations since the Second World War have spent more money on social assistance than on effective reintegrating rehabilitative programs is thus not an indication of anything intrinsic to either approach to policy. It is not as if, for example, social assistance is administratively more efficient than rehabilitation. Rather, what it points to is a persistent feature of labour markets in these nations, namely, that it is cheaper to keep people out than to bring them in.

Thus, as a theoretical matter, the economic model of disablement does indeed generate a rational, consistent, and cost-effective decision procedure for disablement policy. Economists insist that whatever anomalies one finds in policy must result from distortions in the operation of economic reasoning, often brought about by gaps in relevant economic information.[55] Or the problem might be that bureaucrats are prone for political reasons to make adjustments in eligibility and other requirements that are not warranted either by economic evidence or by the policy adjustments being made in other programs by other bureaucrats. Or, again, the problem might lie in the growing tendency to 'constitutionalize' social security benefits to turn them into legal entitlements. Creating rights to benefits, from an economic perspective, is a recipe for disaster, since a court of law cannot be expected to make rational macroeconomic policy decisions.[56]

When it is laid out in this fashion, there is no doubt that economic analysis is tempting. Bureaucratic behaviour, political pressures, and judicial intervention have indeed contributed to the complexity and incoherence of disablement programming. None the less, it would be quite wrong to conclude that, freed from all these distorting influences, pure economic decision-making would produce a unified conception of the social problem of disablement or, for that matter, unambiguous interpretations of the goals of disablement policy. I say this because, whatever the contribution of economic reasoning to social policy formation, this approach has absolutely nothing to say about disablement policy as such. From the perspective of economic analysis, to be blunt, disablement has no inherent social significance.

To see this one need only recall that the governing goal of economic analysis, at least as far as social policy is concerned, is efficiency. As it happens there are numerous interpretations of this apparently straightforward goal, and it could not be said that there is total agreement among economists on what exactly efficiency is, not to mention any agreement why it is a goal to be valued in the first place. Almost everyone would agree, though, that efficiency is,

at least, a standard for comparing policy objectives in light of predicted capacity to maximize the excess of benefits over costs. But
even understood in this simplistic way, there is no guarantee that
any social response to disablement will be judged better, on efficiency grounds, than the 'response' of ignoring disablement entirely. It
all depends on the benefits and the costs.

Although this might seem to be a purely theoretical quibble, it is
not. The economic justification for social insurance schemes is fragile
at best. An economist would ask whether individuals in a wholly
private insurance market would freely buy that measure of insurance
against income loss caused by accident or age that satisfies standards
of social efficiency. If so, and only if so, an arrangement of regulated
and compulsory disability or unemployment insurance would be
efficient. Though there are seemingly powerful efficiency arguments
in support of social insurance and pension programs of the sort we
enjoy in this country, there are also efficiency arguments supporting
the opposite conclusion. From an economic perspective, the prudent
judgment to make is probably that the case of mandatory disability
insurance is an uneasy one.[57]

If anything, the efficiency argument for non-contributory, social
assistance schemes is less predictable. One of the arguments in favour of this sort of programming occasionally suggested by economists is that, insofar as the costs of impairments are independent of
the environment in which they arise, and are randomly distributed
throughout the population, the problem of disablement must be a
social problem best – that is, most efficiently – dealt with at the level
of social policy.[58] But this is plainly not an efficiency argument, since
it makes no mention of the connection between the decision to make
disablement a social issue and the prospect of benefits exceeding
costs if one does. The argument implicitly relies on the secondary
economic goal or standard that economists call 'equity' or 'social
justice.' Social justice concerns are external side constraints on states
of efficiency, not preconditions for them.

In the end, the only plausible efficiency argument for redistributive social assistance programming is the national efficiency argument. Thus, to cite another example of this impressionistic argument,
Nicholas Barr has claimed that when poverty or some other social ill
is uninsurable, the state must still respond on efficiency grounds,
since letting some portion of its citizenry face the risk of starvation
'would have a variety of *efficiency* costs including social unrest/crime

among those facing starvation; the death by starvation of dependants including children (the future labour force); and the fact that malnutrition causes poor health, thereby raising health care costs and lowering the capacity of adults to work and of children to absorb education.'[59]

The problem with this argument is obvious – it is entirely speculative. Until these extremely difficult calculations are carried out we have no way of knowing for sure whether any positive social response to poverty, disablement, or any other social ill is efficient. And what of the Malthusian response? Is it not 'economically reasonable' that some form of painless euthanasia would be far, far less costly?

There is a variant of the national efficiency argument for non-contributory, redistributive schemes that economists occasionally find especially convincing.[60] It goes like this. Disablement is not a form of personal misfortune; it has various 'spillover effects,' or externalities. In particular, human beings are so constituted that the plight of people with disabilities will automatically generate compassion. For an economist, compassion is a cost, indeed a cost that will likely produce other costs in the form of charity (that is, contributions that assuage one's conscience). But, the amount of charity required to meet the cost of compassion is, in part at least, a function of what one knows about what other people will give to the unfortunate by way of charity. Charitable giving, in other words, has the standard characteristic of a public good: each individual benefits both from giving and from knowing that others are also giving. This being so, the optimal level of 'collective compassion' can be attained only if all those who benefit from being relieved of the burden of helping those who are pitied are made to contribute jointly to this benefit. And this optimum can only be achieved by some form of social assistance.

Although it is tempting to dispatch this whole line of thinking as unbecoming of people to whom we entrust our social institutions, the most decisive objection to it, as an argument for social policy, is that it too is unverifiably speculative. Once again, would it not be more cost-effective (by far) to simply remove the cause of all this compassion, or perhaps instruct people in ways of dealing with these 'costs'? In any event, how could the presumed efficiencies here even be estimated, let alone calculated?

The point to be made here is just that the governing goal of cost-benefit reasoning or efficiency makes it inevitable that whatever social policy response to disablement passes economic muster will do so not because it is a response to disablement, but only because the economic results of the response take a certain form. The economic model tends to view unemployment and poverty as the genuine social ills that need to be addressed and treats disablement as one, among several, incidents of poverty. It is ironic that though the economic transformation of disablement, in conjunction with other developments in rehabilitation and social welfare programming, created aspects of disablement policy that were not there before, it also fundamentally distorted disablement by focusing exclusively on the economic problem posed by workers with limited repertoires of productive capacities. Disablement became, in other words, a supply-side labour-market issue, nothing more nor less.[61] This is amply reflected in both the rationale and the regulatory structures of the three basic components of modern social security programming.

Why exactly has the demand side of the labour market been ignored? Making changes to the demand side would, of course, shift the focus of disablement policy to the social environment, that is, the obstacles, which partially constitute disability. The 'employment situation,' broadly construed, can be changed either by altering the overall profile of productive capacity of the workforce *or* by altering the physical, organizational, and attitudinal structures of the workplace. People can be made suitable for work, or work can be made more suitable for people. But if there is this rough symmetry, why has the economic model wholly ignored demand-side solutions? Why must people fit the job, but never the reverse?

Recall that in the biomedical model the focus on the individual and his or her medical problem was inevitable given the ontological 'location' of impairments. This inevitability does not prevail here: disability is an interactive notion and disabilities are not 'in' people or 'in' the social environment, they arise out of the relationship between the two. Therefore, the economic model can, in principle, make the shift in focus from person to social environment, from supply to demand side. It has not done so, however, because economic reasoning makes it all but inevitable – at least in realistically normal social conditions – that disablement programming will have a supply-side bias.

The reason for this is not difficult to see. There are many possible demand-side solutions to the unemployment problem of people with disabilities: the removal of architectural barriers, the provision of a wide variety of accommodations in the workplace, recruitment and employment policy changes to encourage people with disabilities to apply, educational opportunities targeting people with disabilities, public-relations strategies to alter employer beliefs about the feasibility of hiring people with disabilities, affirmative employment programs, antidiscrimination legal enforcement, and on and on. These are all forms of accommodation, although they differ greatly in focus and effect. But they all share one feature, compared with standard supply-side programs: they are all obviously more costly.

Consider what undoubtedly is the most contentious demand-side solution – affirmative action employment schemes. There is considerable variation here, ranging from quota hiring programming and employment equity legislation to direct government subsidies and job creation. Some of these approaches envisage a close working relationship with the private sector, others are more coercive and adversarial. There is very little research available about the actual economic costs of any of these affirmative schemes, and opposition to them, especially in the United States, has been so unrelenting that it is unlikely that there will be any program in existence to study. Yet, it is safe to say that no one, whether economist or non-economist, would be willing to claim that the purely economic benefits of this type of demand-side programming outweigh the costs.[62]

It is true that as a group economists are not unified in their opposition to employment equity, equal access, or any other affirmative action arrangement. Yet when defended by economists the argument given is that policies that require structural social change and ongoing, open-ended government intervention into the market cannot be fairly assessed on economic grounds alone, since their rationale is both political and economic.[63] Thus, the 1984 Abella Report argues that 'the pursuit of policies that permit everyone who so wishes access to the realization of his or her full employment potential is not one that ought to be tied to an economic divining rod.'[64] And it is true that economists who recommend against affirmative programming do so entirely on economic grounds.

Now the economists' traditional modesty about the scope of economic reasoning and the importance of efficiency as a social goal is another way of acknowledging that the economic model is incomplete as a policy tool. Still, this modesty cannot be taken at face value because like the processes of medicalization, the 'economicalization' of disablement has obvious hegemonic tendencies. Although the economist will insist that all he or she is concerned about is the economic side of policy, economic reasoning leaves very little room for any other concern.

For it is essential to economic reasoning that there be a countervailing relationship between efficiency and equity or social justice – this is perhaps the most powerful ideological commitment of modern economic thought. Because of this dogma, the economic model entails that the social injustice of handicapping phenomena such as stigma or discrimination, while 'politically' important, is 'external' to the core analysis of disablement provided by economic rationality. Thus, economists often complain that legal protection of rights in general and the enforcement of antidiscrimination provisions in particular are 'irrational' constraints on policy formation that can only lead to economic aberrations. There has been in recent years a growing scholarly interest in the economic analysis of the law itself, an analysis which, among other things, would recommend that judicial decisions with respect to rights more closely reflect the economic perspective.[65]

It is important to be as precise as possible about the way the economic model distorts disablement policy. For in its defence could it not be said that all the model requires policy analysts to do is 'cost' our social response to disablement policy, something that is surely appropriate? If that is distorting perhaps we should alter our political agenda and our policy goals.

Still, an important part of what costing entails is putting an economic price on handicapping phenomena such as attitudes and practices of stigmatization and discrimination. Once one accepts this move the inevitable next step is to compare these costs with the costs that might accrue if steps were taken to remove the handicaps. Again, as with demand-side solutions to the employment situation, since handicapping phenomena are entrenched and systemic, policy directed at their removal will *always* be expensive, especially since the economic benefits of implementing it, the national efficiency argument notwithstanding, are so speculative.

Thus, it is not strictly true to say that the economic model of disablement *ignores* the role of the social environment in the production of disabilities or treats handicapping phenomena as irrelevant to disablement policy. Rather, it distorts policy since, on economic grounds, the argument in favour of the demand side policy options is extremely difficult to make out. The advocate of antidiscrimination laws or affirmative action initiatives is forced to plead for 'equity and social justice,' notions that are never explained clearly or fully and which, compared with the no-nonsense quantitative and precise standard of economic efficiency, seem almost amorphous.

In addition, one feature of the economic approach, usually thought to be one of its principal virtues, contributes to a persistent misunderstanding of handicapping as a social issue. That is that economic analysis understands cost-benefit relationships to be 'symmetrical,' in the sense that there is no social event or relationship that is inherently costly or inherently beneficial; it all depends on how the costs or benefits compare with alternatives. Thus, for example, workplace discrimination is not prima facie objectionable, since even unfair relationships are symmetrical: the costs to the worker of being unfairly denied employment and the costs to the employer of being forced, through state action, to change this discriminatory policy are, for the economist, fully commensurable. Economic analysis pre-empts any judgment about the discriminatory practice prior to a comparison of these costs.

This is not to say, dogmatically, that a discriminatory employment practice that victimizes (to take the easiest case) *qualified* people with disabilities could not possibly be justified on grounds of cost alone. Of course it could. The point that needs to be made, rather, is the converse. Given the nature of discriminatory practices and our culture's growing concern about them, an argument based on cost alone does not automatically justify such practices; from a social-policy perspective, we must look at other considerations.

To be sure, it is important not to treat the 'economic approach' as monolithic, for just as there are internal doctrinal disputes among those who would medicalize disablement, so there are disputes among economists over the character of efficiency and its relationship to equity.

Perhaps the most obvious controversy is whether, as an economist would say equity and efficiency are in a zero-sum relationship, so that it is an inevitable fact of social existence that disablement policy must always weigh equality against cost-effectiveness.[66] Economists who adopt this view argue that the goals of disablement policy – participation, accommodation, and respect – are in effect mutually exclusive commodities: one may have to 'pay' for participation in units of respect, or sacrifice a high level of accommodation in order to afford some measure of participation. Other economists, though a minority, argue that the standard view is an illusion, and as a society we do not have to trade efficiency for equality.[67]

It is difficult to see how, even if the minority view in this dispute is successful, the basic character of the economic model might be altered. It is difficult to conceive of an economic perspective reconciling efficiency and 'social justice' considerations when nothing very substantive seems to be meant by the latter.

On the evidence of existing programs, however, the economic model is committed to two priorities: that of work disability in the conceptualization of disablement and that of efficiency as a standard of policy assessment. Taken together, these priorities are undoubtedly responsible for some of the more persistent anomalies of disablement programming.

Consider one of these anomalies, directly linked to the economic model, involving the goal of accommodation. Once disablement is transformed into an economic phenomenon it is reasonable to ask of each variety of disability what the upper cost bounds of accommodation are. If the economic model is right and disablement should be an economic phenomenon, then this question is not only answerable, it must be empirically decidable. It must be a scientific question that can be scientifically answered.

The task of determining this upper bound is strictly analogous to the task, made intelligible by the biomedical model, of providing a 'whole-person' impairment rating. And, like the biomedical question, the economic question is arbitrary and fictional. Realistically speaking, no amount of money could accommodate a person to being blind; there is no upper bound, since there is no functional correspondence between money and a limitation on positive freedom. Yet since the economic model demands a solution to this problem, one has to be invented. So it is that economists rely on imaginary lotteries and counterfactual bargaining experiments in which one asks how much the 'reasonable person' would pay to be blinded. These imaginary experiments generate functional correspondences between degrees of impairment and sums of money, since that is what they are designed to do. But no one could plausibly suggest that they have any empirical basis whatsoever. They are merely necessary fictions, although fictions with practical impact.

Another, less localized, policy anomaly concerns the peculiar property of the economic model to perpetuate the social problem it ostensibly seems to resolve. For example, it is a common and well-documented complaint that social security programming in general, but most particularly the 'welfare' components, stigmatizes and humiliates recipients of the benefits. It is difficult to believe that these forms of handicapping are wholly unintended, since there is an obvious economic rationale for limiting access to cost-generating programs. But, whether intended or not, perpetuating handicapping phenomena within disablement programming is anomalous and self-defeating, since it contributes to a social environment that is responsible for creating the needs the programming is presumably designed to serve. Programming that emphasizes the non-normal or atypical character of the benefits received merely entrenches the social belief that those who benefit are 'special cases' who are dependent on the state to meet their needs. But what could be more counterproductive to disablement policy as a whole than perpetuating a 'culture of dependency'?

Demonstrating that the economic representation of disablement tends to perpetuate rather than relieve the 'problem' of disablement, by in effect sustaining handicaps, is one of the achievements of the third and final model I want to consider, the social-political model. First though, we need to focus more directly on an aspect of the economic model that has so far only been hinted at, namely, its normative consequences with respect to disablement theory.

The Economic Model and Disablement Theory

To sum up the previous section, the economic model is founded on the socially contingent and interactive dimension of disablement called 'disability.' Led by the logic of economic reasoning, with its goal of efficiency, the model has historically served to bring disablement policy within the bounds of social policy by creating the economic representation of work disability. Although the model has no difficulty subsuming the impairment dimension of disablement, the effect of economic analysis has been to reduce disablement to an economic problem, principally involving the supply side of the labour market.

Now it has been argued that one of the major flaws of the model is that its conception of normality – namely, a specified repertoire of productive capabilities – reflects assumptions about the nature of work that are no longer tenable. This standard repertoire, the criticism goes, is far more appropriate for manual labour than for the delivery of personal services, especially those that make use of so-phisticated technology.[68] Programming to further the goal of partici-pation, based on this out-of-date characterization of employability, will create disablement ghettos and distort judgments about the costs of making changes to the workplace. While it may be extremely costly and inefficient to make it possible for someone in a wheelchair to work on a road-repair crew, it need not be costly to enable that individual to work as a receptionist at a law firm or, for that matter, as a lawyer.

It is important to appreciate that this particular criticism, though initially powerful, does not touch the economic model itself. Quite the contrary, a sensible economist would favour a highly dynamic conception of the 'normal' repertoire of capabilities, one which would keep pace with the actual dimensions of the labour market. Anything else would be irrational, since an invalid operationalization of work disability would be a self-defeating normative feature of the eco-nomic approach to disablement.

It is also frequently remarked that just as the biomedical model focuses on a set of problems that are not always dominant in the life experience of people with disabilities, the economic model is also fatally unidimensional. People with disabilities are not always over-whelmed by the fact of limitations on their productive capacities, or even their unemployability. The actual experience of disablement is, some have suggested, an experience of handicap more than disability, since one's day-to-day life is shaped more by the attitudes and prejudices of other people than it is by one's general economic condi-tions.[69] To this criticism advocates of the economic model would likely respond that the notion of work disability remains the appro-priate focus for social policy. This is a fair point, since it would be wildly inappropriate to propose a comprehensive and unified dis-ablement policy that did not take work disability into account.

Although advocates of the economic model can dodge both of these criticisms, the critiques still have force since the model's com-mitment to efficiency ensures that it will always have a conservative influence on policy. Although the point is somewhat speculative, it is safe to assume that the more a policy reform package requires extensive and radical change to existing social structures, both public and private, the more costly it will be. And for this reason, the model will always favour a cautious flexibility and counsel against all forms of intervention into the working of the market. But, of course, the economist/policy analyst can then respond: Why should social policy for people with disabilities purport to 'change their world'? Should not social policy have modest aims, and be one-dimensional if that makes its objectives more feasible?

Still, the reluctance to sacrifice efficiency for other values is responsible for the specific concerns I have outlined above: the inability of the model to take seriously the need for demand-side accommodations as a way of furthering the goal of participation; the way it transforms policy putatively designed to meet the needs of people with disabilities into an economic regulatory instrument for the labour market as a whole; its inability to respond to handicapping phenomena; and the way it creates, or at least perpetuates, handicaps in the practice of identifying people with disabilities as generators of special economic costs.

Normatively speaking, in short, the model *conditionalizes* its loyalty to the goals of disablement policy. Although it has no difficulty presenting a coherent account of these goals – one that posits participation as the prior goal with accommodation instrumental to, and respect an inevitable product of, participation – this account is conditional upon efficiency. This means that efficiency, not participation, is the governing goal: a program that fully integrated people with disabilities into the economy, but which was far too costly, would on the economic model be a failure of policy. The economic model put disablement policy on a firm footing as social policy, but only at the cost of transforming it entirely into economic policy.

It is easy enough, therefore, to describe in a few words the normative consequences for disablement theory of the economic model. First, in this model whatever benefits flow from programming to people with disabilities are not benefits enjoyed as of right. Disablement entitlements, as far as the economic model is concerned, are entirely derivative from and conditional upon some level of macro-economic analysis founded ultimately in considerations of efficiency.

One might even say that the benefits that flow to people with disabilities, by virtue of their disabilities, are not strictly speaking entitlements so much as beneficial consequences of policy decisions motivated by economic considerations completely independent of disablement. Bluntly, people in need do not have any claim upon social resources by virtue of their need alone, but only, indirectly, by virtue of the instrumental value that satisfaction of those needs represents to the economy.

Second, economically rational disablement programming cannot be legally committed to the achievement of any objective in furtherance of participation, since such a commitment would remove the flexibility needed to respond to changing economic conditions. In the same way that it would be economically absurd to give people the right to demand a particular rate of inflation or a lending rate, since the Bank of Canada and the Minister of Finance need to be able to respond as they see fit to overall economic conditions, so too in the economic model no one would have the right to any particular form of disablement programming.

Finally, the economic model, constrained by the aggregative and reductive logic of economic analysis, seems absolutely wedded to some version of the net social benefit or national efficiency standard as a basis for evaluating the achievement of policy objectives.

Historically and conceptually, in sum, the normative basis of the economic model has been supplied by economic analysis itself. This is the normative principle of *welfare maximization*, the principle that policy and other social action be designed to maximize the welfare of as many people as possible. Whether disguised as a form of rationality (as it frequently is) or acknowledged to be a moral and political normative theory, welfare maximization is a consequentialist account which, as we shall see, does provide a normative basis for disablement theory. In practice as well, though, the economic model often finds it necessary to rely on one or another manifestation of compensatory or corrective justice, either as embodied in a torts scheme for fault-based compensation or as presupposed by the insurance principle of risk-pooling. Both of these normative bases are embedded in welfare maximization.

The economic model of disablement, possessing as it does both an analysis of disablement and a normative basis for policy, constitutes a complete disablement theory. For many policy analysts the economic model is the only practicable and concrete approach to disablement policy there is. But though the model does indeed explicate disablement, and does provide a normative grounding for an important version of one dimension of disablement – work disability – it has increasingly become the object of criticism among disablement theorists because of its patent failure to acknowledge or deal with the dimension of handicap. This criticism has, almost without exception, come from writers and advocates who have adopted the social-political model of disablement, to which we can now turn.

5 The Social-Political Model of Disablement

Handicaps and the Genesis of the Social-Political Model

It would not be inaccurate to describe the biomedical and the economic models as the 'standard' models of disablement. Both have their roots in mainstream disciplines, the biomedical sciences and economics; both rely on discourses of expertise that occupy an unchallenged position in modern culture; and both offer representations of disablement and people with disabilities that are intuitively understandable and commonplace.

The social-political model, by contrast, is both younger and more revolutionary, and in many respects less coherent and stable. There is no appeal to a single discourse or expertise, no single theoretical framework that ties components of the model together, and no uniform representation of disablement or people with disabilities. Nor could the social-political model be called 'standard' – even though some policy ramifications of it are now permanently entrenched in our law. The model has always been critical of the 'standard' models, and adherents have made a point of presenting their understanding of disablement as iconoclastic.

Although the social-political model is not one but many related models, and although the genesis of this approach to disablement involves a bewildering array of theoretical perspectives and unabashedly political agendas, like the other two models there is at the core of this approach an insight about disablement that is both overwhelmingly intuitive and essential to any attempt to construct a theory of disablement. Since it is quite possible to become lost in the jungle of competing sociological, sociopsychological, and sociopolitical theoretical frameworks used to substantiate the model, it will be helpful to begin by looking more closely at this insight.

Consider the physical condition of short stature. Being short is an impairment (if by 'short' we mean something biomedically significant) and may also be a disability in some contexts, both work- and non-work-related.[1] But there is plainly more to the experience of being unusually short than this. Being shorter than the norm is a modest, one might even say negligible, disability. Yet, because of the social reception of the impairment the experience of being short can involve a substantial limitation on one's positive freedom.

Among children, for example, it has been found that short stature is associated with a wide range of behavioural disorders, including social isolation, depression, low self-esteem, and an increased incidence of somatic complaints. Longitudinal studies that have tracked these children as they age indicate a pronounced level of scholastic underachievement (which cannot be linked to mental impairments attributable to syndromes that include short stature). And studies involving adults show a correlation between short stature and a host of psychosocial problems, such as an inability to sustain supportive relationships, problems obtaining and maintaining jobs, exaggerated extroversion, and a host of other socializing deficiencies.

It is no mystery how these psychosocial disadvantages come about. The nature of interaction between children, and between children and adults, is determined in part by an estimate of the age of the child, usually based on physical appearance. In the case of short children, of course, age tends to be underestimated, and the child is 'infantilized' by parents, peers, and teachers. Short children repeat grades far more often than other children, though the reason given is immaturity and small size rather than scholastic ability. Short adults experience psychosocial difficulties that arise from the reactions of other people rather than from their impairment, which in all but the most extreme instances has almost no disabling consequences at all. These disadvantages are manufactured (though not intentionally) by the attitudes and behaviours of others. They are neither medical problems nor functional limitations; they are socially constructed disadvantages.

To call these 'socially constructed' may conjure up a quasi-mystical act of creation by an amorphous entity.[2] But the meaning should be clear: at the level of the experience of people with disabilities there is a range of disadvantages and limitations that have everything to do with how people react – their attitudes and their behaviours – and nothing to do with one's incapabilities. To say that disadvantages are socially constructed means that these experiences could be altered, remedied, or ameliorated without making any change in the physical condition of the individual. This is the insight of the social-political model.

The implications of this insight are obvious. For one thing, research possibilities immediately present themselves. Should we not investigate what attitudes are responsible for infantilization and what their long-term consequences are? Are there any linkages between the nature of the impairment and the characteristics of these attitudinal reactions? Can these attitudes be overcome, downplayed, or eliminated? How socially or culturally persistent are attitudes and prejudices about height? Are they similar to prejudicial responses to other forms of human differences, such as sex, race, colour, or nationality? And, at the end of the day, why do human beings have this reaction to difference in the first place? Is it some sort of inborn characteristic explainable by evolutionary theory, or learned behaviour, or a bit of both?

We would normally not think of these research questions as requiring, or even being amenable to, biomedical explanations; and economic theory does not seem at all relevant either. For the most part these are questions for sociologists, social psychologists, and psychologists. What is at issue here are attitudes and social responses; we want to know how people react to impairments, and why.

Moreover, once the empirical results come in, and theories explaining the data are suggested, social scientists may find themselves turning into social activists. After all, the prejudices and stereotypes and stigmas that go to make up so much of the experience of disablement are totally unwarranted and socially destructive. Inasmuch as these unjustified reactions seem to be part of the social fabric, suffusing social institutions and private relationships alike, and directly interfering with the lives and well-being of people, they are morally pernicious. Should they not be eliminated if possible, or at least their effects minimized? And since these attitudes are so pervasive, is not the appropriate response some form of direct political action – organization, mobilization, lobbying, and the like?

As we shall see in the next section, in a nutshell this is a fairly accurate description of the evolution of the social-political model of disablement. The basic insight that there must be a third dimension to disablement, namely, handicap, seems to have motivated social-scientific research aimed at getting clear about the nature of the social processes of handicapping. These results were then placed in a wider sociological context by researchers who sought to draw together all forms of discriminatory and stigmatizing social treatment within a single theoretical framework. As this work was going on, though, other researchers saw the need to politicize their research, both as a theoretical exercise and as a prelude to political action by and on behalf of people with disabilities.[3]

As with the economic model there are risks in treating the development of the social-political model as if it involved a tidy, sequential process. Moreover, unlike the economic model, the social-political model is very much in the process of development so, though I want in a moment to identify some of the major intellectual influences of the model, the synergy of these, often extremely diverse, influences cannot be easily described.

One methodological reason for this complexity is that this model is absolutely resistant to the convenient expository technique of drawing a line between 'hard facts' about handicapping and theories of what handicapping involves. An investigation into the theoretical significance of this dimension of disablement must, indeed, be premised on two interlocking claims: that handicaps are socially constructed and that *accounts* of handicaps are socially constructed. In other words, the question of whether handicaps exist, and what form they take, is not a purely empirical issue: it is an issue that derives its significance from normative assumptions about proper and improper responses to human differences. Thus, handicaps are not only social constructs; one can make them disappear by altering one's account of political morality.

The best way of putting this point is: there is no scientific, factual, 'objective,' or value-neutral way of distinguishing disabilities from handicaps; the distinction we draw in particular cases follows from implicit or explicit normative judgments that we make about which disadvantages in life one must put up with and which one need not. These judgments indicate, in part, where the boundaries of our social responsibilities to people with disabilities lie. Since no disability is in principle beyond accommodation – even people who are blind could drive cars if things were *very* different from what they are now – to judge a social consequence of a disability to be a handicap is to identify the obstacle in the social environment, rather than the impairment in the body of the individual, as the problem. The decision *not* to accommodate becomes a manifestation of unequal, discriminatory, treatment that stands in need of a justification. Thus, the line that separates disabilities from handicaps is drawn with the help of political morality, in the form of a judgment about society's obligations to people with disabilities.

Consider the case of short stature again. It may be thought theoretically perspicuous to group together the character disorders and other social consequences of infantilizing and call these the 'disabilities of short stature.' To be sure, each of these psychosocial characteristics has an effect on one's ability to fulfil the normal social roles of student, worker, spouse, parent, and the rest. And we could easily imagine their economic ramifications. So, why not pursue this theoretical classification?

The only reason for not doing so is that the normative assumptions it relies on are objectionable. Since infantilization is a behavioural response of others to short stature – and one which, presumably, can be avoided – it strikes us as manifestly unfair that disadvantages that some people must struggle with in life, created by others, should not be addressed by policy.

As a general matter, *every* disadvantage or loss of positive freedom associated with disablement can be viewed as a disability or as a handicap by shifting perspectives. An employer who refuses to hire an otherwise qualified person with cerebral palsy will cite physical incapacity as grounds for the decision, insisting that this is not a case of discrimination or prejudice, since, as a matter of brute and unalterable fact, this individual lacks the repertoire of productive capacities required for the job. The employer's decision is thus made on grounds of a real and relevant physical difference. And from this perspective, the only relevant social policy would be one which seeks to alter the person's repertoire of capacities or else to make it feasible to remove the worker from the labour market entirely.

Yet if we change the perspective a very different result follows. Since being unemployable is not an intrinsic feature of the profile of physical dysfunction in a person with cerebral palsy, the social disadvantage represented by the employment decision is the direct result of the social reception of the impairment, not the impairment itself. This reception is not cast in stone, simply because changes can be made to the workplace or the job description that would accommodate the limited repertoire so that the individual could become productive and employable. The failure to do this (as well as the judgment that it is not 'feasible' to do so) is a handicap.

Both the biomedical and the economic models of disablement, although for very different reasons, structure the disability/handicap distinction so that it is inevitable that limits on positive freedom such as arise from stature disorders will be understood as disabilities rather than handicaps. The biomedical model makes no room for socially constructed aspects of disablement at all, so must treat these disorders as impairments. The economic model, while it could in theory locate the responsibility for these disorders in the social environment, will resist this move since its governing normative principle deems it to be an intolerably inefficient policy solution.

Thus, we come to the distinguishing feature of the social-political model. This model represents the 'problem' of disablement in handicap terms, which is to say, in terms of the social construction of unwarranted disadvantages. The 'location' of a handicap is always *in the social environment*, never in the individual. So there is no such thing as a warranted handicap. The governing normative stance of the social-political model flows directly from the normative character of handicap, providing the analysis of handicapping as social process and the broad outlines of the political agenda for dealing with handicaps.

But what of our person of short stature who, solely by virtue of infantilization, has developed a severe character disorder? Obviously, the social-political model does not suggest that changes to the social processes that created this disorder, even radical changes, need have any effect on existing disorders – the damage has been done. What the model does demand is that the *responsibility* for such disorders be understood to lie with society. This is crucial, since it entails that accommodation for the disabilities associated with short stature is a social obligation, and the failure to respond to this obligation is a handicap.

Etiologically speaking, it would still be correct to say that stature disorders arise from an interaction of impairment (or perceived impairment) and social environment. But in the social-political model to leave it at that is wrong. For the problem of disablement, and so the nature of disablement policy, must focus on the fact that such disorders, and all the other social disadvantages that may result from them, are handicaps that stand in need of positive social responses to alter the processes that created the handicaps and to accommodate those who have already been harmed by them. Therefore, the characterization of short-stature character disorders is a matter of judgment grounded not in biomedicine or economic analysis, but in political morality. The social-political model is therefore unavoidably political.

To be sure, many proponents of the model are not fully aware of the normative commitment that their analysis of disablement requires of them. In part this is because the model enjoys an impressive social-scientific basis that greatly strengthens the argument for a handicap focus to disablement policy.

The Social-Scientific Roots of the Model

As with the economic model, the successful emergence of rehabilitation therapy had a powerful influence on the development of the social-political model. What set rehabilitation apart from other health professions was its recognition that an effective therapeutic response to impairment must be sensitive to the environment in which the person with the impairment lives and thrives. This insight, as we saw, helped to instil the disability dimension of disablement into program rationale and design. It also sets the stage for the revolutionary proposition that the proper role of the therapist must be to orchestrate environmental modifications as well as to assist people in modifying their capacities or changing their aspirations.[4]

Another influence, beginning in the 1950s with Talcott Parsons's work on the 'sick role,' was the trend among medical sociologists to think seriously about the social ramifications of being perceived as having a medial problem.[5] Though Parsons's work was controversial,[6] as we have seen, it gave critics of the biomedical approach to disablement a valuable tool. The inappropriateness of the sick role in the case of permanent disability suggested the need not merely to modify the biomedical model, but to investigate the mechanisms by which handicapping phenomena of the sort implicit in the sick role were socially created. It seemed to some that it was but a short step from Parsons's analysis to the claim that disablement is itself a form of social deviance.[7] If normal variations in physique are important factors in personality formation, surely visible impairments are bound to have an even more potent effect on one's social relationships. Moreover, since it is obvious that atypical appearance attracts negative social evaluation, it was thought that much could be learned about disablement by closely studying its overall social reception.

It was also noted that people with disabilities, like racial and religious minorities, are subject to group stereotypes and deeply ingrained cultural prejudices. Anthropological cross-cultural studies emphasized the variety of stigmas associated with disabilities, as well as the sometimes astonishingly different cultural views of what disability is.[8] Seeking a background explanation of these diverse data, some researchers began to apply Erving Goffman's classic description of the causes and effects of stigmatization to the case of disablement.[9] According to Goffman, all forms of stigma identify an undesired difference that serves to separate the stigmatized individual from the rest of society, or at least from those who are not similarly stigmatized. Once the stigmatized individual becomes aware of this social label, his or her self-perception is altered by the fact that the stigma is invariably discrediting.

Spanning the decade of the 1960s, two ground-breaking treatments of the social psychology of disablement appeared whose very titles signalled the new approach that was developing: Beatrice A. Wright's *Physical Disability – A Psychosocial Approach* (1960, reissued in 1983) and Constantina Safilios-Rothschild's *The Sociology and Social Psychology of Disability and Rehabilitation* (1970).[10] Wright's work was premised on the view, revolutionary for the day, that 'the source of obstacles and difficulties, that is, what actually handicaps a person, cannot be determined by the disability alone.'[11] For her part, Safilios-Rothschild argued that the primary contribution of social psychology to the investigation of disablement should be that of identifying the social and psychological characteristics of the 'disabled role.'[12] These works heralded the emergence of social-psychological research into physical and mental disablement. Both authors were eager to apply to disablement the most current and potentially helpful background theory available in their disciplines: and that was deviance theory.

Very roughly, deviance theory holds that behaviour is deviant when it does not conform to social norms or expectations, and so is behaviour that most people (or at least those with the power to have their views generally accepted) find offensive in some way or other. Deviance is a social label applied to individuals or groups as a designation of an attribute (or perceived attribute) that is rule-breaking or norm-violating. Of course, this label is anything but a neutral designator, since whatever is labelled 'deviant' is always understood as discreditable in some way. As a consequence, deviants will be assigned a lower position in the social-status hierarchy.[13]

Deviance theory developed out of studies of criminals, drug users, prostitutes, and others discredited because of their 'voluntary' rule-breaking.[14] But from the outset, some researchers thought there could be research potential in viewing people with disabilities as 'involuntary deviants.' As stigmas go, the stigma of disablement has had a long history, fuelled, some speculate, by the fear or anxiety that impairments produce in others.[15] Highly visible impairments were at one time thought to be literally stigmatic, that is, signs of sinful and blameworthy behaviour. This may explain some of our current social attitudes towards people with AIDS.[16]

Although the evolution of medicine helped to undermine this view of impairments, as far as the deviance theorists are concerned the social stigma of disablement remained. They reasoned that disablement is a socially created category applied to people with disabilities by 'normals' in order to discredit them indirectly by justifying prejudice, stereotyping, and misperceptions. Though disablement may no longer be viewed as the mark of sinfulness, it is still a stigma of inferiority, neediness, and dependence. People with disabilities are thus like members of discredited races: they share the same social conspicuousness (an identifiable difference that sets them apart from the 'normals'), the same sense of being prisoners to the misperceptions of others, and the same kinds of systemic discrimination.[17]

The principal drawback of the deviance approach to disablement is that it is riddled with internal, methodological, and theoretical controversies. Some commentators suggest that these disputes represent different perspectives on the same social phenomena about which there is agreement. Others argue that the real problem is that the various alternative conceptual frameworks proposed have not been fully integrated.[18] Unfortunately, this more optimistic assessment overlooks the fact that the disputes sometimes involve deep-seated controversies about the political analysis to be given to the processes of deviance creation,[19] while others raise very broad epistemological issues, such as whether the focus of the theory should be sociological or psychological.

In any event, most researchers who have applied deviance theory to disablement have made use of the so-called labelling paradigm, a popular, social-psychological version of deviance theory that stresses the importance of social categorization in the creation of forms of interaction and self-perception.[20] The labelling paradigm – an offshoot of symbolic interactionism – emphasizes the highly contingent and 'constructed' nature of social roles, shared meanings, and other representations of people and groups. As one of the early theorists in this tradition argued, 'the deviant is one to whom that label has successfully been applied; deviant behavior is behavior people so label.'[21] Though contingent, the processes of social labelling are extremely powerful and have an impact on social institutions and individual consciousnesses alike.

The principal theoretical claim of the labelling tradition is, therefore, that shared meanings arising from shared representations of deviance and deviants, constantly reinforced, not only determine how 'normals' interact with people who are so labelled, they also determine how those labelled view themselves. Deviance is a 'master status' that pervades social life. Being possessed of a deviant characteristic makes one a *deviant person*, an individual whose social identity is exhausted by deviance, as in the case of those who are labelled 'mentally ill.'[22]

Labelling theory in particular and the deviance approach in general hold out the prospect of explaining the processes by which impairments become handicaps. The theoretical contribution of labelling theory in this regard has been to support research into the experience of being labelled deviant as well as research into the social processes of differentiation that create deviant social roles.[23] This research stresses the interactive character of deviance processes, and in particular that deviant outcomes – both social and psychological – 'emerge from the continuous interaction between the individual's behavior and the response of others.'[24]

Yet, it is one thing to posit this interactive relationship and something very different to explain it. Though more sociological and psychological research has come out of the labelling approach than from any other model of deviance, the background interactionist theory has been subjected to powerful criticism from nearly every major school of contemporary sociology.[25] The reason why the labelling paradigm attracts this criticism is not difficult to see: the metaphor of 'interaction' is far too mysterious and undefined to carry the theoretical weight it must if this approach is to have any explanatory power. But, its inadequacies as a theory aside, there is no doubt that the empirical research carried out in its name has given considerable factual support to the insight that underwrites the social-political model.

On the sociological side, there have been various attempts to document the experience of becoming deviant and to determine which social institutions and processes may be responsible. The earliest and still the most persuasive of these studies is set out in *The Making of Blind Men* by Robert Scott.[26] Scott shows that the status and social role of being a blind person is learned and not at all an inevitable psychological consequence of the impairment itself. The relationships between sighted and blind people create and reinforce the blind-person role in countless ways, primarily because, Scott argues, many of the norms that assess the conduct of ordinary interactions are governed by visual clues. Thus, relationships with people who are blind are idiosyncratic and stressful, and the blind person discovers early in life that encounters with the sighted are facilitated if he or she acts like a blind person, that is, in accordance with stereotypical representations.

More troubling though, Scott discovered that the total network of agencies, organizations, and programs for people who are blind serves to complete the production of the blind-person social role. And this is done so thoroughly that blindness becomes the primary factor around which people who are blind must organize their lives and relationships. Their blindness overwhelms their social existence.

More recently, David Thomas has collected together autobiographical descriptions by people with various disabilities of their experiences of being handicapped.[27] These accounts show the variation in societal reaction to different forms of impairment, as well as the diversity of handicap situations, from the trivial and benign to the highly debilitating and discriminatory.

Sociological research of this sort, of which there has been much in recent years,[28] helps to make the experience of being handicapped accessible to others. Significantly, all of this valuable research is founded on the interactionist principle that, since handicapping is the product of a relationship between an impairment and the social environment, the perspective of the person with disabilities is as informative about the nature of disablement as the perspective of those who study it from the outside.

On the psychological side, there has been a great deal of empirical research into the dynamics of stigmatization. Building on early research involving the techniques for the 'management' of strained interactions,[29] important work has been done on the role of stigma in face-to-face encounters between people with visible or noticeable disabilities and normals.[30] The work suggests that the imputation of deviance in the case of disablement emerges from psychological reactions to interpersonal contact – in particular, embarrassment, pity, fear, avoidance, and repugnance – rather than from deeply enculturated or conventionalized attitudes of the sort that seem to be involved in racial deviance.[31]

Pursuing the interactionist model, some researchers have focused on the stigmatized side of interpersonal encounters.[32] Evidence here suggests that people with disabilities often seem to resort to a variety of 'self-presentational strategies' to cope with the reactions their impairments produce in others. When concealment of 'passing' is not possible, the person may attempt to ease tensions in social interactions by 'covering' the impairment, that is, by reducing the salience of the stigma by emphasizing normal attributes. In other circumstances, especially when the individual is required to emphasize the disability in order to be eligible for social programs, there is likely to be role acceptance, a demonstration of inferiority, even self-imposed infantilization. And in yet other circumstances the individual may adopt a more confrontational strategy and resort to self-promotion, exemplification, or some other device for emphasizing the limitations imposed by the stigma in order to support a claim of admirable moral strength.

Although each of the competing psychological 'grand' theories – motivational, psychoanalytic, behavioural, and cognitive – has offered theoretical explanations of the development of the psychology of the person with disabilities,[33] by far the most influential is an approach that builds on the interactionist insight itself. Thus, the somatopsychological approach, suggested by Beatrice Wright and others in the early 1960s,[34] claims that the psychological dynamics of disablement can be explained in terms of an interaction between physique or body image and its social reception. Psychologically, that is, disablement is dominated by the need to adjust to the expectations and attitudes of others and thereby to cope with the implicit image of inferiority conjured up by these attitudes.

It is now acknowledged that the vast literature on the relationship between disablement and personality, the product of intense research in the 1960s and 1970s, did not support the hope of some researchers that correlations could be found between kinds of impairments and personality types. Although all of the studies indicate that people with disabilities manifest introversion, anxiety, frustration, depression, and lower self-esteem, there is also considerable variation among people with the same impairment.[35]

On the other, 'normal' side of the interaction, somatopsychological attitude studies have used virtually every attitude measurement technique available – from social distance scales, sociometrics, semantic differentials, picture and storytelling stimuli, to direct physiological measures. Much of this work has focused on children, in the hope of tracking the social factors that are responsible for the origins of handicapping attitudes and beliefs. There has also been work on the attitudes of health professionals and parents.[36]

Though there is this enormous wealth of information available, nearly forty years' worth, most researchers are extremely cautious about generalizing the results. There are notorious difficulties in providing realistic interactional settings in controlled environments and in separating intrapsychic, experiential, and social components of attitudes, as well as determining the relative degree of the influence of each. And though attempts have been made to isolate and measure demographic and personality correlates of attitudes toward people with disabilities, these results are inconclusive and disappointing. None the less, one of the leading researchers in attitude studies, Jerome Siller, has felt confident enough about trends in somatopsychological research to set out the general structure of attitudes to people with disabilities.[37] Siller claims that there is sufficient evidence to suggest that there are seven basic 'attitudinal components' that shape the social reception of many visible impairments:[38]

1 Interaction strain: a general uneasiness in the presence of people with disabilities and uncertainty as to how to deal with them
2 Rejection of intimacy
3 Generalized rejection: a more pervasively negative and derogatory attitude that tends to favour segregation
4 Authoritarian virtuousness: an ostensibly positive attitude that reveals itself to be an authoritarian call for treatment that is less than benevolent
5 Inferred emotional consequences: a hostility to the character and emotions of people with disabilities
6 Distressed identification: anxiety about one's own vulnerability to disability
7 Imputed functional limitations: a devaluation of the capacities of the person with disabilities.

What is significant about this list is that it provides us with concrete examples of stigmatizing attitudes – that is to say, examples of attitudinal handicaps. Thus, attitude studies provide the link between the concept of handicap and observable and measurable empirical phenomena.

Attitude studies also make it clear that handicapping is a *systemic* social process and not a matter of the ignorance, intolerance, or prejudice of particular individuals. Although attitudinal handicaps are attitudes that individual people express, these individuals do not create them; they are social products. Child research suggests, for example, that from a very early age children seem to learn to react to people with visible impairments in ways that are very similar to the ways of their parents. No somatopsychologist would pretend to be able to explain how and why this happens – we are still at the stage of training ourselves to see the phenomenon for what it is. But some social psychologists are confident enough in their research to see the need to track the various attitudes that Siller identifies in our social practices. Eventually, we may be able to see how our social institutions are shaped by them as well.

There is another important aspect of attitude research that can be gleaned from Siller's summary. That is that no one could plausibly suggest that the language used to set out these seven components is normatively neutral. Of course, there were normative presumptions built into the deviance approach from the beginning, though this was vigorously denied by researchers. In any event, recent trends in deviancy research that frankly and openly adopt a political position on the injustice of deviance-creating processes are merely making explicit the implicit political agenda of the interactionist tradition.[39]

The fact that there are normative presumptions invoked in the deviance approach has led a handful of writers, generally sympathetic with the economic model, to complain about political bias. They have argued that the deviance model wrongly assumes that every social response to disablement creates stigma, when, for example, rehabilitation therapy is not some sort of conspiratorial mechanism for keeping people with disabilities out of the social mainstream.[40]

Deviance theory has also been criticized for worsening the social condition of people with disabilities, a criticism potentially far more damning. In his monograph *Attitudes and Disabled People*, Victor Finkelstein claims that as a social-scientific endeavour the deviance approach perpetuates, when it does not create, the stereotypes it is purporting to investigate. Finkelstein argues that, rather than increasing our social sensitivity to attitudinal handicaps, the deviance approach defuses our normative response: 'During the past two decades the concept of "stigma" has come a long way in making "prejudice" socially acceptable and in enabling bigots to deny responsibility for their attitudes.'[41]

Although Finkelstein overstates his case by refusing to see a distinction between disability and handicap, the thrust of his critique is very telling. For even when research is intentionally aimed at exposing handicapping phenomena as a social ill, there remains an assumption that the social problem of handicapping lies *both* with the person with disabilities and with the environment. As Finkelstein notes, the problem is that the theoretical presumption of deviance theory is *interactionism*, so that however much the deviance theorist insists that handicaps arise from stigmatizing attitudes, he or she must acknowledge that these attitudes are about something, something which is intrinsically located in the stigmatized individual. In other words, the deviance approach is not fully aligned with the concept of handicap. As such the theory cannot provide the foundation for the social-political model.

If we were to make the alignment complete, handicaps and handicapping could not be viewed neutrally as products of impersonal, perhaps inevitable, social processes – which is presumably what true, objective scientists would be obliged to do. To do that, however, is tacitly to endorse or at least condone, the political arrangement that produces and tolerates handicaps. Tolerance of handicaps and handicapping is, as mentioned before, a kind of second-order or meta-handicap. Pursuing this line of reasoning, several writers have come to realize that, if it is to be distinguished from the other two models of disablement, the social-political model must take the next step and *politicize* disablement; and this is precisely what has occurred.

The Politicization of Disablement

The politicization of disablement was not an incidental feature of the development of the social-political model: it created the model. Although the array of sociological and social-psychological research in the past four decades served to ground the model empirically, it also revealed the need to transcend the putatively normatively neutral and scientific mode of investigation and embrace a political agenda.

In yet another instance in the evolution of disablement, where it is difficult to identify what was cause and what effect, the theoretical development that crystallized the social-political model arose simultaneously with the rise of political activism among people with disabilities.

It has been argued, and seems reasonable, that in North America political activism for people with disabilities became a viable and attractive option as a direct result of the civil rights movement in the United States.[42] Political unrest, fuelled by optimism from successes in combating racial discrimination, coupled with the dynamics of political protest and persuasion, created a vehicle for the expression of discontent among people with disabilities and their advocates.

Disablement advocacy has for decades taken the form of voluntary and charitable organizations. These societies – like the Canadian National Institute for the Blind in Canada – tend to be organized around impairments and are predominantly staffed by people with professional or personal links to their constituency. These societies direct public attention to the welfare of people with disabilities and, as charitable organizations, have been effective in addressing some of the needs of people at the local level. Since they often need to maintain good relations with government agencies, they shun political radicalism. Because of this, when activism was in the air, a new breed of advocacy organization evolved in the 1960s and 1970s in order to express the new political consciousness.

A recent study suggests that there are now at least five kinds of advocacy organizations at work in North America and Europe.[43] The voluntary or charitable organizations have been joined by lobbying organizations (usually single-issue efforts restricted to particular impairments), consumer and self-help organizations, collective action / consciousness-raising organizations, and umbrella or coordinating groups.

There is some evidence to suggest that in Canada it was the so-called consumer movement that had the greatest effect on the creation of the current range of advocacy organizations.[44] For example, one of the more influential of Canada's umbrella-type organizations, the Coalition of Provincial Organizations of the Handicapped (COPOH), was organized in 1975 expressly to coordinate consumer activist groups throughout the provinces. COPOH was very active during the hearings before the Special Joint Committee of the Senate and the House of Commons on the Constitution of Canada (the

Hays-Joyal Committee) when section 15 of Canada's Charter of Rights and Freedoms was being considered in 1980–1.[45]

The guiding rationale of consumer and self-help groups, whatever the clientele, is empowerment. It may have been inevitable, therefore, that a group of people characterized, both professionally and socially, as 'dependent' would have been drawn to a political movement that stressed the right of self-determination and control. Without a doubt the most dramatically successful example of consumer organizations is the American independent living (IL) movement[46] which originated in 1972 with the opening of the Center for Independent living in Berkeley, California. The aim of the center was to provide people with severe disabilities with a wide range of services designed to increase their independence – peer counselling, advocacy services, attendant-care referral services, health-maintenance training, wheel-chair repair, and the like. The center continues to this day to be managed by people who have disabilities.

From the outset, IL was conceived to be far more than a service broker. The founders very deliberately tried to create an alternative model of disablement service delivery. Because of their practical emphasis they tended to express this in rehabilitative terms and were especially quick to identify the biomedical model as the principal source of handicapping. The effect of that model, they believed, was to reinforce dependence.[47] These activists aligned themselves ideologically with what has come to be called the principle of 'normalization,' a parallel revolution that was taking place in the area of developmental disability.[48]

In addition, the IL movement saw itself as influenced by, and complementary to the civil rights movement of the 1950s and 1960s. This meant, among other things, that members of the movement saw their task to be a broadly political, indeed revolutionary, one. While considerable effort went into service design models (producing some of the best and most innovative examples of supportive environments available), skills training, and other self-help programming, energy also went into direct political action. For example, the IL movement was active in the lobbying efforts that culminated in the 1978 Rehabilitation Act Amendments.[49]

Taken together, these two facets of the IL movement highlight the wholehearted adoption of the discourse of political rights. The IL movement and its offshoots around the world are committed to exposing disablement as a socially created form of institutionalized oppression and responding to this oppression by empowering people with disabilities in securing their rights. Although there are different responses to oppression, this political representation of the 'problem' of disablement is a characteristic feature of the social-political model.

As these developments in the politics of disablement were unfolding (and perhaps because of them), social theorists sought an alternative representation of people with disabilities. Clearly, the social-scientific findings were not compatible with the biomedical representation of people with disabilities as locations for medical problems, or the economic representation of them as supply-side labour-market problems. The alternative was obvious. If, as the activists were insisting, disablement is a socially constructed form of oppression, then people with disabilities must surely be *oppressed people.*

Despite its political content, this characterization flowed quite naturally from the social-scientific accounts of disablement. The deviance theorists in particular had set the stage by providing a vocabulary for describing social inequality as the transformation of difference into deviance. The next theoretical step, motivated by the theory and practice of politicization, was to represent people with disabilities as a minority group, a marginalized population experiencing systemic discrimination.

Although what is sometimes called the 'minority-group analysis' is not without its problems, it is now a central feature of the social-political model. Indeed without it – or some other similar characterization – the model would be highly unstable. This is because the minority-group analysis provides a way of dealing with an ambiguity briefly mentioned in Chapter 2. To recall, the problem with handicaps as social disadvantages associated with impairments is that we are tempted to think that at least some of the disadvantages are warranted or justifiable. If so, then we seem to need policy criteria for distinguishing disadvantages to which society has an obligation to respond and those to which it does not.

Political theorists will recognize this problem as an instance of a perennial worry about social inequality: given the brute and unalterable fact that people are not equal in countless ways, which detrimental inequalities are unfair, and thus candidates for remedial collective action, and which are just bad luck? If I am born lacking in the sort of artistic ability that would enable me to launch a highly profitable artistic career, the inequality does not seem to be socially unfair, however unfortunate. But so too, apparently, being born blind this is not socially unfair. These misfortunes represent losses in the 'natural lottery,' they are but bad luck – which does not offend our notions of political equality.

But if all of this is granted, what do we make of *consequential inequalities*, those that result when differences in natural endowment interact with existing social attitudes, practices, and institutions? An individual with extraordinary artistic ability becomes fabulously rich; a person who is blind is denied privileges and advantages. What do we do with these inequalities?

On the face of it, one would normally say that even inequalities that arise within society can be justified under certain circumstances. But, the problem for equality theory (as we shall see below) is to describe and justify those circumstances. This enduring problem is especially troublesome in the case of disablement, since we tend to believe that impairments justify unequal treatment, even when it is highly disadvantageous to the individual. We are easily seduced into thinking that since impairments are the product of the 'natural lottery,' some or all of the social inequalities that result are just bad luck and society has no *obligation* to respond to them (granting, of course, that it would be a good thing if it did).

Now, the minority-group analysis of disablement gives us a way of determining which social disadvantages are society's responsibility. The analysis insists that the 'location' of handicaps is *always* in the oppressive social environment inasmuch as handicapping is almost exclusively a systemic phenomenon. Society as a whole provides a climate of discrimination that makes the disadvantageous social consequences of impairments appear to be natural or un-changeable 'facts' about the world. Yet once we appreciate that the true social problem of disablement is systemic, group-based discrimi-nation, stigmatization, and marginalization, then handicapping ceases to be a matter of bad luck and becomes a social evil for which society as a whole is responsible.

A systemic social process of stigmatization or marginalization can only be identified by its adverse impact on a class of people, since there is no single 'culprit' whose intentional or culpable conduct was responsible for it. The fact that a public building is inaccessible to people with mobility impairments is not the product of a conscious and intentional decision on the part of any particular individual. Indeed, it would be perverse to blame one person for this handicap situation, since the true cause is the attitude that the building's inaccessible design is perfectly appropriate.

Systemic handicapping processes can be manifested in any number of ways. There is such diversity that we might think that some of these must be trivial, others justifiable, and still others worsened by background factors, including the psychology of the individual. But, the minority analysis responds, this judgment itself is a metahandicap traceable to pervasive discriminatory attitudes that have yet to be exposed for what they are. Common sense, it was once said, is nothing more than public laziness. Here common sense takes the form of an unwillingness to scrutinize opinions about what society owes people with disabilities.

Thus, to return to our earlier example, if the socially created stigma of short stature produces character disorders, our common-sensical judgment that an employer would be justified in not hiring the individual because of these disorders must be scrutinized. After all, these disorders are a manifestation of handicapping, a concomitant of systemic stigmatization, and as such, whether the employer is justified or not is of little interest, since from a social point of view the employer's conduct is handicapping with respect to the class of people of short stature. Social policy must respond to those disadvantages that accrue to marginalized groups in society, that is primary; what happens at the level of individuals is secondary.

By transforming handicaps into truly *social* phenomena and insisting on a class or group focus for policy, the minority-group analysis provides the social-political model with its political character. Without it there is always the risk that the distinction between handicaps and disabilities will be undermined, and the model will lose its centre of gravity.

In one form or another, the minority-group analysis has been in the background of nearly every social-scientific investigation of disablement since the late 1940s.[50] It was suggested as a possible paradigm for sociological explanation by both Wright and Safilios-Rothschild in their early work,[51] and John Gliedman and William Roth in their ground-breaking treatment of children with disabilities use the analysis as a basis for criticizing the biomedical and the economic models.[52]

Significantly though, whenever the minority-group analysis is raised, the theorist who does so concedes that people with disabilities are an unlikely minority group. True, like racial minorities, people with disabilities must contend with ignorance, prejudice, and bigotry; that is obvious. But it is also obvious that people with disabilities have no uniform set of stigmatizing characteristics parallel to visible racial characteristics. Nor is there a single culture of disablement similar to that defining, say, an ethnic group. People with disabilities lack a language, a tradition, a history that unifies them, since, among other reasons, it is rarely the case that members of the family of someone with disabilities share that status. And it is equally rare for people with one disability to feel much comradeship or common cause with people with different disabilities: the experience of being blind is very different from that of being of short stature, having cerebral palsy, or being HIV-seropositive. On the whole, adherents of the minority-group analysis do not view these differences as relevant to the point of the analysis. They argue that one need not expect every marginalized minority group in society to follow the patterns of racial or ethnic or sexual minorities. All that the analysis requires is that the social processes of marginalization and stigmatization be analogous, and there is every reason to think they are. At the same time, there is evidence of a developing 'Deaf culture,' although the impetus for recognizing this as a discrete minority came from within and was motivated by desires of solidarity and mutual support.[53]

In the end, though, these worries may be beside the point, since the minority-group analysis is not so much a descriptive hypothesis as it is the basis for a political agenda. Advocates of the analysis ask us to see people with disabilities as minorities in order to focus attention on a general approach to social policy. The aim of the analysis is to draw attention to the futility of dealing with disablement on a case-by-case basis – as if handicapping were the product of the particular acts of prejudiced individuals. Rather, disablement policy must see its objectives in systemic terms.

What this implies for the social-political model is that the goal of respect should govern disablement policy, where respect is understood broadly to include emancipation by means of self-empowerment. Once released from the chains of social oppression, people with disabilities as a group will be liberated from the handicaps that stand as obstacles to participation and accommodation. These latter goals are obviously important, but they are secondary to respect in that any attempt to reach them without first securing respect through social liberation will only serve to further entrench handicapping phenomena.

The political dimension of the social-political model, underwritten by the minority-group analysis, is acknowledged by all adherents of the model. Theorists also recognize that the model is both a scholarly tool for understanding and explaining disablement and a framework for a political movement. This point is most explicitly made by Michael Oliver, an English sociologist whose recent book *The Politics of Disablement* represents the cutting edge of the social-political model.[54] For Oliver the recognition that disablement is a social construction alone commits the social scientist to political activity. Of course, the question of the form that this political activity should take remains a matter of some dispute among adherents of the model. Oliver, for example, does not put much stock in the political strategy of the independent living movement in the United States, since he believes it reflects the American penchant for seeing all social problems in terms of legally enforceable individual rights.[55]

For his part, the American political scientist Harlan Hahn, who in a series of papers has done more than any other researcher to clarify both the complex structure of disablement and the minority analysis,[56] seems fully committed to the individual rights approach. Thus, he has argued that central to the social-political model is the realization that 'the primary problems confronting citizens with disabilities are bias, prejudice, segregation, and discrimination that can be eradicated through policies designed to guarantee them equal rights.'[57]

While the dominant American response to the political mandate of the social-political model involves the civil rights approach, recent work by Canada's leading exponent of the minority-group analysis, Evelyn Kallen, may suggest an alternative, Canadian approach to the politics of disablement.[58] In her most recent book, Kallen explains that she and others working in the area of minority studies have come to an important realization about the scholarly understanding of stigmatized non-ethnic minorities such as gays and lesbians, alcoholics, and people with mental and physical disabilities. Scholars should not be deceived into thinking that the deviance approach (let alone the biomedical approach) is somehow value-free and purely scientific. Quite the contrary, she argues, by focusing on deviance as an attribute of individuals, the various sociological theories about minorities inadvertently 'blame the victim' and serve to reinforce the very prejudices and stereotypes they describe. Kallen's solution is to adopt the minority rights analysis as an advocate rather than as a putatively neutral observer. It is only in this manner, she argues, that the entrenched legitimacy of the processes that create deviant minorities can be called into critical question.[59]

As a result of this methodological stance, Kallen characterizes minorities explicitly in terms of *systemic* human rights violations. Her definition is instructive for disablement theory, since it combines descriptive criteria – the social status and disadvantaged position that these groups occupy – with normative criteria – the rights which, when violated, create the defining social oppression:

The concept 'minority' refers to any social category within a society 1/ that is set apart and defined by the majority as incompetent/inferior or abnormal/dangerous on the basis of presumed physical, cultural, and/or behavioural differences from majority norms; 2/ that is categorically and systemically discriminated against by majority authorities and is thereby subject to some degree of oppression (denial of political rights), neglect (denial of economic rights), and/or diminution (denial of social rights/ human dignity); and 3/ that, as a consequence of the self-fulfilling prophecy of systemic or structural discrimination, comes to occupy a socially subordinate, disadvantaged, and stigmatized position within the society.[60]

Although from this definition it would appear that Kallen's analysis is expressly rights-based, it is not, as in Hahn's case, *individual* rights-based. Kallen argues that stigmatized minorities such as people with disabilities are primarily collectivities rather than aggregations of individuals. Pulling together the strands of deviance theoretical accounts, Kallen argues that both self-identity and social representations flow from an individual's minority status. Moreover, while it is true enough that individuals with disabilities are, as individuals, regularly denied their human rights, social policy ought not to be aimed at that level. Violation of individual rights is merely a manifestation of the true social problem, the oppression created by systemic violation of group rights.

When an individual with disabilities is discriminated against by an employer, she or he has a valid legal complaint, specifically a claim under a human rights code. Yet, from a policy perspective, the real complaint does not lie with the actions of this particular employer; it is a social problem. Thus, Kallen argues, minority rights are primarily collective entitlements directed against society's systemic, minority-creating processes.

Now Kallen's version of the minority-group analysis, in which the locus of entitlement is the group rather than any particular individual, is arguably far more consistent with the other features of the social-political model than the more traditionally liberal approach of Hahn and others. If nothing else, her approach provides a suitably broad entitlement basis that can generate a wide range of social programming. Besides legal protections against discrimination, Kallen argues that social obligations to people with disabilities (among other groups) must extend to all the other manifestations of social oppression, including denial of political, economic, and social rights. These rights seem to cover all that is included in the broadest interpretation of the disablement goals, with respect (or as Kallen puts it, destigmatization) being primary.

The social-political model of disablement is still in the process of evolving, and there remains considerable controversy, even among its staunchest supporters, over the social-scientific basis for the model and the political agenda it mandates. That it is a distinct model, and one that sees handicap as the true centre of gravity of disablement, is clear enough. But what are its virtues? Why should it attract our attention at all?

Virtues of the Model

As often happens in the evolution of social policy, the value of revolutionary new approaches to persistent social problems is not as apparent in the specific reforms it suggests as in the shift in perspective it makes possible. In the case of disablement policy, the rejection of the biomedical and economic approaches was animated by a *cri de coeur*: policy must respond to actual lived experiences of people with disabilities. This was not a plea for sympathy or compassion, it was a demand for a shift in perspective, a demand that the social 'problem' of disablement be approached from the point of view of those who experience it.

The wealth of social-scientific research that gave credibility to the social-political model also made the experience of disablement accessible to others. To be, and to be perceived to be, a handicapped person is to experience a social status, a role reinforced by the attitudes and beliefs of people as well as the practices and institutions of society. This status creates an identity, a pervasive role which, as David Thomas has aptly said, 'is seen as a central organizing factor around which explanations of the person are constructed, a construction prejudicial to people so perceived and which neglects the weight to be given to the relationship between the person and society.'[61]

Shifting the perspective of policy to that of the person with disabilities dramatically reorients the social significance of disablement. It is not as if the able-bodied cannot imagine what it is like to have a chronic illness, a memory impairment, or a facial deformity, although it would strain the powers of most to put themselves in the shoes of people with very severe impairments. Nor is the worry that unable to accomplish this feat of imagination, people without disabilities are unsympathetic. The importance of shifting perspectives is that it brings into relief how pervasive and various the circumstances of disadvantage are to those who experience them day by day.

Whether anyone can pretend to know how attitudinal and institutional obstacles are created and sustained, much is gained merely by shifting the focus of policy from impairment and disability to handicap. As the 'location' of the social problem shifts from the individual to the social environment, deep assumptions about what responses are appropriate are challenged. No one disputes that if a qualified worker is confined to a wheelchair and the workplace is inaccessible the social disadvantage the worker experiences is socially constructed. But it is all too easy to assume that it is the worker, or his or her aspirations, that must be modified rather than the environment. We tend to think that the workplace, and the world in general, is immutable and that people with disabilities have to take it as it is.

The principal virtue of the social-political model is that it challenges that assumption. This has had the effect of broadening the range of appropriate objectives for disablement policy. Although the economic model created disablement policy – since it directed attention to the *impact* of impairments on society – the social-political model has liberated that policy. The model jarred social policy analysts out of well-worn paths and demanded imaginative solutions to handicap situations.

One can easily see the effects of this liberation in recent government reports, such as *Obstacles, Transitions,* and *Equality for All,*[62] all of which are products of a political climate that the model helped to create. These reports are provocative, not because of the goals they identify but because they make it clear that the difficulties people with disabilities actually experience involve a far greater part of their social existence than was previously acknowledged. The reports argue for an expanded range of policy responses to the variety of obstacles that people with disabilities confront. In particular, *Obstacles* set out 130 specific recommendations concerning employment, income support, communications, housing, independent living, access to public buildings and facilities, transportation, sports, education, public attitudes, statistical database development, and basic research. Some of these recommendations have been taken up over the years; some are found in the 1992 omnibus legislation Bill C-78.[63]

The social-political model has been responsible for the liberation of policy both because it has politicized disablement and because it has highlighted the reasons why this is necessary. Social-scientific data enable an adherent of the model to do more than identify handicapping phenomena; they provide us with an appreciation of why handicaps are unwarranted social disadvantages, unfairly visited on a segment of the population. That is, the political agenda of the model is not purely ideological, nor is it idealistic: the empirical underpinnings of the model ground the political judgment that there is a social ill to which social policy must respond.

As noted in the previous section, the recurring theme of social-psychological research is that handicapping is a multifaceted and systemic phenomenon, a function of attitudes, practices, and institutions, rather than a manifestation of individual intolerance or malevolence. This theme is at once both encouraging and discouraging. On the one hand, it is obviously not welcome news that handicapping is part of the cultural fabric of society and built into the very institutions we rely on. The social problem would be far less ominous – although undoubtedly still difficult to deal with – if it was entirely the product of individual ignorance or ill will. But, on the other hand, the fact that handicapping is systemic is also encouraging because in that case the social problem may be solvable by means of a suitable social policy.

This last point raises another dimension of the social-political model that is of considerable value. Already the representation of disablement the model sets out has greatly assisted people with disabilities in mobilizing themselves as a political force. Political activism among people with disabilities may have come as a surprise to the general public, but it was inevitable. In the United States in particular – where grass-roots activism is more common than it is in Canada – the past decade or so has seen a spectacular growth of lobbying, educational, and advocacy organizations. Activism seems to have been responsible for considerable legislative activity, not the least important of which is the Americans with Disabilities Act of 1990.[64]

The power of the social-political model to mobilize people with disabilities – perhaps the model's most practical result – is linked to its overt normativeness – undoubtedly its greatest theoretical contribution. The model clearly displays, in its genesis and evolution, the need to abandon, both in theory and in practice, normative neutrality. I have suggested above that, in fact, neither the biomedical nor the economic model is without normative content, though it is part of the ideology of these models that their aim is only to describe disablement, scientifically, objectively, and neutrally. It is precisely this dubious presumption that the social-political model rejects.

This point needs emphasis since it is tempting to split the social-political model in two and set the social-scientific data apart from the process of politicization. But to do so totally misconstrues the general theme of the social-scientific research, namely, that handicapping phenomena are not inevitable, natural, or unavoidable consequences of impairments and disabilities. In the social-political model disablement is not, so to speak, a brute fact about the world, it is a social problem amendable to social solutions.

Perhaps this is another reason for viewing the model as essentially encouraging, even optimistic. In this model, that handicaps exist and that attitudinal, structural, and institutional processes sustaining handicaps exist are at bottom the result of unstated political judgments. As a society we *allow* handicaps to exist by refusing to pay the price (or even to investigate the price) of removing them. Handicaps, therefore, are our social responsibility. Or, in the words of *Obstacles*, 'All Canadians are responsible for the necessary changes which will give disabled persons the same choices of participation that are enjoyed by those who are not disabled.'[65]

Thus it is that the social-scientific analysis of handicapping and the politicization of disablement are not severable; they are intrinsically linked by the notion of collective responsibility. The social-political model brings disablement into the political arena, where disablement becomes a political issue, an issue roughly expressed as: Should we as a society allow handicapping to continue? As such, every social response to disablement – including doing nothing at all – presupposes an answer to the normative question of what society owes people by virtue of their disabilities.

The biomedical and the economic models resist the politicization of disablement – the first by representing disablement as a fact of biological life, the second by representing it as a fact of economic life. But on the social-political model, as a society we have no option but to acknowledge the political decisions we make in our disablement policy, since what we are dealing with is neither inevitable nor natural but the product of our political will. In the end, the realization that as a society we create and sustain handicap situations is the central virtue, and emancipatory message, of the social-political model.

Effects of the Model on Policy

Because of its revolutionary and liberating character, the ramifications of the social-political model for policy are diverse. Since it has yet to stabilize, many of these effects are still to be felt. Looking at *Obstacles* again, one can see a variety of policy themes and objectives brought out by the model, such as accessibility, independent living, equal benefit and protection of the law, and improved quality of life. In practice though, there is but one resonating theme of the model, and that is that disablement is a rights issue.

Since the language of rights is both familiar to us and considerably more complicated than is usually believed, we have to be careful when characterizing the rights the model has introduced into disablement policy. For rights, of one sort or another, have long been part of policy. To take the obvious example, compensatory rights have long formed a part of that aspect of policy concerned with the culpable creation of disablement. And, like everyone else, people with disabilities enjoy all of the rights that flow from the rule of law: the right to be fairly and impartially treated by the state, the right to have one's case heard, the right of legal standing, and so on.

Without in any sense undervaluing these fundamental rights, it has long been realized that they are not of particular relevance to disablement policy. These are rights citizens have independently of any specific attribute or characteristic, which is precisely why they are important political entitlements. One has a right to compensation for unjustified harm, or to impartial treatment under the rule of law, regardless of one's personal attributes, race, creed, colour, sex, or age. Though as vital to people with disabilities as they are to anyone else, these legal rights are not rights people with disabilities acquire by virtue of their disabilities.

But should we recognize such rights? In the social-political model we must, for obvious reasons. The experience of being handicapped is the experience of being treated unfairly *because* of one's personal attributes and circumstances (perceived or real). Therefore, if policy were to ignore these attributes and circumstances, it would compound the unfairness. This is why it may be profoundly handicapping to treat a person with disabilities *equally*: it does no good to have, with everyone else, the right to climb up a flight of stairs in order to reach a government office if one is confined to a wheelchair.

Moreover, the right to be fairly treated when it comes to enjoying the benefits of a law or program for which one is eligible is not a right *to* those benefits. If the state decides not to provide *anyone* with a range of benefits or services, then no one's rights of impartial treatment have been violated. The right of fair treatment is not *affirmative* and does not require the state to provide any service or benefit, whether desperately needed or not. Such a right demands only that *if* the state gets into the business of providing benefits or services, it must provide them fairly and impartially.

The effect of the social-political model on policy, therefore, has not merely been to make disablement a rights issue, but to make it an issue of rights over and beyond basic legal rights. What these other rights are is another matter. In the United States they are often called 'civil rights,' probably because of their association in the public's mind with the civil rights movement of the 1950s and 1960s. The phrase 'human rights' has been made popular by a series of United Nations declarations that have enumerated these rights.[66] And the Canadian writer Evelyn Kallen has referred to them as 'minority rights.'

I prefer to call them 'equality rights,' since they rely upon a commitment to (some interpretation of) political equality. Still, they are also legal rights, or perhaps more precisely, legally enforceable rights, rather than purely moral rights. From the point of view of policy a right or entitlement that has a moral status but has not been legally recognized is of limited interest. One writer has suggested that purely moral rights should in this context be called 'manifesto rights,' since they function to express a call to reform existing legal and political structures.[67]

Though equality rights, legally recognized and enforced, represent the principal impact of the social-political model, it is not the case that *any* interpretation of these rights will be consistent with the political agenda of the model. Quite the contrary, some interpretations are flatly inconsistent with the model. And there is no better way to see this in context than by briefly recounting the American experience with a variety of equality rights, usually called antidiscrimination, that were expressly designed for people with disabilities.[68]

The American Experience

The social movement for desegregation and basic political rights for black Americans produced, among other reforms, the Civil Rights Act of 1964. Title VI of this federal act set out the legal formula for antidiscrimination that soon became the model throughout the United States. Title VI prohibits any recipient of federal funds from discrimination on the basis of race, colour, or national origin. Although the provision has been applied to a wide range of U.S. federally supported agencies and programs, its most well-known use was that of assisting in the desegregation of public schools. Supplementing the constitutional guarantee laid down by the ground-breaking legal case of *Brown v. Board of Education*,[69] Title VI provided a powerful executive-branch enforcement mechanism, the believable threat of withdrawing federal funding in offending localities.

When in the early 1970s changes were being suggested to the Vocational Rehabilitation Act, which had existed in one form or another since the 1920s,[70] the growing activism of people with disabilities made it inevitable that discrimination against them would be on the agenda. After much debate, section 504 of the revamped Rehabilitation Act of 1973 was added; it mirrored the language of the antidiscrimination provision of Title VI: 'No otherwise qualified handicapped individual in the United States ... shall, solely by reason of his handicap, be excluded from the participation in, be denied benefits of, or be subject to discrimination under any program or activity receiving federal financial assistance or under any program or activity conducted by any executive agency or by the United States Postal Service.'[71]

From the moment of its enactment until very recently there has been judicial and legislative activity concerning this much-heralded antidiscrimination provision. Amendments and judicial pronouncements have dealt with issues ranging from the breadth of coverage (who counts as a 'qualified handicapped individual' and what class of federal activities are covered) to the means available for administrative implementation of the antidiscrimination guarantee and the nature of the obligation that is created.[72] As these themes were being worked through, especially in the employment and education contexts, nearly every state in the United States responded by enacting statutory provisions prohibiting workplace discrimination and repeating the language of section 504.[73]

The history of the judicial interpretation of section 504, and the response of the Health and Welfare Department and Congress, though convoluted, have centred on precisely the same questions which, I have been insisting, stand in the way of an adequate disablement policy. That is, there has in the United States been considerable discussion about the nature of disablement and the scope of the social obligation to respond to the plight of people with disabilities.

As for the first of these themes, legal controversies surrounding the phrase 'handicapped individual' have tended to reproduce tensions between the economic and the social-political models of disablement. The original 1973 definition set out the economic interpretation of disability which had long been associated with vocational rehabilitation law in the United States. But by the next year, in a belated recognition of the rationale of section 504, the definition was modified in two major respects: first, the context of disability was expanded beyond employment to include any 'major life activity,' and second, the definition was expanded to include those who were 'regarded' as being handicapped. This second modification (which recognizes medically groundless handicaps) shows the impact of the social-political model.[74]

In 1978 Congress further modified the section 504 definition in order to exclude alcohol and drug abusers, 'where current use of alcohol or drugs [either] prevents such individual from performing the duties of the job in question or ... would constitute a direct threat to property or the safety of others.'[75] In 1988, after a bitter debate, this exclusion was extended yet again to cover individuals with a 'currently contagious disease or infection' in order to capture HIV seropositivity. Many of the issues that have been raised concerning the definition and scope of the phrase 'handicapped individual,' both in the United States and in Canada, are now being played out with AIDS in mind.[76]

The second theme of section 504 jurisprudence has been the significant one as far as the social-political model is concerned. The controversy here, which will undoubtedly be repeated as courts begin looking at the Americans with Disabilities Act of 1990, is whether the goal of legislation is merely to combat individual instances of discrimination or something more systemic. This debate only arose in the first place because the Rehabilitation Act of 1973 was influenced by the social-political model and as a result understood handicapping as a society-wide, systemic phenomenon. This is evident in the wording of section 504, which speaks of the *exclusion* of people with disabilities, as well as three other, less well-known provisions of Title V, sections 501, 502, and 503. These latter sections require the federal government, and contractors working for the government, to take affirmative action in hiring and promoting people with disabilities and mandate the removal from federally funded facilities of architectural and transportation barriers.[77] These social responses are, obviously, aimed at perceived systemic problems, not individual cases of prejudice or ill-treatment.

The legal controversy that arose in the interpretation of these sections involves one of the most important conflicts in American constitutional law on equality rights. More concretely, the controversy focused on a fundamental ambiguity in the wording and intent of section 504. The section begins, as already remarked, by prohibiting any *exclusion* of people with disabilities from participation in society; but it then appears to qualify this by referring explicitly to 'discrimination.' Since one can be excluded from participation for various reasons – such as neglect, ignorance, or economic conditions – to make sense of the section we need to know what was the perceived social evil to which section 504, and the Civil Rights Act of 1964 on which it was based, was aimed.

There are two possibilities. The social evil may be discrimination in what might be called the primary sense of that word, that is, the intentional mala fide exclusion of people from education, employment, and other benefits and opportunities because of an attribute such as race, creed, sex, or disability. Discrimination in this sense is an individual and intentional (or at least culpable) act of invidious prejudice and unjustified exclusion. The other possibility is that the targeted social evil was indirect, systemic, or as it is sometime called, 'adverse effect' discrimination. In this sense the focus is not individual misconduct but the exclusionary and disadvantageous impact, on identifiable groups, of attitudes and social practices and policies.

What does section 504 contemplate, and more generally, what is the point and rationale of antidiscrimination provisions? A historical case can be made that, since most instances of racial discrimination were overt acts of racism and conscious prejudice, it was the primary sense of discrimination that the legislators had in mind. However, there is also considerable evidence that the aim of section 504 of the Rehabilitation Act of 1973 was to address systemic discrimination, or, as one of the sponsors of the act stated, the aim was to 'launch a national commitment to eliminate the "glaring neglect" of the handicapped.'[78]

In a recent article, Judith Welch Wegner pursues this latter interpretation of section 504 and argues that the section creates a powerful notion of antidiscrimination encompassing three categories of concern in the operation of social policy: exclusion (for example, the adoption and application of program eligibility criteria unfairly disqualifying people with disabilities); de facto denial of benefit; and discriminatory treatment (treating equally qualified individuals unequally).[79]

Wegner's analysis is interesting to us because it is firmly grounded in the minority-rights analysis. She argues that if the aim of antidiscrimination policy is full participation and meaningful equality of opportunity, then that policy in practice must be sensitive to the defining characteristics of the group that bears the burden of systemic discrimination. Therefore, handicapping, as a form of discrimination, is different from, say, racial discrimination, in ways that must be taken into account when one interprets and implements an antidiscrimination provision. In particular, people with disabilities, though rarely the victims of individual malevolence or ill will, instead suffer systemic consequences of benign neglect.

As a matter of jurisprudence Wegner's proposition entails that, for example, a judicial requirement that the victim of discrimination prove 'discriminatory intent' on the part of an employer or service provider is both inappropriate and unfair. Such a requirement is itself a handicap, since it perpetuates a misconception about the dynamics of handicapping.

Now, although Wegner's analysis is not without support in judicial decisions,[80] as a strictly legal matter the better analysis is probably that section 504 is ambiguous and thus susceptible to conflicting judicial interpretations. There is some reason to suspect, moreover, that this ambiguity was quite intentional. For example, the section makes a point of saying that those who are protected against discriminatory practices are 'otherwise qualified,' a phrase that raises the question of whether the treatment was truly discriminatory (because unwarranted by the disability) or justifiable (because it was based on the 'neutral' judgment that the person was not qualified because of the disability).[81]

At any rate, since the mid-1970s shifts in the political climate of the United States have threatened to undermine section 504. In 1981, for example, President Ronald Reagan signed Executive Order No. 12,291 requiring the Department of Health, Education and Welfare to review section 504 regulations, specifically with respect to whether the provision would 'maximize the net benefits to society' and, if not, whether there may be 'alternative approaches ... involving the least net cost to society.' The executive order soon produced a Department of Justice regulation that eliminated any duty to take action in situations that 'would result in undue financial and administrative burdens.'[82] Since then courts at various levels and in various jurisdictions have considered whether, and to what extent, *the cost or administrative burden* of the changes required by section 504 should influence the decision to act or not. The cases have gone in a variety of directions.[83]

The cost or 'undue burden' argument, which also plays an important role in Canadian jurisprudence, seems perfectly designed to bolster the view that section 504 concerns discrimination in the primary sense only. Indeed, the argument has been made that people with disabilities can legitimately lay claim *only* to the legal protection against discrimination that a racial minority can. The social evil of racial discrimination involves the practice of evaluating people for benefits and opportunities on irrelevant and prejudicial grounds, namely, the colour of their skin. The proper response to this evil is, the argument goes, equal treatment (colour-blind treatment, so to speak). It is this kind of equality right and protection against discrimination that people with disabilities should also be guaranteed.

An equal-treatment interpretation of antidiscrimination law understands discrimination to be a matter of irrational classification – making and acting upon distinctions that are demonstrably irrelevant to the point of the policy, law, or practice. The classic statement of this interpretation of discrimination in American law is found in the 1971 racial discrimination case of *Griggs v. Duke Power Co.*[84] Speaking of the rationale of Title VI of the Civil Rights Act of 1964, the U.S.

Supreme Court said in that case that the prohibition of discrimination in employment, as a social goal, is a matter of promoting the distribution of jobs on the basis of talents and merits and eliminating 'artificial, arbitrary and unnecessary barriers to employment.' The court went on to hold that an employment policy or practice that specifies a job qualification that bears a 'manifest relationship' to the nature of the employment cannot be viewed as discriminatory.

It is vital to appreciate that in the social-political model an antidiscrimination provision designed for people with disabilities interpreted in this way is worse than useless. For there are very few obstacles to full participation that people with disabilities face that are self-evidently 'artificial, arbitrary and unnecessary.' Since handicapping is systemic, not intentional, obstacles seem to be natural or 'just the way the world is.' Because of this, putting the onus on people with disabilities to show otherwise limits their chances to prove discrimination. Indeed, having such a legal protection in place is arguably itself a metahandicap, since it attracts attention away from systemic discrimination.

But what of the much-trumpeted Americans with Disabilities Act of 1990?[85] Will its interpretative history follow that of its forerunner? There is no doubt that the ADA represents the culmination of the civil rights approach to disablement issues in the United States. The act extends more or less the same protections against discriminatory treatment in employment, transportation, and public accommodation to people with disabilities as are already in place for women and racial minorities.

There are a number of features of the ADA that reflect the influence of the social-political model, features which push the interpretation of its antidiscrimination mandate away from the 'equal treatment' paradigm. For example, the act's definition of 'discrimination' in section 102 is extremely broad and goes far beyond the primary sense of the notion. One discriminates, the act tells us, when one limits, segregates, or classifies a job applicant or employee in such a way that 'adversely affects the opportunities or status' of an applicant or employee who has disabilities. One also discriminates if one uses standards, criteria, or methods of administration 'that have the effect of discrimination' or 'perpetuate the discrimination' of people with disabilities. And, finally, it is discriminatory not to make reasonable accommodation available for the known limitations of an otherwise qualified person with disabilities. As well, the act's characterization of 'qualified individual with a disability' makes it clear that qualification for employment is not contingent on the need for accommodations, rather the employer must demonstrate that the individual would not be qualified for the job *even if* reasonable modifications were made to the workplace and the job.

Despite this language, however, currents in the American political climate are exerting a very powerful force away from an interpretation of antidiscrimination rights consistent with the social-political model, including recent amendments to the Civil Rights Act of 1964. The ADA specifies that the remedies and procedures available to individuals who have been subjected to discrimination are just those set out in the Civil Rights Act of 1964, the source of all the remedial and procedural authority of the ADA – making it clear that the current administration has no intention of recognizing the systemic sense of discrimination in practice. The proposed Civil Rights Act of 1991[86] provided for hefty fines for an employer who discriminates, but only when that discrimination is *intentional*.

In the United States it appears that while the language and spirit of its antidiscrimination law harkens to the social-political model, the political agenda of the model has been blunted by countervailing political forces. Are there lessons here for Canada?

The Prospects for Canada

First of all, Canada's constitutional structure, and present uncertainties about the division of powers between federal and provincial governments, make it dangerous to apply the American legal experience here. Although in many respects our antidiscrimination provisions are similar, for jurisdictional reasons there could be no Canadian analogue of the Americans with Disabilities Act of 1990. Instead, in Canada we have for the most part relied on the more conciliatory mechanisms of human rights codes, and only relatively recently have we begun to explore the scope of the constitutional guarantee of equality found in section 15 of the Charter of Rights and Freedoms.

There are also important, though perhaps ephemeral, differences in the political traditions of the two countries that make a difference in our legal characterization of antidiscrimination provisions. Although this is a topic for later, there is in this country far less ideological objection to more direct and affirmative social responses to systemic discrimination. One cannot survey the recommendations of the 1984 Abella report *Equality in Employment*, the provisions of the Canada Employment Equity Act, Quebec's Loi assurant l'exercice des droits des personnes handicapées,[87] or indeed section 15(2) of Canada's charter, without seeing a difference in political tradition that sets Canada apart from the United States.

It would also be wrong to leave the impression that the only impact of the social-political model on disablement policy in Canada has been the introduction into policy of the discourse of equality *rights*. For there has always been implicit in the model another strategy. The disablement social movement of the 1970s and 1980s was notable for its focus on self-help and self-empowerment. Although the movement expressed its demands in the language of equality rights, it also pursued various forms of direct political action, such as sit-ins and boycotts, demonstrations, and lobbying activities. What is significant about activism of this sort is that it is intended to be a counter-hegemonic political response to handicapping, rather than a legal institutional response.[88] The difference between a demonstration in the streets and a lawsuit may seem to be merely a matter of strategy, but we should not lose sight of the fact that there is a difference between an attempt to destigmatize a group through political empowerment and an attempt to seek specific legal remedies for an individual.

By its nature, counter-hegemonic politics is far more revolutionary than political agitation directed at specific legislative or policy ends. The aim of the former is to attack, directly and dramatically, a dominant societal framework, rather than to use it and the social institutions that make it up in order to win favourable concessions. The aim of the independent living movement in the United States was to wrest control away from existing social structures and professionals. This is not, or at least need not be, expressed as a strategy of combating discrimination, in either sense. It is more like rebellion and secession. Of course, precisely because of this feature of the counter-hegemonic strategy, it is not easy to see what impact it could have on policy, other than making clear the need for a social response to the demands of a politically empowered minority. At the same time, the call for counter-hegemonic revolution may itself be an effective (and greatly needed) strategy for turning attention to policy issues.

There always has been the possibility, if not the immediate prospect, of this manifestation of the social-political model taking root in Canada.

Why the Model Is Distortive

It should be clear from the tone of the previous section that it is somewhat problematic to describe the effects of the social-political model on policy. Since the model is in ascendancy, moulding public opinion and policy in Canada and elsewhere, as well as animating advocacy groups and government agencies, it is difficult to step back and critically assess it. Moreover, all criticism of the model necessarily embodies a political stance of some sort. Still, with care, it is possible to draw attention to inherent distortions and dubious assumptions of the model without having to commit oneself to the normative bases suggested by the other two models of disablement. It is arguably possible, in other words, to criticize the model from within in much the same way that has already been done with the economic and biomedical models. At any rate, that is what I propose to do here.

It is clear, first off, that adherents of the social-political model often succumb to rhetorical excesses in their critiques of the other two models. In order to distance themselves from both the biomedical and the economic approaches to disablement, many of the writers and scholars already quoted have tended to greatly underestimate the importance of both of these dimensions. A good example of this can be found in the otherwise superb work of John Gliedman and William Roth in the area of education rights for children with disabilities.[89] As already mentioned, the authors object to the biomedical model because of its imposition of the 'sick role' on people with disabilities. Unfortunately, though, their critique goes far deeper than this. They also argue that the biomedical model is a mechanism for legitimating handicapping inasmuch as it provides the lay culture with a scientific gloss on their prejudices, in effect a licence to discriminate and treat people with disabilities as inherently inferior.[90]

The difficulty with claims like this is that they assume that modern health care possesses but one therapeutic model, that based on the acute illness paradigm. Gliedman and Roth write as if gerontological, palliative, long-term attendant care, and other chronic care therapeutic models do not exist or are professionally undervalued. This is unfair. Partially because of the realization that chronic illness and disability are more prevalent health care issues than acute, infectious, or parasitic illnesses, health professionals have spent considerable energy developing and implementing chronic care servicing.[91] Health services patterned on chronic care models are perfectly appropriate biomedical responses to disablement. These services seek to establish long-term care environments in which the focus is on coping rather than curing and the goal is self-empowerment rather than dependency, goals that are fully compatible with the other core doctrines of the social-political model.[92]

Gliedman and Roth are not wrong to object to the biomedical model itself since, as I have argued, it does make presuppositions about the nature of disablement that are problematic. What is troubling in their critique is the assumption that the biomedical approach is monolithic and cannot be modified to take into account the legitimate political demands of people with disabilities. There is in this a failure to distinguish between the biomedical approach to disablement, which of necessity concentrates on only one dimension, and the biomedical model, which insists upon the ultimate priority of that dimension.

A similar, but far more extensive critique can be found in some of the recent work of Harlan Hahn. Hahn has come to see disablement theory as being dominated by only two 'competing paradigms.' One of these, the 'functional limitation model,' combines what I have called the biomedical and the economic approaches; the other is essentially the minority-group analysis discussed above.[93] Hahn feels obliged to reject the former and embrace the latter because he holds out no hope that these competing paradigms can be synthesized into a single coherent theory. In his view – one commonly held by disablement rights activists – in order to realize the dream of full participation and respect for people with disabilities, we must make the political choice of abandoning and rendering harmless the 'functional limitation paradigm.'

But even as a matter of political strategy Hahn's radical suggestion is dubious. Bringing disablement theory wholly within the political arena by detaching the concept from this biomedical and functional moorings could easily harm the interests of people with disabilities. Why should we think that the cause of people with disabilities will be served if disablement policy is understood to be entirely open to political manipulation? To be sure, the present impasse in disablement policy with be resolved, but only at the considerable price of reducing disablement to a political symbol or token to be moved back and forth according to the relative success of lobbying efforts.

Another way of putting this worry is to ask more directly what the limits of effective social policy are for people with disabilities. That is, is it truly in their interest, let alone the interest of society at large, to project an ideal of disablement policy that extends over every possible aspect of the lives of people with disabilities? Can, and should, social policy attempt to eradicate, ameliorate, or compensate every form that stigma takes in society? These are difficult questions to answer; it is a serious worry that policy may attempt to do too much, and as a result achieve too little. But the complete politicization of disablement only multiplies these concerns by, in effect, eliminating a non-policy domain in which disablement needs might be more effectively met.

Hahn's radical program also displays a dangerous assumption about disablement theory that is characteristic of the social-political model. Like many adherents of the model, Hahn recognizes that the tensions and anomalies in disablement policy are caused by ambiguities in the concept of disablement itself. And indeed Hahn's analysis of the concept was the one I have presented here. Yet, instead of suggesting a way of resolving the conceptual conflict, he opts for an extreme form of conceptual relativism, arguing that 'the disparity between these concepts underscores the fundamental fact that disability is ultimately defined by government policy. In other words, disability is essentially whatever public laws and programs say it is.'[94]

If Hahn were suggesting by this that we must be realistic about where and how conceptual decisions are made, or if he were saying that handicaps are whatever public laws and programs say they are, then perhaps his point could be taken. But in the context of other remarks Hahn makes it clear that he wants to say much more than this. He believes, as do many activists guided by the social-political model, that at the end of the day disablement itself is a creation of the political process.

It is not difficult to find similar remarks in the literature, remarks which seem to be about handicapping but, perhaps in the rush to make a provocative point, actually speak about the 'arbitrary' or socially constructed character of disablement as a whole. Consider the following comment made by two labelling theorists.: 'the distinction [between normality and handicap] is not "given" so to speak, by reality. Instead, salient and socially meaningful differences among persons (and acts) are a product of our ways of looking, our schemes for seeing and dealing with people.'[95] Or remarks made by a legal writer on disablement issues: 'In a sense, therefore, *handicapped* is an artificial grouping created by the labeling process in our society. From the broad spectrum of human characteristics and capabilities certain limits have been singled out and called handicaps. The fine line between *handicapped* and *normal* has been arbitrarily drawn by the "normal" majority.'[96]

In context it is clear that each of these quotes tries to characterize disablement itself, not just handicap (for example, the first passage quoted goes on to cite blindness as an example of a socially created 'handicap'). More recently, in a report of Canada's Standing Committee on Human rights and the Status of the Disabled, the claim is made that 'The category of "disabled person" is ultimately an arbitrary classification.'[97]

Now, always discounting for rhetorical flourish, these remarks are extremely worrisome. They amount to a denial of what I earlier called the assumption of biomedical grounding, the assumption that the concept of impairment, which denotes biomedically identifiable and explainable phenomena, is intrinsic to the concept of disablement, insofar as it is distinct from social, social-psychological, or political phenomena. These remarks contradict this assumption by claiming, or implying, that disablement is an 'arbitrary,' politically manipulable category. Though there are medically groundless handicaps (which are, in some sense, arbitrary), the concept of disablement is not itself medically groundless or arbitrary.

One can easily see how a person committed to a social and political movement of the sort suggested by the politicization of disablement would be tempted by the suggestion that disablement is a product of the political process. No one wants to engage in a futile attempt to unseat a conception that is rooted in physical reality. A political activist would doubtless feel invigorated and empowered by the claim that disablement is a political product, especially one the activist could come to influence. Unfortunately, the social-political model often seems to have incorporated just this view as an ideological first principle.

Occasionally a particularly provocative and perplexing manifestation of this ideological claim finds its way into the writings of advocates, namely, the suggestion that severe impairments are not disadvantageous in any sense. Some more radical elements of the emerging 'Deaf culture,' for example, have argued that their deafness is not a disabling condition but a positive, cohesive force that identifies their language, past, and community.[98] A past president of an American blind organization has also been quoted as saying that we must guard against overblowing the importance of sight, which is, at most, 'enjoyable, useful and convenient.'[99]

The worry here is that advocates of the model seem to be claiming that disablement itself is socially constructed and arbitrary, the product of forces rather than biological fact. But the more one relies on this sort of claim the more problematic the policy consequences of the model become. For if handicap supplants impairment and disability as a way of characterizing 'people with disabilities,' it will be in principle impossible to distinguish people with disabilities from, one would presume, the considerably larger class of people who are socially disadvantaged. Racial and sexual discrimination do not completely coincide with handicapping or discrimination on the basis of disability. If there are important differences in the manner in which groups are stigmatized and marginalized, then it is reasonable to trace those differences to the object of the systemic discrimination, namely, the attribute or manifestation of difference that elicits the discriminatory response.

If the social-political model is to guide us in the formulation and implementation of policy, it must, at a minimum, assist us in characterizing those who are to benefit from the policy. What is required is a relatively stable, objective, non-arbitrary, and non-circular criterion for identifying, among the class of those who are socially disadvantaged in one way or another, those who are socially disadvantaged by virtue of disablement (granting the obvious that an individual might be disadvantaged by two or more classifications at once). This task is usually performed using instruments of biomedical assessment or disability evaluation, neither of which (whatever other difficulties they may have) treat what they assess as 'arbitrary' or the product of the political process. Although these instruments must be used with care, how can policy analysts do without them?

But there is more trouble to come. Even if the social-political model *could* successfully characterize the population in an appropriate fashion, it could not avoid another major policy dilemma.

According to the model, handicapping is socially constructed stigmatization that manifests itself as obstacles to the goals of respect, participation, and accommodation. This suggests that disablement policy should be devised so that, to the greatest extent possible, all decisions regarding employment, education, communications, and other benefits and opportunities will not depend on whether a person has (or is perceived as having) a disability. In other words, social justice demands that the stigma of disablement be utterly neutralized.

Yet, insofar as handicapping also involves the failure to meet needs and accommodate disabilities and impairments, disablement policy must also – and with respect to the same general goals – acknowledge and address the fact that a person *has a disability*. Therefore, it appears that social justice sometimes demands that the physical fact of disablement be fully acknowledged.

But which is it? If people with disabilities have been handicapped by virtue of their (perceived) physical differences, must we treat them the same as everyone else (since, by definition, equal treatment cannot possibly be stigmatizing); or must we treat them differently? Should social policy be geared to ignore, or to emphasize, physical difference? This powerful and pervasive dilemma has recently come to be called the 'dilemma of difference.'[100]

The dilemma has long been recognized by stigma theorists. In the early 1960s Erving Goffman noted that those who seek a political solution to their stigmatized social status will find themselves confronting two equally self-defeating options: demands for integration seem to require the 'deviant' to draw attention to the stigmatizing difference, while attempts at segregation seem to legitimate, and reinforce, the labels that created the deviant status in the first place.[101] More recently, it has been argued that political activism, which must be highly public if it is to be effective, carries with it the cost of entrenching the categorical social difference of being, say, poor or black of disabled.[102]

Another version of this dilemma surrounds the often-misrepresented 'principle of normalization' that has dominated the literature in developmental disability for decades.[103] When first proposed, the objective of 'normalization' was to break down those forms of institutional segregation that were stigmatizing and resulted in inferior services for people with various forms of mental disability. That objective was immediately associated with another, that of restructuring service provision so that these individuals could live in 'normal' settings.[104] Unfortunately, moves toward community-based service provision, deinstitutionalization, and other 'normalizing' policies were often interpreted as justifying cutting back on service provision since, taken literally, the principle seems to suggest that it was stigmatizing and 'non-normal' to cater to 'special needs.'[105]

Yet another version of this dilemma involves the exceptional achievements of individuals like Terry Fox, Steve Fonyo, Rick Hansen, and Mark Wellman (an American paraplegic who in 1990 climbed the 3,500-foot face of El Capitan in California). What are we to make of these remarkable athletic accomplishments? On the one hand, people with disabilities proudly point to these individuals as examples of what can be done and what obstacles can be overcome. Unfortunately, on the other hand, this much-needed image adjustment can easily backfire when these same accomplishments are taken to represent a plausible standard of achievement that *any* individual with a similar disability *should* be able to reach. People who fall short of this standard may be perceived as responsible for their own disability, even their own handicap.[106]

The dilemma of difference, as I shall argue later, is ultimately a problem about the nature of equality and as such is not simply the product of the social-political model. But the model succumbs to the dilemma in the policy arena – where the dilemma can do the most harm – because the model does not do justice to the multidimensionality of disablement. Like the other two models, the social-political model tries to extend and stretch an important intuition about the nature of disablement in order to distil a complex notion down to one of its component dimensions. In the case of the social-political model this has had the result of undermining, or simply rejecting, the assumption of biomedical grounding, with potentially disastrous results.

In the end it is ironic that the social-political model is structurally more closely related to the biomedical model than it is to the economic model. Where the biomedical model locates the essential difference of disablement in the individual, the social-political model 'locates' it in the social environment. But in so doing both deny the *interactional* character of disablement. Perhaps this is understandable given the limitations of the metaphor: it strains one's imaging powers to try to 'locate' disablement in a relationship between a medical and functional problem and the social responses to it, as the concept of disability requires.

Because the social-political model has not yet stabilized, in time it may be able to produce an account of disablement that is truly interactional. There is no doubt though that the social-scientific and political background to the model, although also in a state of flux, has made a lasting contribution to the study of disablement. Part of that contribution has been to suggest a powerful normative basis for disablement theory.

The Social-Political Model and Disablement Theory

Nearly every feature of the social-political model – its social-scientific foundations, its focus upon socially constructed handicapping, its prioritization of the goal of respect, and its inherently political character – points to the normative dimension of political justice. Indeed, in one way of looking at it the model merely fleshes out the single intuition that the social problem of disablement *is* a problem of social injustice.

As we saw, the biomedical model does not raise questions of justice because it represents disablement as a fact of life, the result of the (amoral) workings of the 'natural lottery.' Nor does the economic model raise justice issues, at least not directly: economists insist that their guiding standard of efficiency is independent of political morality. Only the social-political model unequivocally shifts disablement into the sphere of politics and political morality. Because of this, the model is immediately in the grips of various entitlement controversies: Should the aims of policy be to remove barriers and actively facilitate full participation, or merely to foster opportunities? Should our policy be geared to objectives aimed at individuals, or to people with disabilities as a distinct group? Should we vest people with disabilities with 'special' rights and entitlements, or merely ensure that they enjoy the rights and entitlements that everyone has? Should these rights be absolute and non-negotiable, or defeasible and contingent on other social considerations?

Policy governed by the model would have to address these and other normative questions; but so too would policy governed by the biomedical or economic model. The difference is that, in the social-political model these normative issues are *part of* disablement policy, since disablement is intrinsically a rights issue. Therefore, while adherents of the economic model will debate whether, in the long run, there are economic advantages to be gained from vesting people with disabilities with rights, adherents of the social-political model will insist that the question is rather what are the best ways of recognizing and giving effect to the rights that are already vested as a matter of political morality.

This means that there are only two possible normative bases congenial to the basic thrust of the social-political model, compensatory justice and equality. All the others, as we shall see in more detail in the next chapter, make the question of entitlement contingent on something other than the fact of disablement.

The association of the social-political model and the compensatory normative basis, though historically explicable, is somewhat unstable. In its purest form, compensatory (or corrective) justice has a limited application to disablement policy, since it requires a scenario in which an injury is caused by a culpable agent, someone who, in justice, must compensate for the injury. Since systemic handicapping processes are not individualistic, it is difficult to see how this normative basis could play an important role in policy (although, *some* room must be found for it, since people *do* negligently cause other people physical injury that may result in disability).

The connection between the social-political model and the normative basis of equality is, however, very close indeed. The injustice of handicapping is the injustice of infringing rights of equality, suitably interpreted. Still, to assert that one's disablement policy is firmly grounded in principles of political equality, as most adherents of the model will agree, is not at all to settle the outstanding normative issues equality raises. As the brief review of American antidiscrimination law suggests, there are competing conceptions of equality and ongoing disputes about the obligations a social and legal commitment to equality impose on the state.

There are, in short, deep and abiding disputes about the nature of political equality. There are also serious questions about how the normative basis of equality could guide the formation of disablement policy. But the prior question is whether, in light of the strengths and weaknesses of the existing three models of disablement, the notion of political equality stands a chance of underwriting an adequate theory of disablement, one that can unify the three dimensions of the notion in a consistent manner. Or, more simply, can equality make disablement theory possible?

I want to tackle this question indirectly by first, in the next chapter, looking at the other normative bases for disablement theory already mentioned in passing and assessing their strengths and weaknesses. Then, in the last chapter, I want to build on these discussions and turn to the normative basis of equality, the best hope for a complete and adequate theory of disablement.

6 Normative Bases for Disablement Theory

Toward Disablement Theory and Policy

The premise of this study has been that the evident, and persistent, impasse in disablement policy, despite overwhelming agreement about the goals of respect, participation, and accommodation, can be explained, not by any lack of policy imagination or goodwill, but by the influence of three highly intuitive models of disablement. These models are each firmly embedded in scientific discourses and world-views that are permanent components of our culture – the biomedical, the economic, and the social-psychological. Yet, no one model alone is capable of underwriting an integrated and coherent disablement policy.

As mentioned in the Introduction, my goal here is to begin the enormous task of clarifying the conceptual and normative foundations of social policy for, and on behalf of, people with disabilities. To complete this task of clarification of policy goals and formation of objectives would require what we do not have, namely, a theory of disablement. This is not my aim; there is far too much preliminary work to do before a conceptually and philosophically adequate account of disablement can be attempted. Nor is it my intention to propose an alternative model of disablement. As should be clear from the histories and consequences of the three existing models, a model of disablement is not something anyone could create, let alone implement. What I have been calling the models of disablement are social artefacts with complex social-historical and social-psychological sources. They are not templates that could mould policy in some determinate fashion, but presumptions and background beliefs that interact with and are shaped by policy and social conditions.

Despite this, though, enough has been said so far to be able to outline with some confidence the guiding presumptions and components of a theory of disablement. These theoretical premises can be derived from reasons for thinking that the three models we have considered are inadequate.

Thus, first off, it is salient to the concept of disablement that it is multidimensional and resists conceptual reduction to some single core dimension – impairment, disability, or handicap. However tempting it might be, it is wrong to think that, at the end of the day, disablement is *really* a biomedical, or an economic and rehabilitative, or a social-political matter. Disablement is an unstable mixture of all of these three.

Second, disablement is an interactive concept, in the sense that it is the product of both attributes of individuals and what for short I have been calling the social environment. In this sense disablement is more like disability than either impairment or handicap, at least as these two notions have been interpreted by the biomedical and social-political models. For whereas with these models some sense could be given to the metaphor of the 'location' of disablement, that way of talking was not of much help in the case of the economic model with its intrinsically interactive characterization of disability.

Therefore, like the concept of (human) difference, properly understood disablement is not a thing, or event, or process, or any other distinct and locatable entity. In precisely the same way that it is nonsensical to say that something is 'intrinsically different,' so too it should be nonsensical to speak of 'intrinsic disablement.' Relational concepts, it is true, are difficult to comprehend and work with: for reasons that may only be explicable by cognitive psychology, we tend to reify relations, to make them into things we can more easily classify and categorize. In the case of disablement, a great deal depends on our making the intellectual effort of understanding and using the concept as a relationship rather than as a thing.

A third presumption is that an adequate account of disablement must have a normative component. In part this follows from the fact that handicap is an essential dimension of disablement, and it is a normative notion. The normative question of what by way of special rights or entitlements follows from the fact that one has an impairment, is disabled, or handicapped is thoroughly integrated with the conceptual question of what disablement is. Disablement theory cannot plausibly be seen as a normatively neutral, apolitical, or purely descriptive account of a feature of the social life of human beings.

It follows, then, that a theory of disablement must be a political-theoretical treatment that provides, and justifies, a normative basis for disablement policy. The enormous social challenge posed by disablement cannot be begun without acknowledging its inherently political and moral character.

To be perfectly clear about these last two presumptions, to claim that disablement theory is inherently normative and embodies a political morality is just to say that it is a theory both about a form of human difference and about appropriate and inappropriate social responses to that difference. A theory that took no account of both of these issues would not be a complete theory about disablement.

Disablement theory must, therefore, have two fully integrated components. First required is an analysis of the concept of disablement. This includes an exploration of the dimensions of the notion and how they are related, as well as a treatment of the dangers of reducing the multidimensional concept to one of its dimensions. The second component is an account of the normative basis of disablement, that is, a consistent, principled answer to the question what we, either individually or collectively, owe people with disabilities.

The path we have followed through the three competing models provides a good beginning for the first component of the theory. The second, normative component is, it need hardly be said, the controversial one. It is, however, much needed, since without it there is no basis for grounding any of the rights or entitlements we believe should be vested in people with disabilities. From the point of view of policy analysis, without the normative component it is not possible to provide interpretations of the general goals of respect, participation, and accommodation that will yield consistent policy objectives and plausible solutions. More bluntly, without the normative component coherent and consistent policy is impossible.

Once again, though it is an enormous task to come up with a theoretically satisfactory normative basis, it is less difficult to outline the entitlement issues it must resolve if it is to have policy applications. Roughly, these entitlement controversies concern the nature and character of what is owed to people with disabilities, by virtue of their impairment, disability, or handicap (taken singly or together). Although it may seem preferable to list them in less confrontational form – says, as policy 'options' or 'alternatives' – that would be to misrepresent them. For these are indeed political controversies, not neutral, administrative options. The policy analyst will be making a politically normative judgment whenever he or she adopts one rather than another of these approaches, a fact that should not be obscured.

Rights or Benefits

The distinction here is the fundamental one as far as policy is concerned. There are various kinds of benefits that might be conferred on people with disabilities – for example, money, services, opportunities, privileges, and exceptions to rules applicable to others. Having a claim on these benefits might be called a disablement entitlement (or entitlement for short). The fundamental normative issue though is: are these entitlements legally recognized and enforceable rights, or merely benefits conferred?

In other words, a normative basis for policy must determine whether a proposed policy entitlement is a claim of right or not. If it is not then the benefit conferred is, so to speak, a mere benefit, a legitimate need partially or wholly satisfied. This is not to suggest that the benefit is not a good and desirable thing for the person to have: we can assume that all policy is designed to advantage people (or rather, if it is designed to disadvantage them, that is a problem of a very different sort). Rather, the point is whether that advantage is an entitlement that the person has of right or not.

Conditional or Unconditional

Being entitled to a benefit is a social status that admits of qualification. One important qualification is whether the advantage is conditional upon something other than one's status as a person in need (if mere benefit) or a right-holder (if right). There are, plainly enough, an infinite number of possible conditions that might be imposed to qualify one's entitlement, so there is no point being very precise about what counts as a condition. We can, though, identify two general classes of possible conditions: intrinsic and extrinsic.

An intrinsic condition is one that pertains to the normative basis for the entitlement. Perhaps the best example of this is the implicit condition upon compensation. On this normative basis one is entitled to a benefit (compensation) only if, and to the extent that, one deserves compensation, which usually means that one has been unjustifiably harmed by the culpable actions or inactions of another.

An extrinsic condition, by contrast, is any limitation upon an entitlement to a benefit that is imposed by external social requirements or otherwise in a manner not linked to the normative basis for the entitlement. For example, it would be an extrinsic condition upon an entitlement to a benefit if one's receiving the benefit depended on the costs of the benefit, the feasibility of providing the benefit in light of other social demands, or the countervailing effects of the rights of others.

We might say that an entitlement that is subject to no intrinsic condition is a pure entitlement, and one that is so subject is a conditional entitlement. Following convention, we might also call a right that has no extrinsic conditions an absolute right, whereas one that is extrinsically conditional is a defeasible right, in the sense that it can be 'defeated' or overridden by competing, external considerations. (Since it is implausible that a non-right entitlement could ever be absolute, this terminology is not appropriate for benefits.)

Positive or Negative

This philosophically commonplace distinction among kinds of political entitlement is highly relevant for disablement policy, since it parallels the distinction made in Chapter 2 between positive and negative freedom. A negative entitlement brings about the removal of obstacles and explicit (although not necessarily intentional) hindrances that prevent people from doing what they would otherwise want to do – hence securing negative freedom. Most of the standard political and legal rights in the liberal tradition are negative. A positive entitlement secures positive freedom and so entitles one to whatever benefit is required in order to create, develop, maintain, or otherwise gain or regain previously absent (or underdeveloped) abilities or opportunities.

This distinction is crucial to disablement policy because it demarks two very different kinds of programming: negatively addressed programming (in particular antidiscrimination law) and positively addressed programming (say, vocational rehabilitation, job creation, affirmative action, or workplace accommodation requirements). Obviously, a normative basis for disablement policy must have something to say about whether policy will involve entitlements (right or non-right) that are merely negative, or positive, or both.

Means or Results

This is the (related) distinction between entitlements that are explicitly designed to produce certain results (say, an increase in the employment level of people with disabilities) and those that merely give people the means to achieve some unspecified result (a skills-upgrading program, for example). This distinction is the basis for the persistent debate, especially in the United States, whether government initiatives should be expressly guided by some benchmark result, but otherwise remain flexible with respect to how that result may be achieved, or else merely aim to provide skills and training, allowing background economic and social forces to work unimpeded.

The means/results dichotomy is closely linked, in practice, to the positive/negative distinction. The link is so close, indeed, that policy analysts sometimes assume that one or the other pair does not represent a normative controversy at all so much as a technical or administrative detail. It is important, however, not to gloss over possible normative judgments or rule out some combinations out of hand. For example, one could argue that the state should not be engaged in positively addressed programming (as this interferes with personal liberty), while not objecting to result-oriented, negatively addressed programming (say, destigmatizing educational programs that are to be in place as long as there is evidence of a certain level of prejudice).

Net Social Benefit or Individual (Group) Benefit

This last, three-way contrast concerns the measure of achievement of the basic goals of disablement policy, whether as a matter of right or not. Here the issue is, roughly, whether social planners should devise and assess initiatives in terms of the actual or potential capacity to increase some agreed-upon social standard of benefit for everyone in society, or just for people with disabilities (taken as a group or individually). Optimally, these three measures would coincide so that, even if the focus of the programming were restricted to, say, improving the employment prospects of specific individuals, the consequences of the program would be to improve the overall economic condition both of the class of people with disabilities *and* of society as a whole. When this coincidence is not likely, however, social choice among these three standards is necessary.

Technically, these standards are examples of an indefinite range of objectives, each of which is an implicit condition on entitlement. One might argue, for example, that a proposal to recognize individual positive rights to suitable employment is conditional upon the result that such a policy produce net social benefit, economic or otherwise. Alternatively, one might qualify a right to a benefit, available to any member of the group of people with disabilities, with the proviso that the right cannot be exercised by an individual if the direct result will be an overall lowering of benefit of the group itself. Other possible standards can be easily imagined.

Obviously by ringing through the changes in these five areas of controversy we could artificially generate a number of possible normative stances – strong individual rights accounts; conditional, negative rights approaches; weak net social benefit, non-rights accounts; and so on. Most of these theoretically interesting permutations would be non-starters, practically speaking. But it is interesting to notice the potentially wide scope for inconsistency in disablement policy. Decisions taken about one or another of these issues in one area can produce policy that conflicts with policy in some other area.

We have already seen in some detail how the biomedical, the economic, and the social-political models each seem naturally aligned with different kinds of normative accounts. It is also true that ideological decisions about the nature of entitlement will affect one's preference for models. If one insists upon the strongest form of rights as a basis for policy, for instance, then one will be very tempted by the social-political model; conversely, if one is inclined to the weaker, benefits approach, then the biomedical model will seem more appropriate. None the less, the models and normative bases are not conceptually linked. Disablement has had a very dynamic evolution. The three models have developed together, sometimes one in ascendancy, sometimes another. The challenge of disablement policy is to isolate and develop a single, unified, and workable normative basis that does justice to the concept of disablement.

It is my contention that there is such a normative basis: it is equality, and in the next chapter I sketch an argument to show why equality is our best candidate. For now, by way of an indirect argument for this contention, I want to show that the normative bases that have already left their imprint on disablement policy are inadequate to the challenge. These bases are built on principles of charity, need, compensation, and welfare maximization. I want to look at these in enough detail to highlight the problems each causes for disablement policy.

I begin, though, with a brief discussion of an older, and darker, normative understanding of disablement, one which might be called 'primitive retributivism.' Though universally condemned these days, it retains, perhaps only subconsciously, a hold on our understanding of disablement.

Primitive Retributivism

Personality theorists offer explanations of the stigmatizing attitudes that all of us have toward people with disabilities. Some argue that these attitudes are signs of immaturity, unexpressed hostility, or fear; others that they are the expression of predetermined social roles.[1] Devaluing attitudes are probably too diverse to admit of simple explanations. But one does not need such a theory to suggest, as many have, that a common theme in attitudinal devaluation is that the disability or impairment is a sign of bad moral character.

These days it is difficult to imagine anyone voicing this view openly, unless the individual with a disability was in some obvious way responsible for the condition. Even then few people would think it appropriate to blame or withhold sympathy, especially if the disability is severe. This is because most of us reject out of hand the normative basis of primitive retributivism.

In a nutshell, primitive retributivism is the view that people who are manifestly defective are living out a just punishment for sins, vices, or other moral faults, known or unknown, that has been inflicted by some powerful and moral force. At most, in this view, these manifest sinners are entitled to our pity; but it is our duty to dissociate ourselves from them.

Although it is comforting to think that beliefs about the 'wrath of the gods' and practices such as the exposure of malformed newborns are all relics of ancient times, long gone, the truth, as always, is more complicated. For the attitudes and practices of the ancients were more ambiguous in their motivation, and there is certainly evidence that we moderns have not shed these 'primitive' attitudes.[2]

In any event, this stance obviously flies in the face of all we know about impairment. Morally innocent people can become disabled through no fault of their own, and it is fallacious, not to say morally pernicious, to think that having an impairment is grounds for deserving one. Therefore, if someone held such a view, we would probably take him or her to be rejecting our common understanding of the way the world works.

Still, versions of primitive retributivism can be gleaned from various sources, some current and very much influential. One version has been particularly well documented, namely, that form of biological determinism that links somatic or anatomical structure, or genetic configuration, with complex human behaviours, including moral character. Stephen Jay Gould's 1981 study of the phenomenon in *The Mismeasure of Man*[3] surveys a range of such views popular in this and the previous century. Theories of human races based on the dubious techniques of craniometry and phrenology, and theories of criminal morphology, such as Cesare Lombroso's infamous theory of the 'criminal type,' are some of Gould's examples of how science can come to the aid of racism, sexism, and other prejudices.

The use of the biological sciences, and most prominently genetics, to elevate ideological conceptions of human nature to the status of a science of human social development has been canvassed by Steven Rose, R.C. Lewontin, and Leon J. Kamin in their 1984 book *Not in Our Genes*.[4] As these authors show, sociobiology assumes that marginalized groups are biologically inferior in one way or another. The policy ramification of this is that it would be futile and socially unnecessary to be concerned about the justice of society's attitudes toward these people, since these attitudes are part of our unchangeable natures.

Once again, it is important to bring such modern examples up to counter the temptation to think that primitive retributivism is no longer with us. Needless to say, of course, the normative view remains part of our religious traditions. Some biblical remarks can only be made sense of in terms of primitive retributivism. Consider, for example, John 5:13 where Jesus says, after healing a man with disabilities: 'Behold, thou art made whole. Sin no more lest a worse thing come unto thee.' In classical rabbinical thought there is the view that human suffering is a sign of having sinned.[5]

Historically, Judeo-Christian doctrine perpetuated the belief that outward manifestations of impairment were signs of inward evil. Thus, congenital deformations of the 'changelings' of the Middle Ages were taken as signs of witchcraft and the impiety of parents; and the infamous *Malleus Maleficarum* of 1487 argued that being able to cure disease was a sign of being a witch, since, having imposed the infirmity as punishment, God obviously did not approve of alleviating it.[6]

Whether based on religious dogma or not, beliefs about impairments as 'marks' or stigmata of moral corruption are the stuff of stereotyping we learn from our nursery rhymes and children's books. And from Chaucer's Summoner and Shakespeare's Richard III, to Dostoyevsky's Karamazov the elder and Captain Ahab, the deformed, the ugly, and the freak as morally flawed individual are not uncommon themes in our literature.[7] Although far more complex, perhaps because more fearful, mental impairment has generated its own range of prejudicial representations in myth and literature.[8]

However handicapping the images of evil or corruption may be, another more recent version of primitive retributivism is much more prejudicial. It might be called the claim of voluntarism, the presumption that because of voluntary decisions people have made, and health risks they have foolishly taken, when disease and impairment result these conditions are deserved.

Susan Sontag has traced voluntarism and other metaphors of disablement in her two thought-provoking books on cancer, tuberculosis, and AIDS.[9] In both studies Sontag explores the cultural representations and theories of these diseases that have transformed illness into moral character. The most persistent of these metaphors transforms disease into a psychological flaw – a personality trait predisposing one to infection. Other metaphors, she notes, have been relied on in purportedly scientific and self-help books alike to make the case for the need to alter one's personality as a preventative measure. The normative implications of all of this are clear; as Sontag puts it, 'psychological theories of illness are a powerful means of placing the blame on the ill. Patients who are instructed that they have, unwittingly, caused their disease are also being made to feel that they have deserved it.'[10]

With its associations with sexual impropriety in general and homosexuality in particular, the assumption of voluntarism in the case of AIDS is considerably more influential. That people with AIDS, or who have tested HIV-seropositive, ought not to qualify for disablement benefits because they have 'brought it on themselves' is perhaps the clearest example of primitive retributionism at work. Significantly, something very close to this has recently been approved by the Supreme Court of the United States.[11]

Why does primitive retributivism retain its grip on us? Some psychologists will argue that it is yet another instance of the 'just world' hypothesis at work: when our children are born with deformities, when disease strikes randomly and without apparent cause, we are faced with 'one aspect of the indeterminable universe that we wish to distance from ourselves.'[12] These things challenge our conception of the world as a safe, secure, regular, and just place. In the face of this challenge we tend to construct boundaries between ourselves and those with disabilities in the hope of identifying what put them at risk and not us. One of these boundaries, reflecting an aspect of life over which we believe we have complete control, is that between the moral and the immoral. In a just world, only those who deserve bad things have bad things happen to them; therefore, to preserve the justice of the world, when disease or deformity strikes it must be deserved.[13]

Whatever the psychological explanation, primitive retributivism, in one guise or another, is not an artefact of an ancient culture, long ago superseded by scientific enlightenment. It is still with us, even though it is unlikely anyone would publicly express the view that, since people with disabilities deserve their fate as natural or divine punishment, society owes them nothing but sanctimonious pity. Yet, if the normative basis itself is discredited, as it should be, we must be vigilant unless less obvious versions of it – such as voluntarism – contrive to exert an influence over our policy decisions.

Charity

Given its longevity and persisting influence the normative basis of charity is undoubtedly the predominant normative understanding of the entitlements of people with disabilities. To be sure, it has been superseded in the era of the welfare state by other normative theories; but at no point has it been supplanted. Indeed, to the extent that some forms of social assistance, in particular 'welfare' or 'the dole,' continue to be conceptualized, if not overtly described, as forms of 'public charity,' this normative basis still holds sway over much of disablement policy.

The long history of charity can be attributed to the fact that it is both a normative theory about the entitlements of people with disabilities and a social-psychological framework for coming to terms with disablement. Most researchers now insist that charity is profoundly stigmatizing, since it creates a chasm between the virtuous 'givers' and the worthy, but utterly dependent, passive, deferential, and humble 'receivers' of alms. Some have observed that it is precisely because of the stigmatization of charity that it has survived for so long.

Because of our own cultural orientation we tend to associate charity with Judeo-Christian traditions.[14] The charitable response is, however, a common feature of most of the world's religions; in the Quran, for example, no duty is more frequently mentioned than charity.[15] In the Christian tradition the place of charity was secured by central aspects of Jesus's teaching, so that by the fourth century Augustine was confident enough to argue that the faithful must on no account deny that anyone born of humans, however odd he or she may look or act, is not fully human.[16] Throughout the Middle Ages, feudal religious charity, either in the form of alms-giving or monastic hospitality, was founded on the canonical principle of the moral innocence of poverty and the inherent virtue of the downtrodden and *pauperes Christi*. But, as has been thoroughly documented, although the religious basis for charity was never explicitly challenged, the moves in the early fourteenth century to organize charity were motivated, not by any belief about the moral status of the poor, but by the perceived need to restrain vagrancy and to stabilize the labour market.[17]

As we have already remarked, the social and economic conditions of Europe as it emerged from the Middle Ages mandated a clear distinction between the worthy and the unworthy poor, between 'God's poor' and the idle, lazy, or otherwise troublemaking 'voluntary poor.' The category of disability – initially, the blind, the lame, and the insane – was the main administrative and ideological device used by English legislators by the late Middle Ages to distinguish those worthy of consideration by charitable organizations and those who were rogues, vagabonds, and 'sturdy beggars' who could be made to work.

The creation of disability as a way of identifying those who could be benefited by charity eventually served other social purposes, including controlling access to needs-based welfare redistributive schemes. But the charitable approach to disablement was also taken up by many non-governmental organizations in pre- and postindustrial Europe: the mutual aid societies, friendly societies, unions, and philanthropic societies. These organizations proved in time to be too inefficient to cope with the concentration of poverty-related social ills caused by the increased urbanization that came close on the heels of industrialization. Thus, in England we find a Charity Organization Society established in the early nineteenth century to coordinate the activities of voluntary organizations and, indirectly, to provide the basis for the development of social work as a profession.[18]

In effect, the Charity Organization Society integrated centuries of Poor Laws with the complex structure of private philanthropy that had slowly developed from the late seventeenth century on. The result was to join ideology with administrative convenience to further ensure that only the deserving poor received charity.[19] In the United States similar notions – arguably strengthened by strains of social Darwinism – led to a reorganization of private charitable agencies. Eventually, much of the administrative control of these agencies was incorporated into the Vocational Rehabilitation Act of 1920.[20] The rationale of this legislation was to provide the worthy poor with the skills and training needed to demonstrate their worth in the marketplace.

That the best form of charity, public or private, should be that which lends a hand to the downtrodden expressly so that they can become self-supporting is a normative axiom at least as ancient as the writings of Maimonides.[21] It was precisely this view of charity that was built into the very bricks and mortar of early Anglo-American and Canadian social assistance programming. Eventually, however, the normative basis of social welfare programming shifted to more needs-based conceptions of entitlement.

Still, the spirit of charity has never been wholly replaced or supplanted in disablement policy. Charitable organizations continue to play a role in disablement policy, broadly construed, with organizations such as the Canadian National Institute for the Blind and other impairment-specific groups being integrated into policy through tax policy. And policy analysts continue to see a role for these organizations, inasmuch as they free the hand of the state to a limited extent.

At a deeper level, too, the charitable organization has had an effect on the social perception of disablement. It is hard to imagine a representation more conducive to the creation of dependency – the principal handicapping factor as some see it[22] – than that of being a 'charity case.' This is certainly confirmed by research that has made us aware of the stigma that is associated with being perceived to be a welfare recipient.[23]

Now conceptually, charity as a ground for entitlement has a fairly strict logic. It makes no sense, without a more extensive story being told, to say that strangers have an *obligation* to give charity to those in need. Coversely, if I wrongfully injure you and attempt to make amends, whatever I do to relieve your misfortune can not meaningfully be called charity. Although the charitable response presupposes a predicament or misfortune of some sort, it also assumes the absence of responsibility for that misfortune. One gives charity precisely when one does not have to give anything, but does anyway out of kindness, compassion, or sympathy.

Moral philosophers put this point more formally in terms of the nature of beneficence, that general category of moral behaviour distinct from, but on a par with, justice, duty, and responsibility. As a moral category beneficence denotes the doing of good and the abstaining from evil. More particularly, within this category two principles are recognized, non-maleficence (do not, by action or inaction, inflict harm or evil on another person) and benevolence (do or promote good). Some philosophers make further distinctions and identify another two intermediate principles: prevent evil or harm, and remove evil or harm.[24]

There are normative and practical differences between the core principles of beneficence. The first, non-maleficence, is primarily a negative obligation that is nearly absolute. That is, *not* inflicting harm is a very powerful obligation admitting of very few exceptions. The intermediate principles – obligations to prevent harm from occurring and to remove it – are more positive obligations in the sense that they would normally require some sort of action or intervention, with attendant risks to the agent. The second core principle, benevolence, is inherently positive and universally identified as a form of virtuous behaviour akin to generosity, self-sacrifice, and altruism. At the same time, though, benevolence is a virtue precisely because it is not obligatory. Indeed, benevolence is usually thought to be the paradigm of supererogatory behaviour, behaviour above and beyond the call of duty.

Charity is the clearest example of benevolence (most writers treat them as synonymous). Thus, charity is a virtue that enhances the moral status of the giver, since he or she has benefited another without having the duty to do so. Even when religious texts specify that charity is a duty it is not characterized as a duty to one in need, but to God; with the result that the charitable are enriched more than those who receive the charity.[25]

Thus, it is said that charity arises from feelings of compassion, and the charitable act is by definition undeserved: no one can meaningfully be said to be owed charity; charity is a gift, not a contractual exchange. The act of benevolence is aimed at benefiting someone whose plight is a hard fact of life – the result of 'losing in the natural lottery'; the charitable giver must bear no responsibility for that plight.

Now all of these conceptual features of the concept of charity can easily be read off the structure and legal characterization of our voluntary charitable organizations. For these are, first off, voluntary organizations: whatever may be one's religious obligations toward the poor and the needy, the social institutions that channel charitable contributions do not represent these contributions as anything other than gifts. More to the point, nearly every aspect of charitable giving underscores the virtuousness of those who give. The organizations are all tax-exempt, enjoy favourable incorporation law and other legal privileges, and generally have a very positive social image. People who give, similarly, are praised for their generosity and allowed the freedom to direct their largesse to whomsoever they choose.

As it happens, there are good reasons for being extremely sceptical of the motives and aims of North American charity-givers. Not only do the wealthy in the United States give a far lower percentage of their incomes to charities than do those who are less well off, but the charity of the wealthy tends to go to art museums, opera houses, private hospitals, and elite universities.[26] The direct and indirect benefits to the givers of charity in fact tend to outstrip the benefits received.

Even when charity is channelled to those in need, however, the financial and other benefits received are not without a substantial price in self-esteem. Whatever the form – be it telethons featuring doe-eyed children in wheelchairs or the blind beggar on the street corner – charity creates a relationship between giver and receiver that is inherently unequal and demeaning. If begging, a performance extracted from the poor by the charitable, is 'an especially painful example of the power of money,'[27] then so too is any performance designed to elicit benevolence.

It might seem somewhat mysterious, if not unseemly, that a virtuous act should have these effects. Why is it that charity breeds deference, passivity, and humility? There is no mystery here. Since a recipient of charity is the beneficiary of another's virtue, a virtue denied to the recipient, charity creates a morally asymmetric relationship. It would be ridiculous to praise someone for *receiving* charity; being in that position is a sign of failure and inferiority. Charity exemplifies dependence and sustains it. The needy recipient, whose needs have not been abated by a single episode of gift-giving, must return once again to the benefactor.

It is, therefore, not surprising that attacks upon social assistance programs are often launched by the rhetorical gesture that welfare is nothing more than public charity. One side of the political spectrum uses this remark as a way of saying that welfare is objectionable because it is coerced generosity: the taxpayer is not allowed to benefit from the virtue of being the author of his or her own largesse.[28] And from the other side, welfare is attacked for creating dependency and making it less likely that people in need will acquire the means to make themselves independent.

Given all this, as a normative basis for disablement theory charity provides the weakest forms of entitlement conceivable. People with disabilities have no right to (or do not even deserve) any kind of need-relieving benefit by virtue of their condition of disablement. Moreover, the charitable entitlement that might be offered is conditional upon the desire of someone to provide the benefit, as well as extrinsically conditional upon any other demand for that benefit from any other source. Any claim, however weak, can trump charity.

In short, then, charity could not conceivably provide us with a coherent and integrating normative basis for disablement theory. Charity cannot make normative sense of handicapping, nor for that matter is it compatible with the notion of disability. As a normative response, charity is at best compatible with impairment, but only if understood as a personal misfortune.

It might be objected, though, that there must be some normative space left for a charitable – or better, an altruistic – response to the state of need created by impairments. If useless as a policy rationale, what could be the objection to private beneficence? Is there any way to, so to speak, redeem charity?

In the normal case when one comes to the aid of another person, spontaneously and without any ulterior motive, no morally asymmetrical relationship is created. As someone who aids another, I need not insist that my deeds place me in a position of moral superiority relative to those I help. So what has gone wrong with charity? It may be that the asymmetric relationship was the inevitable product of the institutionalization of the assisting relationship; but in any event there is no reason to believe that what has happened to charity is intrinsic to benevolence as such.

Acts of altruism (or even acts of charity) would neither create nor sustain dependency and stigmatization if they took place against the background of equality. When my actions are not a demonstration of my power, prestige, or virtue, and yours are not a demonstration of your dependency, impotence, and inferiority, then my assisting you cannot be construed as an action that creates inequality. That is, sometimes altruism presumes that *anyone*, including the person who is in need, could have found him or herself in the role of altruist, and *anyone*, including the present benefactor, could have been in the position of need. Thus, equality redeems charity.

Need

Political and moral philosophers insist that it is important to distinguish reasons and justifications when mapping out basic normative principles.[29] While any number of considerations about the human condition might count as reasons in favour of a policy, not every such reason will reveal basic goals sufficient to justify it. Claims about human needs show the importance of this distinction: it is hardly a matter of much dispute that people have unmet needs, or that this is a relevant reason for government action and policy. Yet, the fact of need alone does not justify anything, it merely describes a condition. Thus, the fact of need alone cannot provide a normative basis for disablement policy.

Even if the command 'satisfy needs' were a suitable normative principle, it would be meaningless without a workable definition of what a need is, and the normative role it plays. Does the fact of need impose an intrinsic or an extrinsic condition on rights to the resources required to satisfy the need? Are these rights positive or negative; are they means- or result-oriented? Are they rights to the satisfaction of all needs, or just some of them; and if the latter, which needs?

Why does need pose these problems? On first hearing, it is very tempting to say that, other things being equal, a person in need of food or shelter deserves these things for no other reason than need. It is commonly said that human need is the primary moral and political justification for the welfare state. But both of these intuitions conflate the basis for a distribution scheme with its justification. Though it is true that the welfare state redistributes social resources on the basis of need, it is not true that it does so because of need.

The normative thesis that need alone creates an enforceable right to goods and services was not part of the policy document which, more than anything else, was responsible for our present welfare state, namely, William Beveridge's 1943 report to parliament entitled *Social Insurance and Allied Services*.[30] Although Beveridge was quick to identify *want* as one of the five 'giants on the road to reconstruction,' he makes it abundantly clear that the justification for any social response to want must be grounded in the normative principle of welfare maximization – a wholly economic rationale. Beveridge appreciated that need alone could not normatively warrant redistribution.

The limited normative authority of need is the result of its conceptual fluidity. Needs overlap imperceptibly with preferences, and preferences know no boundaries: does one *need* a new stereo system because one wants (desires or prefers) one? Nor is it clear whether needs are a matter of psychological dependency, the contours of which differ from person to person, or whether they have a more predictable and universal character. Are 'true needs' deficiencies in important things, things that people must have rather than merely want? And if food qualifies as a true need, what sort of food? The blood of cattle is a need for a Masai, but not for a Buddhist monk who needs a bowl of rice and vegetables.[31]

Although this indeterminacy may seem semantic it has powerful political consequences. In our liberal political tradition we insist that respect for personal autonomy means that each person must be treated as the best judge of his or her own welfare. That being so, social policy designed to enhance aggregate welfare must take into account personal understanding of needs. But then a needs-based distribution system is thoroughly anomalous, since anything could potentially count as a need. Thus, on classical liberal grounds, needs are not only elusive and subjective, they are also expansive and expensive. Needs are voracious; they eat up resources.[32]

The theoretical solution to this problem is obvious. We must distinguish between subjective (or preference-like) needs and objective needs and then focus on the latter. Thus, the literature on needs is filled with definitions of 'basic needs,' needs that every human being may be expected to have at some stage of life;[33] or needs that it is rational for anyone to have;[34] or needs that are socially recognized;[35] or needs that are basic social indicators.[36] The point has been to find some commodity or social good the possession of which provides a minimum guarantee of welfare. Thus, basic needs are thought to include minimum levels of food, accommodation, medical care, education, leisure, and so on. The move to 'basic needs,' everyone agrees, is essential if the notion is to be employed consistently and helpfully in social-scientific contexts.

There is no doubt that most accounts of basic needs seem very plausible indeed. One can hardly dispute the claim that water, food, shelter, and the like are human needs that are utterly independent of cultural differences or individual preferences. None the less, the move to objective or basic needs does not alter the normative inadequacy of the justificatory force of need, and, in the case of disablement policy, in some ways it makes it worse.

The problem is that, however objective and universal our list of basic human needs is, the mere fact that these needs are unmet does not itself provide the normative basis for requiring society to meet them. In part this is because the more basic the need the more it becomes an instrumental rather than an intrinsic good. It is, to be sure, a good thing to eat, but not because food is an intrinsic good. Eating is an essential prerequisite for living and achieving whatever one values. Therefore, even with a list of wholly uncontroversial basic needs at hand, there is a normative gap between the fact of need and the obligation of society to satisfy it.

Put another way, needs-satisfaction is a form of beneficence, captured by the principle that preventable harm ought to be prevented. If one argues that the political justification for redistributive policies is that the state has the obligation to meet basic needs by virtue of its broader obligation to prevent preventable harm – which indeed has been argued[37] – one is then required to show at least two things. First, one must show why unmet need constitutes a harm, and a preventable one. Then one must show why, granting that it would be a good thing if the state prevented harms, the state is obliged to. But answering these two questions would be no easier than answering the original one of why need alone justifies social response.

This issue aside, the notion of basic needs is potentially damaging to disablement policy because it reinforces, rather than reduces, the stigma attached to the administrative category of disability. The motivation behind seeking out careful definitions of basic needs is to ensure universality, and so avoid indeterminacy. In order to do this successfully, though, needs become more abstract and less sensitive to individual variation. Since basic needs are usually understood as commodities (goods, services, resources) rather than physical or psychological experiences (health, prosperity, happiness), the more 'basic' the need the more likely it will obscure individual differences. The 'normal' health care resource requirement (or worse, the statistical average use of resources) will end up determining the 'basic health care need.' In this way, the requirements of people with disabilities become, not basic needs, but 'special needs.'

Why not characterize the needs of people with disabilities as 'special'? This innocuous label is potentially disastrous if the normative basis for policy is need. Since 'special' needs are by definition not 'basic,' they fall outside of the justificatory theory for social provision of needs, thereby disentitling people with disabilities, who are then stigmatized as those who cannot 'get by' under programs designed to meet basic needs.

This is no theoretical worry. The criterion of need is used extensively at the operational level of social assistance programming. In various programs across Canada eligibility and allowance level decisions are determined by needs tests set out in so-called liquid asset and earning exemptions.[33] Because of the general administrative tendency towards standardization, these needs tests, unless explicitly offset by other provisions for 'special needs,' ignore or are insufficiently sensitive to the genuine needs of people with disabilities.

There are, in short, at least three substantial obstacles to a needs-based normative account of entitlement for people with disabilities: the conceptual fluidity of need; the normative incompleteness of the notion (that is, need is a reason for redistribution but not a justification of it); and the difficulties the notion creates when used as an administrative test. Conceivably all of these obstacles could be removed by using a theoretical reconstruction of the notion of need, a project that Canadian philosopher David Braybrooke has attempted with impressive results.[39] Whether Braybrooke's efforts are successful or not, his motivation for pursuing this project is well founded. Whatever its problems, the concept of need is a core concept in political theory generally and welfare policy specifically, and it would be ground breaking if it could be rescued.

Still, the substantial obstacles just mentioned teach us at least two important lessons about the needs approach. First, as a basis for describing the purpose of disablement entitlements, needs are not intrinsic; and second, as a basis for a normative theory, the concept of need must be embedded in some other, more satisfactory, normative basis.

The first lesson is the locus of a major dispute in welfare economics. The issue is what welfare is and what its economic significance should be. One side – 'welfarism' as it has come to be called – is the traditional economic view that welfare is a subjective state of some sort, like happiness, contentment, desire satisfaction, or (the catch-all) 'utility,' and the aim of welfare economics is to maximize this state across the population. This, in essence, is the normative basis of welfare maximization that will be considered below. Opponents of welfarism argue that the real measure of welfare is the extent of control over resources or basic social commodities. This approach tends to underscore the importance for welfare economics of minimum standards of resource allocation. These standards, not surprisingly, have often been expressed in the language of 'basic needs.'

Although I want to return to this debate below, for the moment it is enough to notice that an objection to resource-based conceptions of welfare relies on an insight about needs-based accounts that is of particular importance to disablement theory. This might be called the 'Sen argument.'

In a collection of seminal articles.'[40] the philosopher and economist Amartya Sen has urged that, although research based on social indicators of basic needs is undoubtedly important, we should not lose sight of the fact that the true aim of social policy – and the proper analysis of 'welfare' – lies not in these needs but in what their satisfaction makes possible. That is, the provision of needs is a means for achieving what is truly of value, an increased capability or an expansion of one's positive freedom. Our ultimate focus in welfare economics, in other words, should be on a standard of living based on 'doings and beings,' the things that people actually can do or be, the things they have a realistic choice between.

As far as Sen is concerned, meeting needs, by providing resources of various sorts, though instrumental in increasing capabilities, is not the same thing. The mere possession of a resource or other commodity will meet the need for that resource, but in real-life situations that individual's capabilities may not increase. Thus, giving people with disabilities money, or services, or even rights – meeting these needs – is an aimless policy if the goal is not an actual, measurable, expansion of their capabilities to do or be. I will return to Sen's argument later, but its consequences for a needs focus in disablement policy should be obvious.

The second lesson learned from the failure of needs-based normative accounts is that some other, normatively stronger and less problematic, account is required to make normative sense of needs. The same was true of the principle of beneficence that requires the state to prevent preventable harms. Both meeting needs and preventing harms strike us as appropriate, indeed vital, social aims. But this is only because we presume a background normative theory in which these goals are given a rationale.

The best way to see this is to shift to a completely private setting, the family, for instance, where there are strong bonds of affection, cooperation, and mutual aid. In this setting there are indeed duties to meet needs and prevent harms.[41] Our law has consistently recognized obligations of this sort on the part of parents towards their children. The normative gap between being in need and the duty to respond to need closes as one approaches the paradigm of the family relationship.

It is a persistent issue in political theory whether social policy could ever, or should ever, be based on an analogous relationship between citizen and state. Can the solidarity created by common concerns and needs be reconciled with our traditional worry about our freedom to make choices independent of a needs-satisfying state?[42] However one stands on this large issue, its very existence suggests that the gap between unmet needs and social duty must be bridged by another normative basis.

Perhaps, then, the proper role for the concept of need, as far as social policy is concerned, is not that of grounding a distinct normative basis for entitlement (since it is hopelessly inadequate in that role) but in augmenting another, more justifiable account. Because considerations of need are only relevant in the context of some theory of distributive justice, it has been suggested by various philosophers that our intuitions about the role of needs most comfortably fit within a general theory of equality.[43] One of the values of a social commitment to equality, in other words, is that it meets legitimate needs. Equality, once again, redeems our intuitions about the normative role of legitimate human needs.

Compensation

Political theory distinguishes three species of justice, variously called legal (general or formal) justice, distributive justice, and corrective (retributive or commutative) justice.[44] Legal justice is thought to embody fairness in process: lack of bias, the judicial temper, and a willingness to hear both sides. Distributive justice concerns the fair allotment of benefits and burdens among members of society. And corrective justice seeks to rectify or remedy inequities that have arisen in dealings or transactions between individuals. Can principles of corrective justice give us a normative basis for disablement policy?

Our political and legal tradition distinguishes two versions of corrective justice, in effect two ways of 'correcting' an inequity. Corrective justice can be punitive or retributive, or else compensatory. In the first case, corrective justice serves to punish an individual responsible for creating an inequity, usually a socially recognized harm of some sort. In the second case, corrective justice serves to rectify an inequity by attempting to bring the ill-treated or harmed party back to the position he or she was in before the unjust act occurred. Punitive justice is associated with the criminal law and compensatory justice with private law, that is, torts, contracts, restitution, and the like. Punitive corrective justice does not have a role to play in disablement policy: thus, we can focus on the compensatory version.

In its most abstract formulation, compensatory justice presumes a particular set of background circumstances and mandates a specific and limited response. The circumstances in which compensatory justice is called into play involve first an original arrangement – say, an allocation of resources between individuals – and, second, an action or inaction by one party that alters this arrangement in ways that are harmful, injurious, or otherwise disadvantageous to the other party. If this disrupting action is wrong and unjustified, then compensatory justice mandates a return to the original arrangement.

Because the aim of compensatory justice is to bring about an equivalent, but reverse, transfer of resources, it has been recognized since Aristotle that this form of justice presumes some sense of equality and the value of equal treatment. At the same time, compensatory justice is not aligned with the demands of equality, since it would justify the restoration of a prior arrangement which was distributively unjust.

The relative simplicity of the formal structure of compensatory justice notwithstanding, theorists agree that, judging by our legal and social compensatory practices, there are at least three kinds of compensation.[45] The first closely follows the structure of compensatory justice and is captured by the tort law principle of *restitutio ad integrum*: what has been lost, as a result of a wrongful act, must be returned, or if not returnable then its monetary equivalent (called damages) must be awarded to the injured party by way of compensation. Tort law recognizes the application of this principle even in circumstances in which what has been lost is not an identifiable or currently existing object. Thus, the loss of one's future earning capacity as a result of personal injury is typically viewed as compensable. The principle also applies when the 'loss' is an addition rather than a subtraction, when, for example, the wrongful act creates an additional cost or unwanted liability. In these cases the pecuniary equivalent of the 'loss' is more speculative, but the goal remains the same: to restore the wronged or injured party to the status quo ante.

The second kind of compensation in effect dispenses with one component of the formal pattern of compensatory justice, the restoration of the original arrangement. In some instances what has been lost is either practically or in principle irreplaceable, either in kind or in monetary equivalent. Compensation for pain and suffering, or loss of enjoyment of life (two standard 'heads' of tort damages), is of this sort. The money awarded is clearly a substitute, a solace for what has been lost. Thus, too, someone who has been blinded cannot be returned to the status quo ante, and it is fanciful to suppose that any sum of money could be equivalent to the ability to see. None the less, substitute compensation, almost always in the form of money, can help to defray the costs of accommodation.

The modification to compensatory justice brought into play with substitute compensation is not of great theoretical significance. No strain on the core meaning of compensatory justice is created by a sense of compensation that abandons the assumption of replaceability, but keeps, as it surely must, the spirit of restoration in the form of a rule of proportionality. Since intuitively it is more of a loss to be blinded than to have an irreplaceable heirloom destroyed, the compensatory response, in substitution, must be commensurate. Since this is usually the case, substitute compensation is merely a variant of *restitutio ad integrum*.

The third commonly used sense of compensation does seem problematic, however. For it dispenses with the highly intuitive requirement that the party to be compensated must have been harmed or disadvantaged by the wrongful actions of another. This is the sense of compensation found, for example, in social welfare programming where 'compensation' is based entirely on the aim of equalizing the position of a disadvantaged person or group with respect to others in society. Here being disadvantaged itself warrants the compensation and provides the basis for 'equalizing' ('restoring' is not the right word) the situation.

It might be objected that equalization compensation, to give it a name, is not really a form of compensation. But why not? After all it involves but one fairly modest step away from the other two forms of compensation already mentioned. That it ignores the wrongdoer is not obviously problematic, since what makes compensation different from the other side of corrective justice – retribution or punishment – is precisely that compensation does not focus on the wrongdoer. The justice of a compensatory response is assessed in terms of its adequacy as compensation to the victim, not as punishment to the wrongdoer. Or to put the point somewhat differently, although compensation is a contingent right vested in the 'victim,' it is not intrinsically a right *against* the wrongdoer. Compensation is not always a matter of 'disgorging wrongful benefits,' to use the law's colourful phrase; sometimes it is simply a matter of making life easier for the party who has lost something. Thus, we normally do not make compensation contingent on proof that the wrongdoer has gained something by his or her wrongful acts.[46]

To be sure, tort law and related areas of private law *do* insist upon a link between compensation and the actions of a wrongdoer. This is the 'fault principle' at work, the principle that has traditionally in our common law been used as both a necessary and a sufficient condition of liability for tort damages. According to this principle it is just that a person who causes harm to another through fault should be made by law to compensate the victim, and, conversely, that a person who causes harm, but without fault, should not be so required.

Nearly every aspect of a tort action is touched by this principle;

the duty of care, standard of care, causation, and defence components of the action all serve to form a link between the plaintiff's right to compensation and the defendant's obligation to compensate. In law the compensatory process is restricted to the extremely narrow arena defined by the transaction that established the relationship between the parties to the litigation. The victim must bear the loss personally if the person who caused it was not at fault. However, the principle entails that the tortfeasor is responsible for all of the loss, regardless of the degree of fault and notwithstanding the hardship this may cause.

Given the nature and rationale of tort law, the fault principle is both appropriate and unobjectionable. In a moment, though, I shall join with nearly every other writer on disablement issues and argue that, because of this principle, tort law is a totally inappropriate basis upon which to build disablement policy. For now it need only be said that the fault principle is a refinement of compensatory justice, not identical to it, and even though there are good reasons of deterrence, certainty, and efficient risk allocation that justify the fault principle for tort law, we need not conclude from this that compensation itself requires fault.

Viewed more broadly, in other words, compensation is more victim-focused than it is wrongdoer-focused. Programs such as criminal injuries compensation, where compensation is paid by the state on proof of injury or death resulting from a criminal action (or incurred while enforcing the law),[47] are compensatory even though the wrong-doer is not involved. If so, then it is but a short step to another form of compensation in which no particular individual can be held responsible for a harm that has befallen an individual or group. This is equalization compensation.

The most interesting aspect of equalization compensation, for our purposes, is that it is etiologically neutral. Just as a physical condition qualifies as an impairment irrespective of how it came about, so too a person deserves equivalence compensation by virtue of a disadvantageous condition of inequality, irrespective of how that condition came about. This feature further distances this form of compensation from the paradigm of corrective justice, as exemplified by tort law compensation.

This is most easily seen by looking at an etiological feature already mentioned: voluntarism. There is very little doubt that compensation in the tort sense is *not* neutral with respect to the past actions of the plaintiff claiming to be wrongfully injured. Quite the contrary, it is a general tort principle that if the injured party brought the injury on, intentionally or carelessly, or contributed in some way to bringing it about, his or her claim to compensation will be seriously compromised. As a tort lawyer would put it, *voluntia non fit injuria*.

The voluntarism rule in tort law is just the converse of one of the circumstances that characterize the abstract form of compensatory justice. In the usual case one deserves compensation only if one has suffered a loss as a result of the wrongful conduct of *another*. Voluntarily induced harm is not something for which another person can be held responsible. Nor, it would seem, could one plausibly claim to be a 'victim' in such circumstances.

For all of these reasons tort law (and to a limited extent criminal law as well) recognizes voluntarism in the form of defences such as consent and contributory negligence. Indeed, the rule that voluntariness precludes compensation is built into the fault principle, since it holds that a person causing harm to another, including him- or herself, should be made by law to bear the burden of that harm. More abstractly, tort compensation is an intrinsically conditional right, one condition of which is that one *deserve* the claim upon the resources of another. Voluntariness undermines dessert.

If equivalence compensation is etiologically neutral, even with respect to self-caused harms and injuries, in what sense can it be a form of compensatory justice at all? One might try to answer this difficult question by noting that the aim of compensatory justice is to annul, rectify, or eliminate unjustifiable losses, and this is also the aim of equivalence compensation. The difference is that it is of the essence of compensatory justice that a loss is 'unjustified' only when it is the result of the wrongful actions of an identifiable agent, whereas this is not even a necessary condition for equivalence compensation. The fact that an individual or group is disadvantaged by virtue of an unequal social position, status, role, or condition makes the disadvantage an unjustifiable loss deserving equivalence compensation. But this difference between the two forms of compensation is not particularly significant.

Is this a good argument? Whether it is or not, a more telling objection to the status of equivalence compensation as a form of compensatory justice is that it is really a form of distributive justice. The injustice of social disadvantages that are burdens not equally borne by all is an injustice of distribution, not compensation.

Equivalence compensation, it would appear, is really a corollary of the distributive principle of egalitarianism.

Perhaps, then, there is a deep ambiguity in the term 'compensation.' Although there seems to be room for a non-corrective sense of the term, compensation is paradigmatically an aspect of corrective justice. Thus, whenever the term is used to describe a program or initiative we will automatically try to fit its rationale into that mould. But if the real rationale is, like that of equivalence compensation, distributive rather than corrective, the program will appear to be manifestly unjust, if not incoherent. This is a not uncommon phenomenon.

Consider any large-scale affirmative action or pay equity program designed to benefit differentially targeted populations, such as people with disabilities. If it is called a 'compensation' program it will invite the criticism that it is unfair for people outside of these groups to be held responsible for the social status of the targeted populations, or to be forced to disgorge potential gains (employment, advancement, or salary) by way of compensation. This violates the voluntariness rule. True enough, if affirmative action were warranted by corrective justice. But these objections miss the mark in the case of *redistributive* programming that aims to spread the burden of unemployment, or the benefits of employment, more equitably.

What of contributory schemes such as workers' 'compensation,' unemployment insurance, pension plan, and the like? In theory all insurance schemes are risk-pooling, risk-spreading distribution techniques, not forms of corrective justice. Moreover, compulsory and contribution-neutral forms of insurance have an intentional redistributive effect that further distances them from compensation. None the less, benefits from these schemes are called 'compensation,' and this practice is so widespread that there is no point trying to change it.

Undoubtedly one of the reasons for this is that private insurance is a form of contract and thus governed by the logic of corrective justice. The failure of an insurance company to pay out under the policy – when the specified conditions are met – creates just the sort of wrongful loss (and wrongful gain) that corrective justice seeks to rectify. Thus, payments under a policy of private insurance, private pension, or the like can properly be called forms of compensation.

It is more difficult to make this argument in the case of social insurance, since the right to benefits under any of these programs is not so much contractual as statutory, perhaps even constitutional.[48]

Moreover, few social insurance schemes are 'pure' insurance plans, since the governing legislation typically imposes other constraints so that they perform several social and economic functions at once. Still, there are two reasons for thinking that, at some level, it is appropriate to call social insurance programming a form of compensation.

First (a point which may only apply to disablement programming), the earliest forms of these programs were based either on private accident and life insurance policies or else on tort principles. With private insurance those who do not insure, when they have the opportunity to, and are injured must, in justice, bear the responsibility for their uncompensated loss. They deserve it. Unfortunately, this aspect of compensatory justice was carried over to the public sphere. When social insurance was first recommended in the English-speaking world by Sir William Beveridge, one of his core arguments for a compulsory and contributory scheme was that citizens ought to contribute to their own protection against accidents and other harms.

Second, many features of existing social insurance schemes continue to display the presumptions of corrective justice as these are played out in tort law. This is nowhere better seen than in workers' compensation which, for reasons already canvassed, bears many structural resemblances to tort compensation.

This said, though, it is clear that as a normative basis for disablement policy compensation cannot be said to generate a single, unambiguous normative grounding for the kinds of entitlements that one finds in disablement policy. There is but a loose family resemblance between the 'compensation' that governs some programs and that which governs others.

If, contrary to the evidence, the notion of compensation found throughout disablement policy were nothing more than a direct application of compensatory justice, then the task of assessing it as a candidate for a normative basis of disablement would be a relatively simple matter: compensatory justice is a wholly inappropriate normative basis and could not possibly make disablement policy coherent.

The reason for this is simply that the principle of compensation only applies to those impairments and disabilities that are directly caused by the wrongful acts of others. To employ this as a normative benchmark would commit us to the irrational distinction between human-created and non-human-created impairments. The victim of an assault who suffers a broken nose would be entitled to compensation, but the person born with a highly disabling congenital disease would be entitled to nothing at all. Even if we were to extend the scope of the 'human-created' category to include all disease, deformations, and other anomalies that might arguably be the result of environmental conditions of which the human race is, collectively, responsible, this would still not include all forms of disablement of concern.

Thus, as has been argued by many scholars, a tort-law-like approach could not be a suitable vehicle of disablement compensation.[49] The causation requirement, which looks for a single, often fictional cause of the impairment, the need to prove that the defendant had a duty to avoid harming the plaintiff and had breached that duty, and in general all of the obstacles to proof of liability make it fair to say that the prospects for a victim of a human-created impairment obtaining tort compensation are slim. As for the 'victim' of the natural lottery, the chances are non-existent.

Would not tort liability be appropriate for those handicaps that result from intentional and prejudicial treatment of others? Yes, but the costs involved in bringing actions, and the uncertainty of being successful, are still major constraints on the usefulness of this approach, even assuming that intentionally created handicaps are, in comparison with systemic handicaps, a significant social problem.

Now it may be argued that it is quite inappropriate to pick on tort law as the paradigm of compensation when assessing compensation as a normative basis for disablement theory. For surely no area of private law could provide a suitable basis for social policy which concerns collective action towards collective goals. This is a fair response; but is there a more suitable paradigm than tort law?

The problem with using workers' compensation as a model of a normative principle of compensation is that, as I have argued above, it is notoriously unclear what workers' compensation is compensation for. Even in those jurisdictions such as Saskatchewan that have adopted the 'two-track' benefit system, which provides benefits for permanent impairment as well as actual loss of wages, it remains unclear which permanent consequences of a work-related injury should be compensable and which not.[50] Impairment-related costs, such as treatment for pain and continuing medical care and the like, form a primary level of consequence, whereas functional limitations of the sort assessed by ADL standards form another. Which is to be compensated? As well, functional limitations usually produce work and non-work disabilities, and compensation for these may be considerably more difficult to assess.

The point here is not just that workers' compensation (and other disability-centred social insurance schemes) relies on an inadequate understanding of the consequences of impairments, although this is true enough.[51] As well, the compensatory rationale of these programs tends to be far too indeterminate to give any guidance on how assessment questions are to be answered. Workers' compensation schemes are obviously not pure applications of compensatory justice, in any case. If they were, they would be totally inadequate. But at the same time their redistributive features are also not clearly set out or motivated.

In sum, advocates for compensation as a candidate for a normative basis for disablement policy are trapped in a dilemma. If compensation is modelled on the abstract form of compensatory justice then applying it to the social issues involved in disablement policy is unjustifiable. As a matter of public policy we cannot draw a distinction between human-caused impairments (including accidents and intentional harms) and other impairments (chronic disease and congenital deformities). However, the further away one moves from the purely corrective justice reading of compensation towards equivalence compensation, the less suitable compensation becomes as a normative basis for entitlement. Tort-like compensation has the virtue of being consistent and relatively coherent; the law gives us a test for identifying the beneficiary, the measure of compensation, and the normative justification for taking money from one pocket and putting it into another. When this structure is abandoned – as it is when insurance principles and redistributive pressures influence the structure of the 'compensation' – important gaps appear. We no longer have a way of identifying what is being compensated and why, let alone who deserves compensation and who does not.

In fact, when opponents of the fault principle and tort-based compensation propose alternative 'compensation' plans for people with disabilities there is a tendency to look elsewhere for a normative basis of the entitlement. Not infrequently when causal criteria are abandoned, and all plans for a replacement or rectification standard for compensation are eschewed, the reform package suggested implicitly adopts need instead. This is true of radical and comprehensive reforms focusing on income continuity,[52] those that focus entirely on the nature of the disability,[53] and those that try to do both.[54]

The mistake here is understandable, since the gravamen of the critique of tort-like compensation is that it fails, in a variety of ways, to meet the real needs of people with disabilities. From there it is but a small, but very mistaken, step to the view that the appropriate normative basis for entitlement is the fact of need alone.

More careful reformers and other commentators realize that the inadequacies of corrective justice schemes for compensation eventually require us to move to a different, and more normatively inclusive, basis for the entitlements of disablement policy. Denaturing compensation by abandoning the principle of fault can only undermine the entitlement that compensatory justice actually underwrites. This very powerful entitlement to compensation derives its normative authority from corrective justice. Unfortunately, need alone cannot fill the shoes left unfilled when corrective justice is evicted.

What can, and should, step into those shoes? In the pure compensation setting an individual complains of unfair, differential, and unequal treatment. The misfortune suffered (at the hands of another) in effect separates the victim from others and justice requires that distinctions which created difference, be eliminated and the original situation restored. But to ask for 'compensation' for disablement as such, however caused, is not at all to ask for reciprocating, difference-annulling preferential treatment, of the sort provided by tort principles. It is rather to ask that the consequences of 'natural' misfortunes, those that are part of what it means to be human and to live a human existence, be spread equally among all people. Loss distribution is arguably a central aim of distributive justice. Thus, it would seem that for compensation to play a role in disablement policy it must be embedded in a distributive justice framework.

The normative mandate to distribute the burdens associated with disablement, however, must be grounded in something other than prudent risk management or economic efficiency. We are drawn to burden distribution when we seek equitable disablement policy because we sense that the social problem of disablement is a problem of inequality. As Atiyah and Cane have argued: 'The justice of loss distribution owes something to the feeling that "we are all in this together," that when misfortune strikes fortuitously and unequally the inequality it creates can be partly removed by the payment of compensation.'[55] Thus, our intuition about the relevance of compensation to a normative basis for disablement theory is redeemed by equality.

Welfare Maximization

The economic analysis of disablement is a dominant policy tool in our political culture, and has been for decades. As that model understands it, disablement policy is in large part policy regarding the economic problem of 'spreading' the costs of disablement so that they do not all fall on the shoulders of the individual with disabilities. As well, since disablement incurs 'spillover' or external social costs, these too must be spread. Thus, we find that although there is policy with respect to medical, special aids and devices, and rehabilitation costs, most policy in this area concentrates on the social costs of disablement in the labour market.

I have already rehearsed the limitations of, and distortions caused by the economic focus on disablement policy: the inevitable reliance on cost-benefit analysis, in the context of supply-side labour-market dynamics, threatens to turn disablement policy into a complex device for regulating the labour market in ways that need not serve the interests of people with disabilities or further the goals of respect, participation, and accommodation. That said, it remains to investigate the background normative position that drives the economic model. Professional disclaimers aside, there obviously is one, since the standard of efficiency, on any interpretation of it, is invariably employed as a norm for assessing the viability and suitability of policy recommendations. In practice, that is, efficiency is a social norm. What underwrites efficiency as a normative standard is another normative principle, one that is wholly result-oriented and committed to net social benefit as the sole measure of policy: the principle of welfare maximization.

Unlike all of the other normative bases discussed so far, welfare maximization – like utilitarianism, its ancestor – has been a basis for social policy rather than individual conduct. Welfare maximization generates and justifies social decisions about entitlements, assesses policies and policy objectives, and generally functions as a guide for all forms of state action. The principle of welfare maximization holds that the measure of achievement of any goal of policy must be the overall and aggregate welfare that accrues to everyone in society as a result of pursuing that goal or policy.

Put this way, it is clear that welfare maximization is really two interlocking normative claims in one. It is first of all a normative claim about what is, from the perspective of social policy, intrinsically of value – namely, welfare. Second, it is the normative claim that since welfare is intrinsically valuable more is more valuable than less, so that policy must aim at maximizing the aggregate sum of welfare.

In philosophical terms, welfare maximization is an example of a purely axiological principle: one based on the moral dimension of 'the good' rather than 'the right,' on the valuable rather than the obligatory. Welfare maximization does not countenance any form of entitlement or obligation-creating privilege, whether in the form of a legally enforceable right or something weaker, unless that entitlement is instrumental to the production of welfare. The notion of inherent or natural rights is, on this account, entirely fictitious and socially undesirable.

Given its nature, welfare maximization provides disablement policy with a powerful normative basis: people with disabilities should be vested with those entitlements, but only those entitlements, the vesting of which maximizes welfare overall. The precise form these entitlements will take (whether positive or negative, conditional or unconditional, and so on) can only be determined if, once granted, the result is welfare maximizing.

Although abstractly the principle of welfare maximization is unambiguous, in application it is something of a chameleon: it will sanction any entitlement at all, not because people deserve it, or society has an obligation to provide it, but only because of its maximizing consequences. Perhaps the best way of showing how the principle works behind the scenes to influence policy formation is to see how it functions as the guiding principle of welfare economics.

Welfare economics is an approach to the achievement of distributive justice with respect to the allocatable resources across a society. It seeks to characterize a just distribution as well as an economy that stands a good chance of achieving that condition of justice. Towards these ends the concept of welfare is posited as standing for that which is of intrinsic value to people, and, of course, something that can be distributed by means of an economic structure. Generally, welfare is taken to be a subjective state of some sort (happiness, desire satisfaction, or whatever) that has the property of being achievable by means of objectively valuable things, such as money, goods, services, and other resources.

The task of identifying the just distribution of welfare is a matter of political theory, which makes it controversial. The economist, even the frankly normative economist, prefers to leave this aspect of the project open and proceed to the second question: What sort of economic structure can achieve just distribution? On this there is consensus: the market is the best social distribution mechanism. Economists then go on to take sides on the subsidiary questions of whether market-driven distributions are inherently just or whether there is a role for the state to 'correct' these distributions in one way or another.

As a group, welfare economists tend to favour, or at least tolerate, state intervention into the operation of the market, in the form of regulation, state entry into the supply side of the market, or direct redistribution. Intervention is justified, when it is, on grounds of efficiency, but efficiency of a specific sort – welfare efficiency or Pareto optimality.

Roughly, welfare efficiency characterizes the best allocation of limited resources given people's own understanding of their welfare. Given any existing distribution of resources, a welfare improvement is any reallocation of resources that improves or increases the welfare of at least one person but does so without at the same time decreasing the welfare of anyone else. A state intervention that procures such an improvement yields a more efficient distribution, on this account, whatever might have been said of the original distribution.[56] Since it would be odd for someone proposing putatively just distribution of resources to refuse to accept a reallocation that made one person better off without reducing anyone else's welfare, it is a maxim of welfare economics that welfare efficiency is a necessary condition for social justice.

But, it is not a sufficient condition. Indeed, some welfare improvements might only be possible at the *expense* of social justice. It may well be the case, as John Rawls has argued in support of his 'difference principle.'[57] that social planners would willingly accept less equality in distribution (or permit more inequality) if that yielded, through increases in economic productivity or other 'trickle-down' systemic benefits, a welfare improvement. Thus, policies furthering social justice or favouring equality of resource distribution may or may not be efficient.

Within these broad parameters, welfare economists have devised policy for the welfare state – policy regulating the supply side of the labour market and redistributing income through the tax system or directly through subsidies. As we have seen, these initiatives form a major part of disablement policy and are all firmly grounded in the principle of welfare maximization.

But there are two things to notice about welfare maximization. The first is that as a normative basis it has no conceptual linkage to the concept of disablement, nor any inherent normative linkage to the needs of people with disabilities. The principle justifies the welfare state but does so entirely in terms of macroeconomic issues independent of disablement. It would be perfectly possible for a distribution of resources to qualify as welfare efficient even though the actual needs of people with disabilities went wholly unmet. Thus, as a normative basis for policy, welfare maximization creates entitlements to benefits that are extrinsically conditional on societal factors irrelevant to disablement.

Second, welfare maximization is not concerned with what might loosely be called the inequities of social organization. When people's needs are ignored because these needs are 'special,' or when people's talents are not developed because it would be too costly to develop them, or when some people are stigmatized and discriminated against because they are different, social inequities result. Some of these inequities are not easily translated into the social costs economists acknowledge; and some may contribute to economic conditions economists would tend to see as favourable. But intuitively, social inequities have an immediate call on our policy, whether or not something can feasibly be done about them. As far as welfare maximization is concerned, though, these inequities are irrelevant to policy.

Does not welfare maximization have these two characteristics, and is it not indifferent to disablement (or any other form of difference), because it explicitly takes everyone equally into account? In a sense this is true: the principle assumes that everyone is a welfare-consumer and as such must be counted. And, like utilitarianism, welfare maximization is an aggregating principle concerned only with the overall welfare result, rather than with what happens to particular individuals or groups.

Now arguably this indifference is no virtue, since, like utilitarianism, welfare maximization will sanction the sacrifice of the welfare of some if doing so will guarantee an increased welfare overall. Nor is this a mere theoretical possibility. There is every reason to think that sacrifice will *always* be prudent in the case of people with disabilities, since their welfare is, per unit, more costly in resources than the welfare of those who are not similarly burdened. After all, from the economic perspective disablement is first and foremost a cost that must be reduced.

Arguably, too, an indifference to the systemic conditions responsible for marginalized minority groups in society is a clear violation of a social commitment to equality. Disablement policy, by contrast, must be an attempt to respond to difference in a context of a social commitment to equality, rather than merely efficiency. Or to put the point more provocatively, were it grounded in efficiency alone, disablement policy would be very different than it is now, since the most efficient response to disablement is to ignore it and sacrifice the interests and rights of people with disabilities.

Now welfare economists usually acknowledge these concerns and, with some reluctance, grant that welfare efficiency must on occasion (for 'political reasons') be sacrificed for considerations of vertical and horizontal equity, that is, equality as between the top and the bottom of the social-economic spectrum and as between those at the same level. For the most part these equities can only be achieved through state intervention, since the free market is indifferent to them. Economists are reluctant to allow these interventions, since they assume that efficiency and equity are at loggerheads and concessions to one must involve sacrifices to the other.[58]

All of these familiar objections to welfare maximization as a policy rationale, unconstrained by other values, apply with more force in the case of disablement policy than anywhere else. But they are all objections based on the maximizing character of the principle. It is easy to show that the principle is also vulnerable to doubts about the notion of welfare. These doubts are potentially more devastating for the principle, since maximization can only be accomplished if what is maximized is a stable, measurable, and fungible commodity. This was appreciated early on when A.C. Pigou, the founder of modern welfare economics, argued that the science requires units of welfare that are intrinsically valuable states of consciousness.[59] This move was fully in line with the 'felicitic calculus,' based on units of happiness or pleasure, of early utilitarianism. The notion of welfare was invented by economists to denote what is intrinsically of value and so the basis for evaluating commodities, resources, services, entitlements, and other 'things.'

The notion has, however, always been somewhat problematic. Is welfare a function of preferences, desires, and wants, or of more particular states, such as contentment or pleasure? Should welfare be analysed factually or counterfactually – as an existing, measurable, subjective state, or as that mental state that *would result* were a person to make one choice rather than another? There have always been worries about the subjectivity of welfare. How are we to be assured of intersubjective comparability? Is it really appropriate to count all preferences and desires (including, for example, the preference that blacks not be allowed to vote, or the desire to harm another)? If we only accept certain preferences and desires as socially valid, in what sense will the standard we use to make this distinction count as a standard of subjective welfare?[60]

Even if all these conceptual questions could be satisfactorily answered there would remain a problem about 'welfarism' as a policy tool that is of particular concern to disablement policy. Any approach to policy that is founded on the principle that it should aim to give people with disabilities 'what makes them happy,' 'what they prefer or desire,' or 'what they would choose' embodies a social-psychological presumption that is both naïve and dangerous. Almost every psychological investigation into stereotyping has shown that people who are subjected to this systemic treatment frequently come to affirm some or all of these views about themselves. Stereotyped and stigmatized minorities tend to behave in ways that are expected of them. People with handicaps act handicapped. In other words, the dynamics of handicapping are perverse and the choices, preferences, and desires of people with disabilities not infrequently reflect the handicapping attitudes policy should be geared to challenge and change. A person told since childhood that it is out of the question for her to become a lawyer, since she has cerebral palsy, may not have the desire to become a lawyer. 'Rugged individualists' for whom anything is possible tend, not coincidentally, to be people who have been brought up to believe that anything is possible. It is thus both naïve and unfair to *expect* people with disabilities to be able to transcend their social environment and 'prefer' or 'choose' what is in their interest.

Even the seemingly self-evident policy aim of making people with disabilities 'happy' or 'content' may be perverse. As Amartya Sen has observed, in his study of the underprivileged in developing countries, 'quiet acceptance of deprivation and bad fate affects the scale of dissatisfaction' and a welfarist criterion for social policy may simply legitimate that distortion.[61] The condition of people with disabilities in ours, the first world, may not be as deprived, but the dynamics of handicapping surely operate in a similar way.

Importantly, Sen also argues that welfare maximization can be rescued from these difficulties and serve a legitimate function in policy analysis once it is redeemed by a broader normative basis founded on equality. If, as in the other normative bases, we are once again led to equality, what normative basis can it be expected to provide for disablement policy?

7 Equality and Disablement

The Normative Challenge

Our disablement policy has been shaped by the biomedical, economic, and social-political models of disablement, and it is therefore not difficult to discern the influence of the four normative bases suggested by these models – namely, charity, need, compensation, and welfare maximization. Each normative basis leaves a distinctive stamp, not only on the rhetoric and public rationale of a policy initiative, but also, at a deeper level, on its structure and administrative detail. Moreover, each basis, in its own terms and within the tightly circumscribed context of a particular policy or program, seems to us both reasonable and morally acceptable. We are swayed by the intuitions that animate a charitable or needs-based policy; we see the rationality and prudence of a compensatory or economy-wide efficiency justification. Thus, it is that these four normative approaches to disablement constitute our cultural understanding of what, as individuals or as society as a whole, we owe to people with disabilities. Yet, as I have tried to show, viewed as theories of entitlement and rationales for policy, these approaches are at odds with each other and point us in very different directions. Hence, the persistent impasse in disablement policy.

Throughout the history of our social response to the problem of disablement, though, there has always been another normative influence, that of equality. To be sure, it has only been fairly recently that policy analysts, politicians, and the judiciary have taken seriously the claim that the entitlements of people with disabilities, or anyone else for that matter, are rooted in our social commitment to equality. This has been the result of the social-political model of disablement, which, by focusing on handicapping phenomena, has provided the theoretical basis for the political rallying cry that the social problem of disablement is a problem of discrimination and marginalization, that is, unacceptable social inequality.

Yet, intuitions about equality suffuse the other two models as well. The processes of medicalization that underwrite the biomedical model are reflections of the commonality of the human condition: all of us are potential victims of the whims of biological fate, disease, abnormality, accident, and impairment. Though, ironically, it is the biomedical model that has entrenched the difference that is disablement, it has also projected this difference against a background of inescapable sameness: human vulnerability and mortality. Thus, when people with disabilities say in jest that the 'normals' ought really to be call TABs – the temporarily able-bodied – they are appealing to a sense of equality at the root of the biomedical model.

The economic model, too, is built upon equality of consideration, the principle that each person counts for one and no more than one. This is the equality inherent in policy analysis which identifies the public interest and ensures that it is not conflated with the interests of an elite group or individual. As it happens, equality of consideration is secured by the economic model by reducing disablement concerns to economic concerns, thus ensuring that the costs of disablement are fungible with all other economic costs. But though objectionable for reasons already given, this reduction is motivated by considerations of equality.

In the last chapter I have also argued that our intuitions about the role of charity, need, compensation, and welfare maximization in disablement policy are redeemable if these normative principles are expanded in light of intuitive principles of equality. The stigmatizing effects of charity can be partially removed if the benevolent impulse is set against the background of equal social standing. The principle of meeting needs, although alone insufficient to justify entitlements, is a suitable measure of what is required to equalize capabilities by removing limitations on positive freedom. Fault-based accounts of compensation, though of little value to disablement policy, prepare the way for the distributive notion of equalization compensation which is both relevant and potentially very useful. And, finally, welfare maximization, viewed as an overarching policy standard, fails to do justice to disablement just in those cases where it sanctions sacrifices to the equal status and condition of people with disabilities.

An optimist might see in the history of disablement policy an evolution in normative understanding – from the fears expressed by primitive retributivism, the benevolence of charity, to the social planning of welfare maximization – an evolution that makes an equality-based model of disablement inevitable.

I share this optimism, realizing as I do that it may be because of my own cultural location in the era of the social-political model. I also strongly believe that a suitable theory of equality is the only conceivable normative basis for a disablement policy, as a matter of both theoretical and practical adequacy. Only equality can succeed in putting all aspects of disablement policy on a firm and consistent footing. Moreover, any theory of equality that adequately accounted for the multidimensional social phenomenon of disablement would probably stand a good chance of making sense of all forms of marginalized human difference – race, colour, creed, sex, and others.

At the very moment that I affirm and revel in this optimism I am mindful of the immense normative challenge that such a theory of equality represents. I cannot help but think that it would surely count as the major intellectual achievement of this century (or more likely the next).

Still, my task throughout has been limited to that of providing clarifications of the normative and conceptual foundations of disablement policy. The practical aim has been to resolve the impasse and to ensure consistent, coordinated, and anomaly-free programming, with unambiguous objectives realistically oriented towards the goals of respect, participation, and accommodation. My argument has been that a unified and unifying normative basis for policy is essential as it provides a concrete response to the question of what, if anything, society is obliged to do for, and on behalf of, people with disabilities.

The fundamental problem with the normative bases of charity, need, compensation, and welfare maximization is not that they are counterintuitive (quite the contrary), or that they do not apply in some cases (they do), or that they could not answer all entitlement questions (they could). The problem is that as a complete answer to the normative challenge, not one of them can be taken seriously. As a society we have tried to avoid the need to come up with an adequate normative basis by, implicitly in our programming, relying on all of these bases, at different times for different purposes. But that tactic only produces confusion, since these bases are not compatible.

Now, as before, this diagnosis of the impasse suggests a way of proceeding. Starting with the hypothesis that a social commitment to equality, appropriately understood, qualifies as a unifying normative basis for disablement policy, can we not learn from the failures of the other bases and sketch out what an adequate basis would accomplish? This would give us the structural requirements for an account of equality suitable to the task of unifying policy. This seems like a reasonable strategy; and, fortunately, the structural requirements are not at all difficult to formulate.

First, an adequate normative theory must be compatible with the concept of disablement and so be able to integrate the three dimensions of impairment, disability, and handicap. Having this characteristic is essential if policy is to represent disablement as a set of related social problems, which affect the lives of people different with disabilities in different ways.

A second characteristic follows immediately: an adequate normative basis for disablement would address the fundamental entitlement controversies that set the agenda for policy development. It is essential that the basis resolve the question whether the entitlements of people with disabilities are enforceable rights or merely benefits that society provides or withholds at pleasure. And it must offer guidance on the normative character of the entitlements that form part of policy: Are they intrinsically or extrinsically conditional? If conditional, what are the conditions? Will these entitlements be positive or negative in function? Will they provide opportunities and other means for individual or group achievement? Will they be designed to secure specific social objectives? And if so, will the standard of assessment be founded upon overall social benefit, targeted-group benefit, or individual benefit?

To insist that an adequate normative basis address these difficult questions does not mean that it must offer a rigid and uncontroversial formula policy analysts can apply mechanically. A formula would be undesirable, even if possible. To recall, the single most distorting feature of the three models of disablement is that each purports to close the debate over what disablement is really about. Thus, an adequate normative basis must *guide* policy development by first identifying what political values are at issue, and then setting out the vocabulary and discourse we need to engage in an ongoing political debate. It must do this without pre-empting that debate.

Taken together these two accomplishments of an adequate normative basis serve to set the stage for policy analysis by, in effect, providing a working characterization of the social problem of disablement. Of course, this is a conceptual characterization only. The extent of the problem, measured by the distance between policy goals and social conditions, can only be determined by factual investigation. None the less, this investigation presumes a characterization of the problem. One cannot go out into the 'field' and count, measure, or assess something until one knows what it is one is counting, measuring, or assessing.

The third achievement of an adequate normative basis is a consistent interpretation of the basic goals of disablement policy – respect, participation, and accommodation. We have already seen how each of the three models of disablement gives priority to one of these goals with the result that some legitimate disablement concerns are ignored. Since an adequate normative basis would incorporate an integrated understanding of disablement, it would not rank policy goals in this way. Instead it would interpret these goals as fully integrated and realistic social aims. The integration of respect, participation, and accommodation would be a substantial policy improvement, since it would dispel the presumption (shared by each of the three models) that gains in the furtherance of one goal can only be secured at the expense of some other one.

At the same time, though, an adequate normative basis would not alter the contentious and politically controversial character of these goals. By their nature, policy goals are open-ended expressions of political value, and our understanding of this value is dynamic. Nothing would be gained by operationalizing, say, respect in such a manner as to pre-empt the political debate about what it entails in practice. And the nature of policy analysis would in no sense be improved if participation were transformed into a precise statement of desired unemployment levels or vocational skill acquisition outcomes (although such precision is appropriate for participation objectives). Political values should remain contentious, and public debate concerning them should be encouraged. The pre-emption of debate by 'experts' is, looking back, one of the flaws that the three models of disablement had in common. Each model privileged an expertise about disablement – biomedical, economic, social-political – thereby removing from the public domain the social problems posed by disablement.

To avoid this an adequate normative basis must, somehow, provide an integrated normative context in terms of which the goals of respect, participation, and accommodation can be treated as compatible and mutually achievable, without pre-empting the ongoing political debate over what these values should commit society to, either politically or legally. The basis must capture an overarching political value that can provide a context sufficiently encompassing to express, debate, and resolve all normative issues, large and small, raised by disablement. As we saw, the normative bases of charity, need, compensation, and welfare maximization are all inadequate in this regard.

This suggests that an adequate normative basis must call forth a core value of our political and legal culture. This value must be broad enough to link the goals of respect, participation, and, accommodation, making them mutually realizable, rather than antagonistic, policy goals. The value must also be relevant to the spectrum of social issues and concerns arising from all three dimensions of disablement. And, finally, the value must not represent some utopian ideal that requires unrealistic or unattainable levels of resources, or profound changes in human nature and the human condition. That is, the value will give us the sense of how much social policy can do and when it attempts to do too much.

The fourth and last accomplishment of an adequate normative basis for disablement is to provide a framework of policy guidelines that put the aspirations represented by the goals of respect, accommodation, and participation into effect. This framework would make it possible to identify plausible policy objectives and formulate, implement, and track the success of specific initiatives for fulfilling those objectives.

This last accomplishment is not one but several interlocking achievements. An acceptable policy framework must provide all the normative material required to guide analysts as they devise specific solutions to policy problems; but there are many facets of this enormous task. To be sure, much of this framework will be provided by answers to the basic entitlement controversies, as well as the integrated interpretation of the goals of respect, participation, and accommodation. But there remain at least two structural issues involved in policy formulation and implementation that an adequate normative basis needs to resolve.

The first of these concerns the allocation of responsibility with respect to disablement entitlements, whatever these turn out to be. If the normative basis entails that people with disabilities have a legitimate claim to the satisfaction of, say, their medical needs, or to a more equitable representation in the labour force, or to the end of stigmatization, who or what is responsible for responding to these claims? As we have seen, some normative bases, while acknowledging that people with disabilities have legitimate claims of this sort, deny that they have a right as against society that these claims be satisfied. Other bases characterize some of these claims as conditional rights, but do not clearly identify who or what is obliged to respond to them. An adequate normative basis can leave none of these questions unresolved or, worse, unresolvable.

Realistically, the issue of responsibility comes down to whether an entitlement is a legally enforceable right or not. From the perspective of policy formation this is an issue of great importance. Indeed, it might be argued that when reports such as *A Consensus for Action* cite absence of political will as the predominant cause of the impasse in disablement policy what is actually being flagged is an administrative failure to clearly demark the spheres of responsibility between society at large (what might be called the political responsibility) and our law and legal institutions (the legal or constitutional responsibility).

The politically charged approach to disablement issues that is the legacy of the social-political model has heightened awareness of this administrative failure. As a rule, advocates of that model put their faith in the legal enforcement of rights, not because they believe that courts and judges are immune to the effects of handicapping attitudes, but because they feel that the law, at least potentially, can protect the inherent rights of people with disabilities more effectively than political institutions can. To be sure, people like Evelyn Kallen, Harlan Hahn, and Michael Oliver, whose views we have already considered, insist on the need for extensive public education and other non-adversarial, destigmatizing activities as well. But, either because of pessimism or realism, these advocates of the social-political approach have looked to the law and legal institutions as the best hope for people with disabilities.

There are, however, potential worries about this strategy, especially in a legal tradition such as ours, which, however the legal question is initially framed, transforms a social policy question into a discrete complaint by one individual against another. Increased reliance on the courts for social and political change is not only risky (the case may not be successful) and costly, it is also likely to perpetuate ad hoc or 'add on' changes to existing laws and policies rather than address systemic issues. The law courts are, by their nature, reactive rather than proactive institutions.

The public may be led to believe, on the evidence of a handful of high-profile legal actions, that society's obligations to respond to the spectrum of disablement issues – from medical and rehabilitative needs to discrimination – have been satisfied. But this can be prejudical to the interests of all people with disabilities. It is one thing for an individual who has been discriminated against by an employer to gain redress by means of a human rights action, but something very different to provide the means for an employer to restructure a job or workplace in order to accommodate a person with disabilities.

The legal approach to disablement entitlements seems essential, however, when the source of the discrimination or marginalization is the laws and actions of the state. While instances of 'facial' or de jure discrimination may be too few to be of much concern, there are countless examples of the invidious application of laws and regulations, not to mention unintended consequences of policies, that are handicapping. Making changes here may require legal action. In addition, an argument can be made that the only effective review mechanism for policy decisions that fail to respond to disablement needs, or decisions of administrative tribunals or agencies that adversely affect the lives of people with disabilities, is judicial review.

Legally speaking these concerns fall within the areas of administrative and constitutional law. Short of political lobbying for legislative change, judicial review of legislation, regulation or state action (or inaction) may be the only plausible avenue for recognizing, refining, and enforcing some disablement entitlements. Thus, in the end, the legal approach to disablement issues may be both inevitable and essential.

This said, the basic structural problem of disablement policy remains. How do we allocate, as between the legal and the political spheres, the responsibilities that are created by the recognition of disablement entitlements. Putting the question this way should not pre-empt the possibility that both spheres have a role to play, since an issue such as employment equity should probably be addressed both as a policy initiative – affirmative employment programming, for example – and as a question of legal rights. The point to make here is that an adequate normative basis for disablement must be able to provide guidance on this structural issue. And, again, it must not do so by removing the question from the arena of legitimate political debate, or by setting out adamantine criteria that forever demark the political from the legal. What is needed is the appropriate normative context for an ongoing political debate. We need to know what political values govern the discussion when we debate whether our responsibilities to people with disabilities reflect our collective commitments to a particular kind of political order, or are captured by common law and the provisions of our constitution.

The second structural issue that must be addressed is that of the proper role of disablement policy in social policy as a whole, a topic I have so far avoided. Disablement policy decisions, plainly enough, cannot be made in a vacuum. There are other calls on society, its resources, institutions, and citizens. An adequate framework for policy decision-making must come to grips with macroallocative dilemmas, and it must shed light on what is to be done about our obligations to people with disabilities, given our other social obligations.

At bottom this structural issue concerns the nature and strength of extrinsic conditions on disablement entitlements. It might be argued that since these are extrinsic conditions they are not relevant to the adequacy of a normative basis for disablement policy. No normative basis could be expected to extend its scope outside of the area of the social policy to which it applies. Nor need the normative basis for disablement policy be a complete political theory of the state and its obligations – a theory of justice, in other words.

This is a fair point, but still an adequate normative basis must be compatible with that part of our culture's understanding of political justice about which there is consensus. The normative basis cannot be so specialized that it applies to the social status and entitlements of people with disabilities, but to no one else; or so focused that it is incompatible with our normative intuitions about other forms of marginalized human difference. An adequate normative basis for disablement must comport with our political and cultural values.

The necessity of this compatibility of value is often ignored by advocates of the social-political model. But a moment's thought shows why, regardless of one's political agenda, the degree of one's commitment to the plight of people with disabilities, or one's concern to avoid the impasse in disablement policy, it is a theoretical and strategic blunder to suppose that the normative framework for expressing the entitlements of people with disabilities calls forth normative principles and political values that are unique to it.

First of all, it is extremely unrealistic to suppose that any of the rights of people with disabilities will be absolute, or extrinsically *un*conditional rights, rights that must be satisfied whatever the costs or consequences. Compromise is inevitable.

Second, the normative basis for disablement must be commensurable with that of other areas of policy, or else there is the alarming prospect of a forced competition between marginalized groups and minorities. Whatever form it takes, advocacy for the rights of people with disabilities must always be tempered by an equal concern – founded on similar grounds – for people of colour and women, for the poor and the elderly. Just as the political power of people with disabilities can be defused by rivalry between impairment groups, so too the common concerns of marginalized populations in our society can be undermined by chauvinism that demands that one's minority group deserves more rights and benefits than another's.

Finally, the political principles and values involved in disablement policy must be of a piece with those found in all aspects of social policy, because the process of disablement policy analysis is never isolated from the larger domain of social policy development. As we saw, the greatest single virtue of the economic model is that, by construing disablement solely in terms of costs, it integrates disablement policy into social policy at large. An adequate normative basis for disablement must accomplish this without, as in the economic model, utterly reducing disablement to some other social concern.

Pulling together these strands we can now create a fairly precise characterization of what is demanded of an adequate normative basis for disablement. A policy so grounded would:

1 Incorporate and integrate the three dimensions of the concept of disablement – impairment, disability, and handicap – in order to formulate a complete representation of disablement as a social problem as well as an appropriate representation of people with disabilities
2 Set out the means for expressing, debating, and resolving the

fundamental entitlement controversies that establish the agenda for policy development

3 Provide an interpretation of the policy goals of respect, participation, and accommodation that integrates these goals within a complete account of disablement, and so provides a normative context for the ongoing political debate over what these goals actually commit society to

4 Provide a broad and flexible, yet practically adequate, framework for policy analysis that offers guidance in the formulation of policy objectives and the implementation of policy solutions, and, more specifically, addresses the structural issues of, first, allocating responsibility between the legal and policy approaches to disablement issues and, second, ensuring that disablement policy is commensurable in aim and outcome with general social policy

Together, these four accomplishments, it need hardly be said, set the level of adequacy for a normative basis for disablement theory and policy very high indeed. What I propose to do is explore the complexities of equality as a moral and political value in order to make plausible the hypothesis that, appropriately understood, equality is our best option for a normative basis that would satisfy these four conditions.

Why Equality?

There is a real danger that the Byzantine complexities of the entitlement controversies and practical necessities of policy development may obscure the problem before us. That is a shame, since we might overlook a simple intuition which, on its own, very nearly makes the case for equality: impairments, disabilities, and handicaps matter to us because they are not merely differences, they are inequalities. Although there are many ways in which people differ, only a very few of these differences matter to us. These are the differences which, so to speak, make a difference; they are differences that make us unequal. Disablement is just such a difference.

Now, like all pre-theoretical intuitions, this one suffers badly under close scrutiny. It is, after all, quite circular to say that impairments are differences that matter because they are inequalities, if an inequality is nothing more than a difference that – as evidenced by the fact that we have a concept for it – matters to us. What difference could there be between two things being 'different' and being 'unequal': they are unequal simply by virtue of being *two* different things.

Though vague and open to these complaints, the intuition about equality gestures toward a truth of great profundity. Disablement, in any of its three dimensions, only raises issues of any sort – scientific, literary, philosophical, historical, psychological – because normatively speaking it is a condition of social inequality. On the face of it, then, the only relevant normative basis for disablement is that founded on equality. Could it be that our cultural reliance on charity, need, compensation, and welfare maximization, each of which can easily be shown to be inadequate, has been the result of our reluctance to grapple with the political value that is really at issue?

There is considerable theoretical value in seeking the grounds for an equality basis for disablement theory in this simple intuition. It may sound naïve to ask why it matters to us whether we have impairments, or why we care about disabilities, or what difference it makes if some people face handicaps. Yes, it is naïve to ask these questions. The central normative question of disablement theory – What, if anything, does society owe to people with disabilities? – is also naïve. That does not mean it has been answered.

Why is it relevant, and important, then, to say that disablement is a matter of inequality rather than (mere) difference? I have already mentioned one reason: inequalities are differences that matter to us because they are socially consequential. Inequalities involve, or lead to, differences in wealth, power, access to resources, status, social role, and other indicia of social importance and individual well-being and self-esteem. Inequalities are more than mere differences because they inevitably involve some form of ranking based on normative distinctions of virtue and vice, superiority and inferiority, worthiness or worthlessness. Whereas differences create distinctions, inequalities create stratifications.

Disablement – for complex reasons involving social and economic forces as well as social-psychological dynamics – is an inequality as well as a difference. As we have seen, the analysis of disablement reveals a complex and multidimensional notion that is irreducibly normative. Although the kinds of inequalities created by the three dimensions differ (for example, the inequality of health and sickness has a different social significance than the inequality of capability and incapability, or the inequality of 'normal' and 'deviant'); each is a form of inequality rather than a normatively neutral difference. It is only by insisting on a wholly abstract characterization of impairment that a measure of normative neutrality can be achieved within disablement; but even this is short-lived. Once we turn to questions of policy we ignore the myriad 'mere' physical differences that the concept encompasses and focus our attention on those that matter, that is, those that produce disabilities.

Social inequalities are problematic because they raise the issue of when differences justify inequality and when they do not – an issue that earlier I linked to the so-called dilemma of differences.[1] We can only justify an inequality by showing that it is a socially relevant distinction founded on a genuine difference, since otherwise the inequality of status, role, or treatment is irrational and arbitrary – a an act of social tyranny. How do we know when, so to speak, a true difference justifies an inequality?

We are tempted to say that we have to first determine when a difference is real or important before we look at the inequality in social treatment in order to see if what makes the difference real and important is (minimally) relevant to the inequality. Thus, 'real and serious' impairments create disabilities that are genuine, and if the difference in social treatment is relevant to the nature of the disability, then, other things being equal, the inequality appears to be justified.

Unfortunately, this intuitive solution is quite unhelpful, even vacuous, without non-circular and independent criteria for determining when differences are 'real' and when forms of unequal social treatment are 'relevant' to them. These criteria are, obviously, problematic, and have long been viewed to be the central theoretical problem with equality as a political value. As Aristotle pointed out, although it is analytically true that equality demands that people ought to be treated differently only if there is some *relevant* difference between them (and otherwise they should be treated similarly), that principle of equality is practically empty if we have no criteria of relevance.[2]

Criteria of the 'reality' of differences raise a host of other problems. As Martha Minow has argued, most of our judgments about the reality of human differences are grounded on spurious or contentious assumptions. We assume that human differences are intrinsic features of the bearer of the difference; that there is an obvious 'normal' point of reference; that differences can be perceived by observers who themselves lack a perspective, while the perspec-

234 Physical Disability and Social Policy

tive of those who are different is of no consequence; and, finally, that
difference exists in a social environment that is itself natural and
neutral.[3]

We have seen close relatives of these assumptions at work in the
social construction of handicapping. This is because the failure of the
intuitive solution to the problem of justifying social inequalities is a
reprise of failures implicit in disablement policy. This is understandable, since disablement policy treats people with disabilities differently
from 'normals' in those respects in which they are thought to be
relevantly different, while ensuring equal treatment in those respects
in which they are equal. In short, the social problem of disablement
is just a problem about what equality demands.

Importantly, however, it is only possible to see disablement in this
way when we insist upon a multidimensional interpretation of the
concept. The biomedical model is attractive to us because it assures
us of the intrinsic and objective reality of disablement as a form of
human difference. By the same token it fails as an adequate model
because, inasmuch as it wholeheartedly accepts all of Minow's
assumptions about human difference, it can make no sense of
interactional disabilities or socially constructed handicaps. The
economic model answers the question of when differences are
relevant to inequalities, but fails, through an inability to shift
perspectives, to appreciate the irrelevance of physical difference in
the creation of handicapping inequalities. The social-political model
explicitly rejects all of Minow's assumptions, thereby making it
possible to appreciate the injustice of handicapping inequalities. But,
ironically, the model accomplishes this only by ignoring the reality
of impairments and disabilities and so the need to provide unequal,
but relevant treatment that is beneficial to people with disabilities.

It is only when these models of disablement are rejected and the
notion is seen as a multidimensional one that the true impact of the
problem of justifying social inequalities becomes clear. Compared
with other forms of human difference that have attracted social
inequalities, disablement is the most resistant to simple solutions. To
be sure, racial and sexual differences are also multidimensional; but
disablement is paradigmatically multidimensional, and the differences it embodies are neither always relevant nor always irrelevant
to socially unequal treatment. In other words, some of the differences
of disablement are undeniably 'real,' at least in the sense that
Minow's assumptions validly apply to them. Policy analysts must not

question the assumption that impairments are intrinsic to the individual, presume a 'normal' point of reference, or privilege the biomedical observer's perspective at the expense of that of the individual concerned. Nor would any benefit accrue to people with impairments if biomedical criteria for unequal distribution of medical resources were challenged as spurious or socially constructed.

None the less there are also many differences of disablement that are not 'real' and about which we regularly make the kind of mistaken assumptions that Minow identifies. The attempts to justify handicap situations can always be challenged on the grounds that what passes as 'reasonable,' 'natural,' or 'inevitable' is in fact a manifestation of systemic social processes of stigmatization and marginalization that can be, and in a just society would be, changed.

To sum up, disablement represents one of the clearest instances of an area of social policy that raises, over and over again in different guises, the single most fundamental issue of equality: When do human differences justify social inequalities? To offer equality as the appropriate normative basis for disablement theory and policy is thus to do no more than to acknowledge the normative background that has always been there, whether appreciated by policy analysts or not.

If principles of equality suffuse this area of public policy and if, as I have just argued, equality can incorporate the multidimensional character of disablement and illuminate the social problem of disablement, it seems safe to assume that equality can satisfy the first accomplishment of an adequate normative basis. But what of the other three?

As for the second achievement – providing the general normative framework in which to express, debate, and resolve the entitlement controversies implicit in policy – it is perhaps enough to say that, as a political value, equality encompasses the domain in which each of these controversies arise. A glance at the standard philosophical literature on equality reveals that it is precisely these kinds of entitlement controversies that have produced the competing theories of equality that are now current.[4] (At the same time, though, as we shall see in a moment, it is precisely because there are several competing theories of equality that this normative basis poses problems for disablement theory.)

As for providing a context for interpreting the three policy goals of respect, participation, and accommodation – the third achievement – it is possible to be more definite. It is an easy matter to interpret these goals in terms of equality, without presuming any particular theory of political equality. Thus, whatever else the goals of respect and participation mean, they at least denote two realms in which human difference should not be allowed to transform into social inequality. As a policy goal, respect captures the insight that people with disabilities are, despite their physical differences, deserving of that measure of respect and consideration that links all of us together as humans. Similarly, the goal of participation includes, at least, our cultural commitment not to allow the differences of disablement to interfere with those opportunities, endeavours, and aspirations that everyone presumptively enjoys.

Interpreted in light of equality, respect and participation mandate the removal of obstacles to services, opportunities, benefits, and other social advantages that have been created, sustained, and purportedly justified by differences associated with disablement. This is precisely how the sub-committee on Equality Rights of the Standing Committee on Justice and Legal Affairs, in its 1985 report *Equality for All* chose to interpret these goals.[5]

Equality also makes sense of the goal of accommodation, and in a way that responds to a common misunderstanding about the rationale of disablement policy. The objection has been voiced that if government expends time and resources improving access so that people with disabilities will become equal to the 'normal' population, why should it also cater to special needs – a practice that guarantees that people with disabilities will remain unequal to the 'normal' population? This objection is not restricted to disablement policy; it is not uncommon, for example, to hear complaints that blacks or women who demand 'special treatment' in the name of equality are contradicting themselves. Though common, the objection trades on an equivocation of equality and identity. There is no contradiction in demanding unequal treatment (and in particular, some form of accommodation) for people who are not equally situated, in the name of equality. Indeed, as the great American jurist Felix Frankfurter once remarked: 'there is no greater inequality than the equal treatment of unequals.'[6] Thus, the equality interpretation of accommodation forestalls objections about the unfairness of 'preferential' treatment by claiming that, sometimes, the unequal treatment of accommodation to difference is both consistent with and a necessary condition of a social commitment to equality.

Equality also makes it possible to explore the scope of accommodation without falling victim to a dilemma. To recall, this dilemma arises because the economic model requires a direct functional correspondence between money and the limitations of positive freedom constitutive of disabilities. Since in most cases there is no amount of money that could, literally, erase the disability, the goal of accommodation seems chimerical.

To deal with this dilemma, we need to view accommodation as a necessary condition of political equality – rather than of identity – so that the goal becomes realistic and feasible. As mandated by equality, the goals of accommodation and participation are integrated and the range of adaptations and modifications required for, say, employment opportunities is not constrained by a dubious standard of success. The point of accommodation is not to make impairments disappear but to facilitate equality of access as required by a social commitment to equality. Thus, even an intuitive and pre-theoretical understanding of equality seems to suffice to integrate the three goals, and to do so in a way that does not pre-empt ongoing discussions about what these goals actually commit society to in more concrete terms.

What then of the fourth and final achievement of an adequate normative basis, that of providing a framework for policy analysis? At first blush, it is difficult to imagine a more pervasive or central political value than equality in terms of which to organize social policy. It provides the vocabulary for expressing and debating all of the issues that disablement raises. An equality-based model of disablement would offer a normative context broad enough to include all dimensions of the phenomenon. But what of the two structural issues outlined above?

On the issue of allocating responsibility as between the political and the legal spheres, equality seems to be of assistance. In Canada, the political value of equality is constitutionally recognized and protected by selection 15 of the Charter of Rights and Freedoms.[7] As well, protection against forms of discrimination involving people with disabilities are found in our provincial and federal human rights codes. Hence, for us, equality is both a political *and* a legal value.

Of course, as the brief review of American jurisprudence in Chapter 5 makes clear, there are many and persistent doctrinal controversies concerning the legal characterization of equality, and many of these can be found in Canadian law as well. However, the controversial nature of legal equality is beside the point. As a normative basis for policy, equality is appropriate because the issue of responsibility becomes both expressible and debatable in our public philosophy, and that is what is important. Disablement policy is not, on this crucial structural question, cut adrift and left to search for ad hoc solutions. Equality puts this structural issue into a pre-existing context; moreover, arguably, it puts it into the only context that is consistent with our political traditions.

Once again, equality provides a normative context, not a collection of rules for deciding this structural issue in particular cases. It will always be open to argument that, for equality's sake, the proper role of judicial review of legislation should be a limited one as far as disablement is concerned. It will also be open to argument that the value of equality is enhanced and reinforced when it is expressed in the form of legally enforceable rights. This debate is left open, as it should be. What is important is that equality supplies the essential normative context against which this debate can be intelligibly carried out.

By the same token, the normative basis of equality makes it possible to situate disablement issues – both theoretical and practical, jurisprudential and administrative, legal and political – into social policy at large. Equality is an ideal normative background for an area of policy involving the problems of a group of people who have been and continue to be disadvantaged because of their differences. In providing a normative basis, equality helps us to fix our attention on the fact that disablement raises issues for everyone in society, not just those who happen to have disabilities.

What we have so far is a strong, prima facie answer to the question with which I began: Why equality? The four theoretical conditions for an adequate normative basis for disablement policy seem to be satisfied, in principle. This argument, it must be emphasized, has been framed entirely in terms of our pre-theoretical intuitions about equality. That is a start, but only a start.

We also have pre-theoretical intuitions about charity, need, compensation, and welfare maximization; but the difference is that for these normative bases we also have relatively uncontentious theories to criticize. Of the four bases, need is the most theoretically complicated, but not so much so that we cannot be confident that we have located its central principles. Equality, as a theory, is very different. The notion is highly contentious, with several competing accounts vying for our attention. More worrisome for our purposes, as we have seen, some theories about equality (that founded on the primary sense of discrimination, for example) are wholly unsuitable for disablement policy.

The prima facie case having been made, what remains is a review of the major contenders. However, this is not a neutral review: there are persuasive theoretical and policy objections to some theories about equality, and we can rely on these to point us, if not to the right theory, then in the right direction.

Which Equality?

One of the lasting achievements of the social-political model is that it characterizes disablement as an instance of what sociologists call 'structured inequality,' a persistent condition of stigmatization and marginalization brought about by systemic attitudinal and institutional forces.[8] Sociologists disagree whether social inequality or stratification is 'functional' or not, in the sense of being both inevitable (or for social Darwinists, 'natural') and useful, or whether instead it is preventable and socially destructive.[9] Most do agree that the presence of structural inequalities is incompatible with our culture's conception of democratic institutions, and that this tension, heightened in recent decades by greater mobility, the pervasiveness of mass media, education, and consumerism, has given rise to political pressure for social equality.[10]

Despite this evidence, though, the hard fact remains that it has proved to be far easier to identify the criteria of structural inequality than to reach a consensus about what equality means as a political value or legal norm. The theoretical literature on equality is, predictably, immense and inconsistent. The same can be said of the literature on the legal interpretation of constitutional and other guarantees of equality.

Those concerned about the abstract character of equality agree on at least this much: equality is not a single concept or principle, with a core meaning that can be directly operationalized into explicit policy guidelines or legal tests.[11] Equality is, rather, the name of a family of related considerations or principles. There are many kinds of equalities and though there is no reason to think that one is more fundamental than the others, there is also no reason to be sceptical and conclude that any interpretation of the notion is as good as any other.

Since it is a professional characteristic of theorists to attempt to transform the complex, if not into the simple, then at least into the orderly, there are various proposals circulating for categorizing kinds or conceptions of equality. Depending on the granularity of the parameters, the number of categories can range from a handful to over a hundred.[12] Of the various analytic distinctions that have been drawn, two stand out as important, not just because they demark competing theories of political or legal equality, but also because they forestall common misconceptions found in disablement policy.

The first of these has already been considered, namely, the distinction between difference and inequality. Although there is a dictionary sense of 'equality' that means identity or sameness, political equality does not fit that sense of the word. It is a silly rhetorical device to be opposed to equality on the grounds that everyone is different, or to suggest that political equality is a subversive notion since it implies making everyone the same. Inequalities are social manifestations of those human differences (intrinsic, contingent, or interactive) that, wrongly or rightly, make a difference. The political value of equality concerns differences that make a difference.[13]

The second preliminary distinction, expressed in these terms originally by Ronald Dworkin but familiar to theorists for centuries, is that between the right to equal treatment and the right to treatment as an equal.[14] This distinction, in its simplest form, marks the difference between a right to an equal distribution of something (benefit, opportunity, resource) and the right to be treated with the same respect, dignity, and concern as everyone else, and to whatever share that entails when it comes to distribution. These are different rights, since, to take the obvious example, if people's needs are radically different, then treating them the same may well constitute differential treatment that undermines, rather than preserves, their dignity.

The distinction is extremely important in the case of disablement, since, as already remarked, this is an area of policy in which the problem of determining when a difference warrants an inequality of treatment looms very large indeed. In many contexts treating people with disabilities the same as everyone else is extremely disadvantageous to them, if not insulting. Were no distinction drawn between equal treatment and equal respect, then every inequality of treatment, such as would be required for an accommodation, would automatically be a violation of equality.

Dworkin's distinction also hints at an account of political equality that should be mentioned at the outset, so we can set it aside. It might be called the presumptive account of equality, and, though it has never been championed by anyone as a complete theory, it is frequently cited by philosophers as a minimal version of what the political value commits us to. The presumptive account states that those who recommend, create, or perpetuate inequalities of treatment have the onus of justifying them. The rationale for this principle is that equality demands the presumption that every member of society counts for one and no more than one, so that everyone at least has the right to a justification for unequal treatment.[15]

The presumptive account of equality is familiar to us because it is the intuitive solution to the social problem of equality mentioned in the last section. Lawyers (quite incorrectly) label this 'Aristotle's formal equality,' and in legal contexts it is sometimes identified by the slogan 'people who are similarly situated should be similarly treated.'[16] Formal equality does not include a description of, and so does not inform us about, the conditions under which a difference justifies an inequality. Presumptive or formal accounts merely insist that *some* difference be set out by way of justification for inequality.

Calling this account 'formal,' though common, is misleading. It has been popular to dismiss equality under this interpretation as 'empty' and superfluous,[17] and similar criticisms have been made about the legal test of 'treating like cases alike.'[18] But the presumptive account, however uninformative, and the legal 'similarly situated' test, however open-ended, are *analytic* descriptions of the concept of equality and as such could not be false. Moreover, no formal account of equality could possibly be rejected by any civilized society or plausible legal system. It would be grossly unfair and a blatant violation of equality to treat people differently for no reason whatsoever. If nothing else, equality demands the presumption that inequalities be justifiable.

As an interim conclusion, therefore, we might say that the presumptive account, and all other related forms of substantively empty, 'formal' accounts of equality, represent a minimum that *must* be included in any theory of equality that could possibly qualify as an adequate normative basis of disablement policy (or for that matter, anything else).

In Canadian constitutional law, and specifically in the language of section 15 of the Charter of Rights and Freedoms, the fundamental legal rights that express the requirements of 'formal' equality have been argued to be included in the right of 'equality before the law.'[19] Significantly, on the wording of that section this is but one of four legal equalities. The other three are 'equality under the law,' 'equal protection of the law,' and 'equal benefit of the law.' Although it is controversial what these three other legal equalities mean, both in jurisprudential and in concrete terms, most commentators agree that they purport to describe forms or varieties of *non-formal* substantive equality, or what in an earlier context I termed 'equality rights.'

This suggests a strategy. Equality theory is replete with principles of equality that, defenders claim, are core or paradigmatic to the concept. There is universal recognition that substantive equality can be interpreted in a variety of ways, given various 'contents,' ranges of application, and, for lack of a better word, 'strengths.' Without doing violence to equality theory as a whole, it is possible to consider these competing interpretations, in order of relative strength. Each of these takes the form of a principle of equality with at least political significance and, in some cases, legal significance as well. In this fashion we can consider the contenders for equality theory.

The obvious place to begin this survey is with a principle of equality that qualifies as the least substantial and 'weakest' of them all.

Equality of Respect

In order to give content to 'formal' equality one must identify an attribute or characteristic of people that makes them relevantly similar in some respect. Since there are many possible attributes, reasons of theoretical simplicity suggest that we pick that one in terms of which people are *necessarily alike*, in every conceivable context. Given what is required, no contingent or even empirical attribute could fit the bill, a realization that has led political theorists since Immanual Kant to argue that the most fundamental substantive right to equality must be the right to that which every human individual necessarily possesses merely and entirely by virtue of being a human individual. Thus, the least substantive account of equality posits a right to the respect and concern owed an entity possessed of moral worth.

On first reading, equality of respect of moral worth – or equality of respect, for short – may seem to be indistinguishable from the formal presumption of equality, since equality in both cases comes down to the basic proposition that everyone counts for one and not more than one. Is not equality of respect as 'formal' as the principle that everyone must be taken into account?[20]

There is a difference, and a fundamental one, for both policy and law. First, equality of respect identifies a respect in which everyone is relevantly equal, a respect which is unaffected (either by being diminished or enhanced) by any manifestation of human difference. Thus, this form of equality constitutes an unconditional or absolute human right, a right, in Ronald Dworkin's words, people possess 'not by virtue of birth or characteristics of merit or excellence but simply as human beings.'[21] In terms of the Charter's 'four equalities,' this principle has been argued to be 'equality under the law,' which is to say, that collection of legal rights that extend mere 'formal' fairness to the substance of laws, policies, or government actions.[22]

Second, equality of respect is not at all contentless. This principle specifies the kind of context of similarity that differential treatment may offend, thereby characterizing treatment that is offensive to equality. Specifically, any treatment that shows disrespect for an individual, or that ignores or undermines that individual's moral worth, is in conflict with this principle. Hence, a law or policy that unilaterally and non-consensually restricts the liberty of some people for the greater, but exclusive, good of others, or that distributes social benefits with the intent of exploiting or ignoring the interests of an identifiable group, is a violation of equality of respect. These inequalities of treatment are instances where some people are being treated as not worthy of consideration or the same measure of respect as others.[23]

The social evil that equality of respect seeks to identify and proscribe is, therefore, discriminatory treatment in what I have called the primary sense of that word, namely, intentional or culpable invidious treatment that disadvantages an individual or group. The content of this principle of equality, though minimal, is sufficient to proscribe at least two classes of inequalities of treatment relevant to disablement policy.

The first class includes all forms of malicious discrimination, where the intent of the state's actions, or the behaviour of the individual, is to harm, malign, insult, or in any of a myriad ways fail to respect the basic moral worth of an individual or group. Discriminatory treatment in this obvious and primary sense might more aptly be described as an assault on dignity, the intentional act of insulting a person, not for anything that person did or merited, but for the failure to qualify as a human individual. No greater disrespect or violation of equality is imaginable than that of refusing to recognize an individual's status as a human being.

The second class of proscribed actions includes all forms of differential and disadvantageous treatment founded on prejudice, bias, or grounds so irrational as to count as fundamentally insulting. This kind of discriminatory treatment may be manifested by gross examples of denial of basic political and legal rights to a population, as in the case of slavery or apartheid, the denial of the right to vote to women, and similar acts. This form of discrimination differs from the first only in not requiring intentional action by specific individuals. Thus, entrenched and irrational forms of differential treatment that divide people into hierarchical structures within society, with the result that one or more of these groups suffers prolonged, unremediable, and unjustifiable disadvantage, would be an example of unequal treatment proscribed by the principle of equality of respect.

Although these two classes of unequal treatment are recognizably different, they are both examples of discrimination in the primary sense. Both of these must therefore be distinguished from what is variously called 'indirect,' 'adverse effect,' or 'constructive' discrimination. The principle of equality of respect makes it possible to distinguish these two categories of discrimination more clearly.

Discrimination in the primary sense is a social evil because it is disrespectful of basic human worth: the dignity of an individual or a group is either intentionally assaulted (as in a racial slur or sexual harassment), or a policy is promulgated that expressly deems an individual or group to be inferior or unworthy of basic human respect. Primary discrimination is inherently insulting. 'Indirect' or 'adverse effect' discrimination, by contrast, is indirect precisely in the sense that it is not disrespectful in motive, intent, or significance. That is, not only is 'indirect' discrimination not culpably disrespectful, it is also not founded on an irrational or factually unsupportable classification.[24]

In other words, equality of respect only proscribes insult and disrespect of a very fundamental sort. It is perfectly possible to know about, but ignore, the needs of people, or to acknowledge, but be unconcerned about, the adverse effects of policy decisions on a specific population, without being disrespectful of the fundamental moral worth of the individuals involved. Indeed, it happens all the time. As a general matter, one can pursue a policy of treating groups differently and adversely, without violating equality of respect so long as the 'difference' upon which one bases the inequality of treatment is not a difference in moral worth.

Thus, equality of respect is an extremely 'weak' principle of equality; though for all that it remains a fundamental principle that must be included in any viable theory of equality. The problem with it is that it suffers from precisely the same difficulties as the normative basis of welfare maximization, with respect to the effects of policy decisions on groups like people with disabilities. Indeed, arguably welfare maximization is a version of equality of respect, namely, the principle that everyone's welfare must be given equal consideration. Unfortunately, giving equal consideration to everyone's welfare is perfectly consistent with a policy that fails to respond to the interests of some, when, for example, doing so is too 'costly' in relation to the overall total of welfare.

As a political value, the principle of equality of respect is generally thought to be limited in ways analogous to the principle of majoritarian democracy. The political manifestation of equality of respect is that everyone must be provided with one, and only one, vote, so that an election is a preference-aggregating device (akin to welfare maximization) that preserves this form of equality.[25] Yet the results of elections, for minorities, may well be disadvantageous in the extreme. The principle of equality would prevent the majority from disenfranchising the minority, and this is not inconsequential. But the principle is far too weak to provide much relief for people who are adversely affected by majoritarian policies, or, as in the case of people with disabilities, systemic handicapping.

Because of its limited scope and power to effect change, there have been various attempts to strengthen this principle of equality without changing its fundamental nature. The favoured approach has been to opt for an inflated conception of what is embodied in the notion of human worth. The accounts of equality that result focus more directly on the social evil of discrimination.

The Principle of Antidiscrimination

While there is little disagreement among scholars that discrimination in the primary sense violates equality, some wish to detach antidiscrimination from equality of respect, treat it as a separate principle, and expand its scope. Thus, some scholars have suggested that adversely differential treatment is prima facie evidence of prejudice, which is in turn conclusive evidence of discrimination.[26]

This expanded principle of antidiscrimination relies on expanded interpretations of prejudice and discrimination, interpretations that have found great favour among advocates for people with disabilities. The reasoning here is clear: if one restricts the notion of prejudice to overt expression of disrespect, then, although there are undoubtedly examples of this in everyday affairs, one would be hard-pressed to find instances of governmental action, law, or policy that were intentionally discriminatory. We learn from the social-psychological data that, for the most part, the stigmatization of people with disabilities involves systemic forces found in unconsciously expressed attitudes and behaviours, and in the structure of social practices and institutions. These forces, by definition, are covert and hidden, not intentional or expressed. Thus, some scholars have been attracted to notions of 'indirect' discrimination and non-intentional 'prejudice.'

A good example of this can be found in a recent discussion by legal theorist Martha McCluskey, who argues that discrimination against people with disabilities ought to be legally analysed in terms of 'prejudice' understood in a vastly extended sense to include not merely expressed and culpable prejudicial conduct, but all forms of disadvantageous classification. In effect, on McCluskey's account, disparate impact alone is a form of prejudice.[27]

McCluskey's argument, read in the context of American antidiscrimination jurisprudence, may make sense as a matter of legal strategy. But as an account of equality it is flawed. Indeed, it is dangerous to conceptualize the social problem of disablement as a matter of a prejudice which, in McCluskey's concluding words, 'fosters the perception that the particular needs of people with disabilities are necessarily 'different' and disadvantageous.'[28] Plainly, if one's primary policy focus is vocational rehabilitation, refusing in principle to characterize the needs of people with disabilities as 'different' would have disastrous results. It is not appropriate for people without disabilities to have an equal claim on these resources. There are occasions when refusing to treat people differently is a clear violation of equality, and this is one of them.

Moreover, even as a matter of legal strategy, McCluskey's version of the principle of antidiscrimination raises legitimate concerns that need to be addressed. In recent years, Canadian courts have, somewhat cautiously, come around to the view that intent is not always a prerequisite of discrimination, as long as there is clear evidence that the effect of the policy or practice has been to exclude a protected group.[29] Although our law seems to have followed McCluskey's analysis to some extent, the evidence suggests that Canadian courts will continue to mark a difference between the remedies appropriate for discrimination in the primary sense and those appropriate for indirect, adverse-effect, or constructive discrimination.

There is a good reason for this. It is a defence to adverse-effect discrimination in the area of employment that a hiring decision is based on a 'bona fide occupational requirement,' an attribute or qualification of the candidate which in the circumstances it is reasonable for the employer to insist on. Obviously this defence could not be available in the case of intentional discrimination. More important, a court would be reluctant to find a duty to accommodate the candidate if the defence is successful, but less so otherwise.[30]

If McCluskey's analysis were to gain acceptance with Canadian courts it is not clear whether their cautious acceptance of adverse-effect discrimination would backfire. If the violation of equality that is at issue is a matter of 'prejudice,' will courts consider it necessary to seek concrete evidence of this prejudice, rather than, as they now seem willing to do, abandon talk of discrimination and deem the fact of unwarranted obstacles to participation, affecting groups in a disproportionately negative manner, to be a violation of equality?[31]

There is another and deeper worry involved in recent attempts to expand the notion of discrimination in this way. If successful, equality and non-discrimination will become entirely reciprocal concepts. As it happens, there is fairly clear Canadian law to the effect that, as section 15 of the Charter of Rights and Freedoms is concerned, legal equality rights coincide with antidiscrimination rights.[32] There may well be good jurisprudential and institutional reasons for limiting the scope of legal equality rights in this way. However, there is no a priori reason for similarly limiting the political value of equality. As far as the normative basis for disablement policy is concerned, there are very good reasons not to.

The most persuasive reason is the following. There is no doubt that many forms of handicapping are instances of discrimination, whether intentional or systemic. Since discrimination is a violation of equality, some version of the principle of antidiscrimination is a necessary component of any theory of equality adequate as a normative basis for disablement policy. But, as I have tried to argue in my critique of the social-political model, there is more to disablement policy than could be caught by the notion of antidiscrimination. Specifically, the policy goals of participation and accommodation require a far broader policy focus than merely protecting against, or compensating for, acts of discrimination.

Since everyone who writes on disablement issues recognizes this, there has been a tendency to further expand the scope of the principle of antidiscrimination by inflating the notion of discrimination. Thus, for example, in the Royal Commission report *Equality in Employment* we read: 'Equality in employment means that no one is denied opportunities for reasons that have nothing to do with inherent ability. It means equal access free from arbitrary obstructions. Discrimination means that an arbitrary barrier stands between a person's ability and his or her opportunity to demonstrate it ... Ignoring differences and refusing to accommodate them is a denial of equal access and opportunity. It is discrimination.'[33] The force of these remarks is that the goals of participation and accommodation are subsumed under a general principle of freedom from discrimination in employment.

What is wrong with this as a normative basis for policy? What is wrong is that it falls victim to the dilemma of difference. If the social problem of disablement is a matter of discrimination then a denial of equality of employment opportunities is discriminatory. What is required to combat this, as we read, is the removal of 'arbitrary barriers' that stand between 'a person's ability and his or her opportunity to demonstrate it.' But how do we identity these barriers?

If the criterion is, as stated, that of 'arbitrariness' then it is hard to think of *any* barrier, limiting the opportunities of people with disabilities, that would qualify. There is nothing 'arbitrary' about refusing to hire a person in a wheelchair because he or she cannot perform the activities required for the job (although the person making this rule may do so arbitrarily). Surely the employer would have no difficulty at all in making out a direct and scientifically accurate argument relating the disability and the requirements of the job.

What the Abella Report wants to say, we might presume, is that the 'difference' of a disability should not make a difference in employability, so that assuming that it does is a kind of obstacle that violates equality. But, then the question is: Why is this obstacle a form of discrimination?

If one insists that it *is* discrimination one is firmly caught in the grips of the dilemma of difference: either discrimination is a matter of making the difference of disability into an inequality or it is not. If it is, then affirmative action programs, or any positive program that relies as it must on the difference of disability as a criterion for destigmatizing or otherwise benefiting people with disabilities is a violation of equality. If it is not, then people with disabilities are not being denied equality by obstacles to employment opportunities.

Now, to be sure, many of the attempts to broaden the notion of discrimination as a legal category – in order particularly to encompass disadvantageous treatment that is imposed on a minority with a history of such treatment – were carefully designed to avoid this dilemma. In American, English, and Canadian human rights law 'discrimination' has become something of a legal fiction as a result. Like 'constructive' contracts (transactions that utterly fail as contracts but are deemed to be so none the less), 'constructive discrimination' has the air of unreality to it. Perhaps if it served a legitimate purpose, no harm would be done. But fictions outside of the refined atmosphere of the courtroom always create problems. This, among other reasons, is why political philosophers, looking for a principle of equality to serve as the foundations for political theory, have turned their gaze onto the next major principle of equality.

Equality of Opportunity

Equality of opportunity is an axiom of liberal democracy, perhaps its *raison d'être*. But it has long been appreciated that it is open to two, quite different, interpretations. These go by several names, but the upshot of the distinction is that between means and ends.[34] We can ask either whether all of us have the equal right to a chance to succeed in the life endeavours we choose to pursue, or whether all of us have the right to an equal chance of success in these endeavours. We might call the first fair competition, the second equality of prospects.

Some writers also suggest that the principle of equality of opportunity rightly understood embodies not just an equal chance to participate and compete, nor even an equal chance to succeed, but also equal outcomes or results.[35] Others have argued that this is an unwarranted extension of the notion of opportunity. There is a difference, they claim, between what might be called 'result-sensitivity' (in which an agency of the state would be charged with the duty to monitor the competition to ensure that, at each juncture, everyone still had an equal prospect of succeeding) and equality of result (in which, presumably, one must abandon the competition entirely and strive for an egalitarian distribution). In any event, as we shall see later, though related to equality of opportunity, equality of result is a considerably stronger principle of equality.

Another way of distinguishing the two standard versions of equality of opportunity is to highlight differences in aim. The aim of the first is to ensure that social inequalities follow directly from differences in ability, talent, and motivation (the so-called natural inequalities). The aim of the second is to engage in a series of adjustments – in the form of redistribution, regulation, and other state interventions – so that the natural inequalities are never allowed to establish unfair and objectionable social inequalities. (Equality of result, by contrast, simply pursues an ongoing policy of egalitarian redistribution.)

In terms of Canadian equality jurisprudence it has been suggested, although with precious little judicial support, that both versions of equality of opportunity are captured by section 15 of the Charter of Rights and Freedoms. Thus, 'equal protection of the law' – a legal phrase borrowed from the American Fourteenth Amendment – is said to embody the principle of equality of opportunity (at least as equality of means), and 'equal benefit of the law' embodies equality of prospects (if not equality of result).[36]

The legal terrain is considerably more convoluted than this, though, because of the assumption noted above that legal equality and antidiscrimination must coincide. American jurists who are concerned to extend antidiscrimination legislation to cover all social inequalities analyse equality of opportunity entirely in the language of discrimination,[37] or more confusingly, in the language of equality of respect.[38] Usually this conflation goes unnoticed until the analysis is used on a program or initiative that is applied absolutely equally (that is, identically) to all, although the effect of doing so is, or so it is argued, an inequality that affects opportunities. At that junction the analysis comes under considerable strain: Can identical application of a law ever be an instance of discrimination?[39]

Despite these complications, the thrust of the principle of equality of opportunity seems straightforward enough. Unwarranted obstacles standing in the way of full participation in the complete range of social activities and endeavours that characterize social life ought to be removed so that all of us have the opportunity to make of our life what we will. An unwarranted obstacle is the product of a difference that ought not to make a difference, differences that are usually called 'morally arbitrary.' Thus, the fact that someone is black is a morally arbitrary difference which, if used (intentionally or not) as a barrier to entry into the labour market, would count as a violation of equality of opportunity.

What exactly is a morally arbitrary difference? Historically, the fair competition interpretation of equality of opportunity has addressed this question most clearly. On that interpretation equality is achieved when 'careers are open to talents' and no socially contingent, or socially constructed, difference prevents one from competing.[40] Equality of opportunity in this sense proscribes distinctions in allocation of social benefits and burdens based on, for example, hereditary class, religious caste, racial or ethnic background, race, gender, and any other difference causally unrelated to 'natural talent and ability.'

The fair competition interpretation, however, does not proscribe, indeed it insists on, the moral relevance of talents, abilities, and motivations (including traits such as ambition, self-confidence, and optimism), for it is these 'natural assets,' and these alone, that should be responsible for all social inequalities of power, wealth, and social position. Equality of opportunity, so interpreted, is a meritocratic principle.

Stripped to its essentials, in other words, the fair competition version of equality of opportunity seeks to remove those limitations on negative freedom it judges to be morally arbitrary. Fair competition is structurally analogous to freedom of speech (as usually interpreted). Freedom of speech implies the absence of prohibitions, bans, and other restrictions on one's right to speak freely. It does not include a right to be heard, the right to be provided with the skills of public speaking, or the right to anything else that might be required to speak more effectively or indeed to speak at all. A limitation of freedom of speech is, in short, an outright restriction on my speech, a restriction which, once removed, does not in any sense guarantee that I will *be able* to speak, speak effectively, be heard, or communicate my ideas.

Analogously, fair competition proscribes those socially contingent restrictions on an individual's right to compete that are arbitrary in the sense that they have nothing to do with what ought to determine success and failure in competitive arrangements. Since differences in 'natural fortune' or an inequality of 'natural assets' are untouched by fair competition, social inequalities (of potentially staggering proportions) are assured. Those with the assets will win in the competition, those without will lose.

It should be obvious that the appeal of this form of equality of opportunity depends entirely on an assumption that cannot be made in the case of disablement, a fact which sets disablement apart from, say, racial or sexual difference. It is plausible to say that the struggle against racism would be over when everyone was able to find his or her own place in society, and be limited only by his or her own ability and ambition. But even if the struggle against handicapping were won, people with disabilities would still be limited by their impairments, including emotional impairments, such as lack of ambition. Although accommodation can, to one degree or another, remove or ameliorate disabilities, the failure to provide an accommodation is not a limitation upon one's negative freedom and so is untouched by fair competition.

Can fair competition be modified to fill this gap? This has been tried recently by Norman Daniels in the course of making a case for a 'legally enforceable right to a basic minimum of decent health care.'[41] Daniels's argument is straightforward: each of us has a range of opportunities open to us, an array of life plans that, as reasonable people, we can construct for ourselves. Although one would expect different ranges of opportunity for different societies, Daniels believes that it is possible to derive a transcultural basic range directly from species-typical functioning. He then argues that diseases and other health problems impair the opportunities available to an individual relative to this range of opportunity. That being so, a social commitment to equality of opportunity must include a guarantee of a reasonable or fair share of the basic opportunity range, and this guarantee can be satisfied in part by a right to a minimal level of health care.

The argument is ingenious, but since Daniels never abandons fair competition he is forced to restrict the scope of the positive right to health care to include only those impairments that impede the range of those opportunities which an individual's 'skills and talents' make it reasonable to pursue.[42] That is, Daniels makes a distinction between limitations on opportunities resulting from deviations from species-typical functioning and limitations resulting from deviations from capability norms.[43] But by drawing this entirely artificial line between impairments and the incapacitating consequences of impairments (that is, disabilities), Daniels retains the basic form of fair competition, but only at the cost of turning disabilities into legitimate and fair limitations on one's 'natural assets.'

There is no real mystery why Daniels, committed though he is to extending the scope of 'unfair' competition to include a subset of impairments, refuses to include disabilities. It is of the essence of the fair competition interpretation of equality of opportunity that some social inequalities are justifiable because they are deserved. In particular, differences of merit ought to make a difference. It is a good thing that there are winners and losers in competitive arrangements. Since any version of meritocracy demands that the grounds of merit be legitimate, allocations of 'natural talents and abilities,' though inevitably unequal, must be unquestionably legitimate. Thus, Daniels's approach cannot salvage the fair competition approach.

Similar objections can be made concerning any other 'means' interpretation of equality of opportunity. To say that everyone is entitled to the means necessary to participate fully in social activities is ambiguous. It either refers to the tools or instruments necessary for success, or else this and whatever else that together would be necessary and sufficient for success. Since the latter interpretation is equivalent to equality of results, only the former interpretation is relevant for the moment. But then what is 'necessary' for success? Usually the answer is that what is necessary are just those instruments or skills that someone with a normal range of 'natural talents and abilities' could use to succeed. Again, this response does not require society to overcome those limitations of positive freedom that people below this normal range confront.[44]

In the end, then, the fair competition and other 'means' interpretations of equality of opportunity are of no assistance to people with disabilities. To be sure, these principles do encompass handicapping limitations, and if Daniels is right they may also be sufficient to ground rights to resources required to meet *some* impairment needs. But they flounder on disabilities. The reason they do is instructive.

The principle of equality of opportunity, as commonly understood, presupposes a social arrangement in which everyone is more or less equal in his or her range of capabilities (and similarly unburdened by 'special needs'). The presumption is not that everyone has the *same* set of capabilities, only that each person's repertoire has, more or less, the same potential social value. The difference between those who succeed and those who fail is a matter of merit, drive, gumption, guts, or some other more or less mysterious *je ne sais quoi* about which individuals are wholly responsible. In this view, it can be plausibly assumed that when unfair barriers to full participation are removed and everyone can compete 'fairly' for scarce resources and social positions, whatever social inequalities result are just and legitimate.

This presumption of equal capability is attractive to political theorists, since it simplifies the theory and minimizes the need for state intervention into the market and other competitive social institutions. As long as the laws, social institutions, and practices are, to use the American phrase, 'colour-blind' (and sex-blind, religion-blind, and so on), social inequalities in wealth, social position, and power are justified. In this way equality of opportunity resolves the fundamental conundrum of equality: When do human differences justify social inequalities?

Yet even if a policy of ignoring race and sex differences was acceptable, and many would vigorously deny that it is,[45] a policy of ignoring disabilities is simply out of the question. For disabilities are limitations of positive freedom, and if there is to be a disablement policy at all it must address these limitations. Moreover, because disabilities are interactive incapacities that arise out of a relationship between impairments and social environments, it is not possible to draw the distinction, essential for equality of opportunity, between differences one is responsible for and differences one is not. It would be grossly unfair to say, for example, that a person with hemiplegia should be able to climb a flight of stairs unaided because, with enough training, gumption, guts, and so on, it is possible for someone with hemiplegia to do so. We do not demand this much effort from people without disabilities. To put this point differently, if we abandon the unrealistic, simplifying presumption of equal capability and refuse to be 'disability-blind' in our policy, does not equality of opportunity still require us to draw a line between those disabilities that are unjust and those that are merely unfortunate?[46] The unjust ones should be accommodated, but unfortunate ones need not be.

How can we make this distinction? Outright fraud and 'voluntarily' acquired disabilities aside – such cases are obviously exceptional – the only guide we have is whether or not accommodation is *required* to increase the scope of one's capabilities. But that is no guide at all, since presumably all, non-fraudulent, disabilities require accommodation.

It makes far more sense to say that the putative distinction between 'unjust' and merely 'unfortunate' disabilities is a charade. Like the notion of social disadvantage discussed above with respect to the concept of handicap, this distinction purports to be empirically based and normatively neutral. But it is nothing more than a disguised judgment about the scope of equality of opportunity (and therefore, given its use, entirely circular). Since no disability is in principle beyond accommodation, the judgment that the social consequences of a disability create an unfortunate, but not unjust, inequality is a normative judgment, and should be assessed as such.

All of these difficulties strongly suggest that a concern about equality in the case of people with disabilities demands result-sensitivity. We need to be sensitive to the effects of impairments on an individual's repertoire of capabilities, with respect to some normal range of social activities. Precisely this insight is the theoretical motivation behind the second of the two interpretations of equality of opportunity, namely, equality of prospects. The rationale here is that by monitoring the careers of people with differences we will be able to determine on solid grounds when opportunities have been restricted by attending to instances where differences actually limit the chances one has to succeed.

As already remarked, there is some evidence that this interpretation of equality of opportunity has left its mark on Canadian law and may well be constitutionally entrenched as one of the 'four equalities' mentioned in section 15 of the Charter of Rights and Freedoms. Unfortunately, equality of prospects, as a reading of equality of opportunity, is not stable.

Equality of prospects purports to identify unfair impediments to equal opportunity a posteriori in terms of the obstacles that actually affect people's chances of success in social endeavour. Thus, if the research is done properly and adjustments are made where necessary to eliminate unfair inequalities, the only remaining social inequalities will be those just and legitimate ones that are deserved or merited. What could these deserved inequalities be? Whatever 'talent' it is that makes this difference (special ability, motivation, gumption, or whatever), it obviously counts as a human difference that makes a difference in one's prospects for success. Can there be any doubt that being lazy, unmotivated, unwilling to take risks, and so on are disabilities, given our social environment? In other words, the equal prospects interpretation, if consistently applied, collapses into equality of results or flounders completely.

To see this more clearly consider those social programs such as employment equity that are, at least implicitly, based on equality of prospects. If the goal of the program is equality of employment prospects we will only know if the program is a success when the *actual* distribution of jobs among our targeted groups changes to reflect demographic distributions. That is, the best evidence of 'equal prospects' is 'equal results.' In that case, why not pursue equality of result directly?

Or consider the developing legal standard for 'reasonable accommodation' in United States and Canadian equality jurisprudence. Courts have held that accommodation in employment settings (the most frequently litigated context) includes the provision of assistive devices and aids as well as job restructuring and rescheduling in order to ensure physical accessibility and eliminate architectural, transportation, and communications obstacles.[47] But when is accommodation reasonable? To begin to answer this question we need to address general issues of expected costs and benefits, but these issues depend on the prior question of when an accommodation, with respect to some disability, is appropriate. The only way we can determine that is by the effects the accommodation will have on the employment record of people with that disability. Again, the test is one of results, not opportunities.

The general and particular inadequacies of equality of opportunity for disablement are not always appreciated because writers have traded on the ambiguities inherent in the equality of prospects interpretation. In its strict sense, equality of opportunity is not congenial to disablement policy goals, most particularly the goal of accommodation, which is concerned almost exclusively with limitations on an individual's positive freedom. Because of this, many writers have felt the need to turn to equality of result.

Equality of Result

So far I have characterized the central problem of equality as that of categorizing human differences into those that ought to make a difference in social treatment and those that ought not to. At this juncture, as we move to 'stronger' theories, it is important to see that this is really two problems wrapped into one. The first is the preliminary classification of kinds of differences. Some people have disabilities that make it difficult for them to get a job, others cannot get a job because their talents are not in demand, others because they have no interest or ambition to use the talents they have that are in demand, and still others because they have 'expensive tastes,' idiosyncratic ambitions, or other personal oddities that interfere with their employment prospects.[48] These are all differences, but which of them should make a difference in employment and which should not? The second problem is whether irrelevant differences are, so to speak, categorically irrelevant or only irrelevant in certain contexts.

Fortunately in the case of disablement, the first problem has a partial solution, and here is where the assumption of biomedical grounding shows its value. As a form of human difference, disablement is conceptually linked to one of the securest bases we have for judging a human difference to be objective and 'real' – biomedical impairment. We lack this connection in the case of motivational differences, or idiosyncratic beliefs, tastes, and ambition, which is why we are strongly inclined to believe that, normatively speaking, people with these differences are responsible for some of the social disadvantages they bring about. In other words, because the dimension of impairment is essential to the concept of disablement, we can be confident that as a form of human difference, disablement is not entirely social constructed. This forestalls the objection, plausibly raised in other contexts, that the relevance of this form of human difference with respect to social inequalities is a judgment made by the powerful and imposed on the powerless.[49]

The second problem as it applies to disablement is more difficult. The problem can only be resolved if we abandon the assumption that disablement differences which are socially relevant (in one context or another) are so because they are intrinsic to the individual and so will always be disadvantageous unless completely ignored. As we have seen, disability is not such a difference. Disabilities are inherently interactional so that a policy of 'disability-blindness' constitutes an infringement of equality.

In general, for interactional differences such as disablement, where there is no a priori method for determining when the difference should make a difference in treatment (and what sort of difference in treatment it should make), a social commitment to equality seems to drive us inexorably to the theoretical position of result-sensitivity. As policy analysts and lawmakers we discover when differences asso-ciated with disablement should make a difference in treatment only when the actual outcomes of policies and programs are known. Thus, the argument goes, equality demands result-sensitivity.

Yet, once we adopt this policy orientation another question looms large: What sort of result or outcome comports with the political value of equality and what violates or compromises it? It is clear enough, first off, that equality of result is a form of egalitarianism. It is a political principle that allocates social resources to the production and maintenance of a social condition of equality. As such, equality of result is a good candidate for the strongest possible interpretation of equality as a political value. But as always, there are various versions of egalitarianism and various conceptions of what this social condition of equality consists in.

Egalitarianism represents a spectrum of political doctrines, defined by degrees of social commitment to redistributive policies that 'remedy' whatever social inequalities arise. At one extreme (usually called 'levelling' by opponents), all social inequalities must be rooted out and eliminated; at the other extreme are 'weak' mandates that may, for example, do no more than vest all of us with a right (to use if we wish) to slip in and out of social hierarchies, thereby eliminating the possibility of a perpetual underclass.[50]

The most widely discussed interpretation of egalitarianism is one we have already examined in some detail, namely, the minority-rights analysis relied on by Evelyn Kallen, Harlan Hahn, and Michael Oliver, among others. Applying this analysis to legal equality, the legal standard for constitutionally suspect social practices would be evidence of persistent disparity in wealth, power, status, or access to benefits in identifiable minority groups.[51] This analysis meshes surprisingly well with legal tests used by American courts to characterize 'suspect' classifications. The most famous of these, which has now entered Canadian law,[52] asks the court to determine whether the complainant is a member of a 'discrete and insular minority' that has been the object of such prejudicial treatment as to relegate the group 'to such a position of political powerlessness as to command extraordinary protection from the majoritarian political process.'[53]

The wording of this test indicates that it is grounded in antidiscrimination law. A class of people is a 'suspect' class when it is the object of social hostility, denigration, stereotyping, exploitation, and scapegoating[54] – that is, handicapping. The range of remedies that are suggested by advocates of this approach make it clear that the social disparity of the group in question motivates legally sanctioned attempts at resource redistribution. Indeed, this is the legal basis for what I earlier called equalization compensation, a policy of redistribution designed to achieve equality of result by way of a corrective response to systemic handicapping. Thus, if a minority group wins its case by arguing systemic mistreatment, it can then fashion its remedies by appealing to equality of result (since an appeal to corrective justice would yield a very different remedy).

It must be said that as an interpretation of social egalitarianism this 'group disparity' legal test is not particularly useful for disablement theory. It attempts to use the injustices of handicapping as a motivation for addressing social disparities caused not just by handicapping, but by disabilities as well. It opens the possibility of adopting the strategy of advocates of the social-political model and arguing that *every* social inequality is itself a manifestation of handicapping.[55] This tactic, however, does not accord well with any version of egalitarianism, since it entails that people with disabilities, as a group, have a stronger claim to resources than other groups who may also have a proportionately unequal share of social resources, although they have not been subjected to handicapping. In other words, if one takes the social egalitarianism perspective seriously one must provide an answer to the 'macro' policy question. As among other groups in society that, for whatever reason, have received and will likely continue to receive a disproportionately smaller share of social benefits, what does equality mandate for people with disabilities? From this global perspective, it is far less obvious why people with disabilities are owed more by virtue of a social commitment to equality than racial minorities, people with unmarketable skills, or the aged.[56]

Though the question is a difficult one, it is encouraging to see that it is the kind of question equality of result should be able to answer, since it asks what equality demands, for everyone, by way of overall social condition. What is less encouraging for disablement policy is that this version of equality cannot answer the question until it comes to terms with the second problem mentioned above: Since disablement is not a 'categorically' irrelevant difference, how do we know when it is and when it is not relevant to some form of unequal treatment?

Plainly, no version of egalitarianism, nor any statement of equality of result, will solve this issue until a decision is made about the nature of the social result or outcome at which egalitarian redistribution should be aimed. Equality theorists call this the 'equality of what?' problem and it is a serious one. If we agree that as a society we are committed to social policies that endeavour to provide every citizen with an 'equal share,' what will this share be a share of?

Egalitarians are often criticized for wanting to eliminate differences between people, thereby creating a bland and homogeneous society devoid of just those individual differences that are responsible for social progress. Although this is an unfair caricature of the egalitarian social agenda, the onus is certainly on egalitarians to be explicit about what it is that is to be 'equalized.' Though this issue is not something that can be resolved here, the theoretical debate has recently produced a novel solution which, because it accords well with the conception of disability offered here, is a fitting way of concluding this review of contending accounts of equality suitable for disablement policy.

Equality of Capability

Modern egalitarians, or at least those who trace their views back to R.H. Tawney's 1931 classic Equality,[57] argue that equality of result must involve political and economic power, since without an equal share of power unjust inequalities are bound to reappear. Egalitarian pluralists such as Michael Waltzer, however, argue that equality is a multidimensional notion, and we should expect different 'objects' of equality in different contexts.[58] Although this debate remains active, when egalitarianism is applied to policy the issue of 'equality of what?' has for decades resituated the debate to one between welfarism and non-welfarism.

As already mentioned, welfarism is the general philosophical position that human welfare, variously understood and operationalized, must be the ultimate basis for value of any state of social affairs.[59] Welfarist egalitarianism is thus the view that society should aim at some version of equality of welfare as an overall policy goal. The weakest form of this account is welfare maximization, which we have already considered and rejected. Another, stronger version, holds that the best distributional arrangement is that which distributes society's resources among the population until no further distribution would leave them more equal in welfare.[60]

Non-welfarist egalitarian views, however, identify some non-subjective good (that is, a thing or attribute as opposed to an experience), and then offer a distributional rule that either immediately secures or aims in the long run to secure equality in the possession of those 'things.' Thus, for example, John Rawls first identifies 'primary social goods' as 'rights, liberties and opportunities, income and wealth, and the social bases of self-respect' and then proposes a potentially egalitarian distributional principle in their terms.[61] And Ronald Dworkin in his theory of equality of resources sets out a series of 'price-setting' hypothetical devices for determining equality of shares of bundles of resources, including any objective good or commodity that is valued in society as an end or a means.[62]

The welfarist/non-welfarist debate is important not merely because it raises the issue of the content of the ideal end-state of egalitarianism, but also because it helps to identify tools for determining 'equality improvements,' advances achieved through the operation of social policy and law. The latter is particularly important, since only egalitarian visionaries believe that the end-state is achievable; most others see the value of egalitarianism in providing a goal that can be approached, incrementally, by equality improvements.

Thus, we would expect a welfarist to seek 'welfare improvements' or increases in overall happiness or satisfaction levels and incremental reductions of 'welfare hierarchies' generated by disparities in the average happiness or satisfaction levels of representative groups, and so on. For her part, the non-welfarist might assess the level of social equality by considering commodity or wealth growth achievements averaged across the population, or growth of gross national product per capita, or a reduction in commodity-possession hierarchies, and the like. In these ever-more-nuanced ways, the amorphous notion of society's 'standard of living' can be given content.[63]

Although these are the major contenders, *both* welfarist and non-welfarist approaches to the 'equality of what?' question are problematic for disablement policy. Welfarist equality, on the face of it, seems to be a godsend to disablement policy because it appears to resolve the puzzle of when disabilities make a difference, and in what respect. Suppose our overall social policy goal, in the name of equality, is to ensure that everyone achieves the same (and a suitably high) level of personal satisfaction, enjoyment, or contentment. Since this is our goal, people with greater needs will require *more* of society's resources in order to achieve equality. It follows that impairments and disabilities will be judged to be differences warranting unequal social treatment when they actually affect individual achievement of welfare, but not otherwise. This makes sense.

In addition, since it is a presumption of welfarism (dubious though it may be from a psychometric point of view) that welfare is quantifiable and measurable, equality of welfare holds out the prospect of a precise, principled, and not ad hoc way of shaping effective policy. The kinds of initiatives that equality of welfare mandates would not be restricted (as they are in the 'weaker' principles of equality of opportunity or antidiscrimination) to removing limitations on negative freedom. The governing policy guideline would be this: look for and implement the social response to disablement that provides the greatest welfare improvement. This guideline would obviously apply to improvements in positive freedom.

But our initial enthusiasm for this approach must be quickly tempered with scepticism brought about by well-known conceptual and practical difficulties with welfarism.[64] To begin with, there is no reason to be confident that equalizing welfare (even if this were feasible) is even relevant to a social commitment to equality.[65] After all, people value enjoyment or happiness differently (some, for example, willingly sacrifice their own welfare for other goals). Moreover, the subjective state that arises from unmet needs and incapacitations is in no sense a function of the severity of those conditions: a blind person with a cheerful disposition would receive fewer resources on this account than a dour and pessimistic person with a slight visual impairment. We cannot justifiably infer need from psychological response to need, since 'mental reactions [to one's plight] often reflect defeatist compromises with harsh reality induced by hopelessness.'[66] Because of this, equalized welfare turns out to be a dubious and unattractive goal for disablement policy.

If we turn to non-welfarist, resource-based accounts of equality we once again confront an insight that seems to solve many of the basic normative problems of disablement theory. If, as seems likely, people derive different levels and varieties of satisfaction from different things, the optimal arrangement as far as equality is concerned is to provide everyone with an equal share of society's resources (or rather an equal share of the overall value of these resources, determined in some objective fashion). If everyone has an equal share then each can decide, given her or his needs, wants, desires, capabilities, and disabilities, what sort of life he or she wishes to lead.[67] With this distribution in place no one could legitimately complain that society has failed in its equality obligations. What better way of dismantling unjustifiable social hierarchies and other inequalities?

Notice though, that if equality of resources is understood to be a 'starting-gate' theory – the theoretical scenario in which everyone is allotted equal shares, guaranteed the negative freedom to apply his or her natural talents to his or her shares, and then let loose to start a society – non-welfarist accounts reduce to equality of opportunity. Therefore, what is needed, as Dworkin makes clear in his sophisticated version of resource equality, is a diachronic social policy dedicated to periodic redistributive adjustments or 'corrections' to maintain equality.[68]

On Dworkin's scheme these adjustments take the form of an income tax that 'will neutralize the effects of differential talents, yet preserve the consequences of one person choosing an occupation, in response to his sense of what he wants to do with his life, that is more expensive for the community than the choice another makes.'[69] This must be accomplished without sacrificing what he terms 'ambition-sensitivity,' the policy requirement that social inequalities of resources that result from differences in ambition and the choices people make *will not* be altered by the tax, inasmuch as these inequalities are fair and do not violate resource equality.

It should be clear that Dworkin's egalitarianism is a modest and qualified one. He feels the need to characterize key productive capabilities ('skills') as mixtures of natural ('genetic') talents and ambitions. Since a disability is a relative lack of skill, by factoring out the ambition component it is possible, or at least Dworkin believes, to set the rates for the income tax by means of a hypothetical insurance scheme. We ask how much insurance would someone buy in an insurance 'auction' where everyone has equal resources to bid, against the possibility of *not* having a particular level of some skill.[70]

If this counterfactual insurance auction can be made sense of, and Dworkin grants that there are several fanciful assumptions built into it, then the result would be a basis for measuring the amount of redistribution – through tax transfers – required to maintain resource equality. Importantly, as Dworkin readily admits, this arrangement would not prevent some people with natural talents in high demand from using their ambition to acquire a level of material wealth far in excess of what anyone would have been able (or willing) to insure for in the insurance auction. This is not a problem, however, Dworkin insists, because resource equality does not guarantee equal shares of resources; it only guarantees that no one will have fewer resources than another simply in consequence of less natural talent.

Dworkin's account of resource equality is worth the time to outline because it represents one of the few treatments of disabilities that recognizes them as interactional phenomena. Dworkin is willing to extend the notion of disability so that, in effect, it merges with an unnamed notion that does not distinguish between disabilities and abilities at all. As Dworkin puts it, there will always be some context in which *any* actual ability will not be enough and will therefore count as a disability.[71] Although one would want to avoid 'capability relativism' (since it contradicts the assumption of biomedical grounding), Dworkin's point is worth making. He is concerned that resource equality treat everyone, and everyone's particular repertoire of capabilities, as amenable to policy analysis. Whether or not the tax and insurance mechanisms he proposes make sense, Dworkin's account of equality does accord with an adequate analysis of disablement.

In light of this achievement, it is all the more ironic that Dworkin fails to see that any scheme for distributing and redistributing resources will from the outset undermine the effectiveness of disablement policy. Stripped to its essentials, Dworkin's scheme is that people with incapacities will, from time to time, be given money in lieu of accommodation, and the amount of money provided will be assessed in terms, roughly, of the amount a person without these incapacities would be willing to pay in premiums for insurance concerning this eventuality. Inasmuch as this is the only possible policy ramification of Dworkin's theory of resource equality, it is hopelessly inadequate as a normative basis for disablement policy. In other words, disability is not like poverty. Given enough money one simply ceases to be poor; money fills a gap, and the gap was the problem. But disability is a limitation of positive freedom and though removing this limitation *costs* money (sometimes) and involves resources (usually), the limitation is not a gap that *any* sum of money or *any* particular bundle of resources automatically fills.

What is required to respond to disability is capacitation and accommodation, and more often than not these things require the creation or strengthening of social relationships that respond to the interactional nature of the particular disability. The lack of physical accessibility in a workplace will create a disability for those workers who cannot walk up stairs. What is required to remove this limitation on the workers' positive freedom is a modified work environment – which may involve any number of possible accommodations, from putting in an elevator to restructuring the job requirements, some costly, some not. Schemes to create a measure of resource equality, although they would obviously *alter* the relationship between impairment and the social environment that creates disabilities, would do so serendipitously and not necessarily in a manner that would address the problem of disability. Resources are not social relations, nor do they necessarily create or strengthen them.

Amartya Sen has done much to highlight these deep and pervasive problems with both welfarist and non-welfarist theories of equality.[72] His objection to both approaches is straightforward: a social commitment to equality must be a commitment to the positive freedom of everyone, but that is not the focus, or effect, of either welfarist or non-welfarist accounts. Welfare is not a reliable, or even relevant, indicator of positive freedom. And theories of equality of resources (in which Sen includes equality of opportunity and other 'means' theories), though attractive because they purport to distribute the means for securing positive freedom, are equally unreliable. Given human diversity of capabilities and needs, levels of resource possession are not functionally or predictably related to levels of positive freedom.

Sen notes that these difficulties tend to be obscured by theorists who rely on 'standardizing' assumptions about human capability and need. But if one turns to concrete situations, say, in the field in which Sen specializes, international development economics, it becomes obvious that one cannot assume that changes in resource allocation automatically lead to meaningful changes in people's lives. Even the impact of food resources on nutrition cannot be predicted without situational information about, for example, knowledge of food preparation, climatic conditions, and the average age and health of the population.[73] Of course, Sen's point is that food resources are not, but nutrition is, interactive.

Thus, welfare assessments can be extremely misleading and attempts to secure equality of resource holdings can go hand in hand with serious inequalities in the actual range of positive freedom enjoyed by people. By the same token, if one wishes to develop a coherent and plausible conception of the standard of living of a country, one must appreciate that 'the value of the living standard lies in the living, and not in the possessing of commodities, which has derivative and varying relevance.'[74]

The political value of equality, in short, is about positive freedom, not subjective experience or income levels. Positive freedom has to do with ranges of options, the things people can do or become. What is required, Sen argues, is equality of capability.

To formulate this account of equality more precisely, Sen defines 'functionings' as the things and activities that people actually can do or become – that is, things and activities people have a realistic choice between. A functioning is not merely a physical and mental capability (or absence of impairment), it is also the set of all the other preconditions to achievement (that is, absence of disability) that infringe on positive freedom. A 'capability,' then, is a set of functionings over which a person has a choice, so that the set of a person's capabilities constitutes his or her actual freedom of choice over alternative lives that he or she can lead.[75]

Sen is clear that capabilities are not 'doings and beings' that people do choose, but those that they can and could choose. The distinction is important since positive freedom is a matter of what one is able to do, not just what one has actually done. Freedom is about the range of one's plausible and realistic options. Thus, Sen claims that 'the capability to function is the thing that comes closest to the notion of positive freedom, and if freedom is valued then capability itself can serve as an object of value and moral importance.'[76]

The category of capability, Sen argues, is also the most appropriate 'result' for a substantive principle of equality of result. An egalitarianism of capability is, in effect, the realization of universal positive freedom. Moreover, capabilities solve the problem of 'equality of what?' since they complete the rationale for equality, as a political ideal, a legal value, and a normative basis for social policy. All of the component principles of equality, in other words, are linked and made coherent by equality of capability. Thus, when we speak of respect for persons what we mean is respect for persons as agents, and equality of respect entails a guarantee of equally attractive ranges of options for all. Interpreting the principles of antidiscrimination and equality of opportunity in terms of capability, we can see how they share a single underlying rationale, namely, furthering the goal of positive freedom for all.

Inasmuch as disabilities are impairment-based limitations on an individual's positive freedom, and disablement in all its dimensions involves positive freedom in one form or another, Sen's theory of equality of capability, schematic though it is at present, is immediately attractive. It addresses, in a suggestive if not complete manner, all four requirements of an adequate normative basis for disablement policy.

Sen's interpretation of equality as a political value accords well with the concept of disablement in each of its three dimensions. Since the interpretation is founded on positive freedom, it is, so to speak, disability-centred. But, unlike the economic model, equality in Sen's sense does not exclude the impairment or the handicap dimensions; the latter because, as a theory of equality, it directly addresses socially constructed inequalities; the former because it requires, as a theory of equality of results, a causal connection between negative freedom-limiting disabilities and biomedically grounded impairments. Like all theories of equality, Sen's account satisfies the second aspect of the normative challenge, namely, that of providing the central political value, in terms of which all entitlement controversies establishing the objectives of policy development can be expressed, debated, and resolved.

Because a concern for capability is a concern for the realization of actual and realistic options to do and become what one chooses, equality of capability holds out the prospect of integrating the policy goals of respect, participation, and accommodation. Positive freedom, like capability, entails respect-building and participatory options. Moreover, the needs for accommodation are plausibly interpreted in terms of improvements on the level of positive freedom an individual experiences.

Sen suggests why goal integration is possible in his account by means of a provocative argument from elimination: 'If it is argued that resources should be devoted to remove or substantially reduce the handicap of the cripple despite there being no marginal utility argument (because it is expensive), despite there being no total utility argument (because he is so content), and despite there being no primary good deprivation (because he has the goods that others have), then the case must rest on something else.'[77] What that 'something else' can only be, Sen concludes, is equality of capability.

As for the fourth aspect of the normative challenge, whether equality of capability could provide the basis for a broad, flexible, and practically adequate framework for policy analysis, the case has yet to be made. Of course, like any account of equality – except, perhaps, the weakest, formalistic ones – the two specific structural issues of allocating responsibility between law and social policy, and determining the place of disablement policy in social policy at large, can be addressed by Sen's approach. Yet there is no doubt that there remains the immense challenge of developing Sen's suggestive remarks about equality of capability in a way that offers a practical framework for policy analysis and so a solution to the impasse in disablement policy.

In the end, though, anyone taking the time to become informed about disablement, both as a concept and as a multidimensional social phenomenon, and who is sensitive to the concerns and needs of people with disabilities, will probably quickly enough see what a suitable and worked-out theory of equality would tells us. Such a theory would make it clear, in the words of A Consensus for Action, that disablement 'is not a problem of "us" versus "them," but a problem of recognizing our common human condition.'[78] Some of us have disabilities now, but, chances are, all of us will have disabilities later on. Emphasizing, even celebrating, the ways we are the same will make it easier to respect and, when necessary, to accommodate the ways we are different. After all, impairments and disabilities are just features of human biological and social existence; only handicaps represent the dark side of human nature and a failure of political will. Seeing all of this might in the end make it easier to imagine the world that Jacobus tenBroek described some years ago, a world in which, as a blind man, he could 'rise in the morning, help get the children off to school, bid his wife goodbye, and proceed along the streets and bus lines to his daily work, without dog, cane, or guide, if such is his habit or preference, now and then brushing a tree or kicking a curb, but, notwithstanding, proceeding with firm step and sure air, knowing that he is part of the public for whom the streets are built and maintained in reasonable safety, by the help of his taxes, and that he shares with others this part of the world in which he, too, has a right to live.'[79]

Notes

Chapter 1

1 This chapter incorporates material I presented on 13 December 1990 to the Standing Committee on Human Rights and the Status of Disabled Persons which can be found in the *Minutes of Proceedings and Evidence of the Standing Committee, Issue No. 42.*

2 Canada, Parliamentary Special Committee on the Disabled and the Handicapped (1981); for similar remarks see Canada, Parliamentary Committee on Human Rights (1985).

3 I am following Deborah A. Stone's characterization of policy analysis (1988).

4 For this notion, see Sen (1984a).

5 Canada, House of Commons Standing Committee on Human Rights and the Status of Disabled Persons (1990)

6 I derive these examples from the following sources: (1) *Globe and Mail*, 'Definition of Handicap Variable,' 25 November 1990; (2) Browne, Connors, Stern (1985), 79–80; (3) *New York Times*, 'Disabled People Say Home Care Is Needed to Use New Rights,' 14 October 1990; (4) *Traynor v. Turnage, Administrator, Veterans' Administration, et al.* 485 U.S. 535 (1988); (5) *Globe and Mail*, 'Thalidomide Groups' Aid Request will be Studied, Beatty Pledges,' 7 May 1990; and (6) *Acquired Immunodeficiency Syndrome (AIDS): Policy Adopted by the Canadian Human Rights Commission* (25 May 1988) and *Ontario Human Rights Commission Policy on AIDS* (November 1985).

7 World Health Organization (1980)

8 Of the several places where Harlan Hahn develops this point see Hahn (1984a, 1984b, and 1987). As I argue in ch. 5, although I am

272 Notes to pages 20–37

greatly indebted to Hahn's analysis, it seems to me clear that Hahn fully aligns himself with the social-political model and so falls victim to the basic misperceptions embodied in it.

Chapter 2

1 Quoted in the *Globe and Mail*, 15 October 1991
2 Kessler (1931)
3 Nagi (1969), based on Nagi (1965); see later refinements in Nagi (1979, 1981, 1987).
4 See, especially, Hamilton (1950), Sokolow et al. (1959), Wright (1983), Sussman (1969), Barry (1971), Haber (1973), Garrad (1974), and Bury (1979).
5 U.S. Department of Health and Human Services 1991
6 Wood (1975); other early writings were Wood and Badley (1978a, 1978b, 1980) and Wood (1980a, 1980b). For Wood's discussion of this history see Wood (1989).
7 See, for example, Jablensky, Schwarz, and Tomov (1980), Duckworth (1983, 1984), Haber (1985), Pfeiffer (1986), Colverz and Robine (1986), Wiersma (1986), Paicheler (1987), and Grimby, Finnstam, and Jette (1988).
8 CSICISH/QCICIDH (1991)
9 See Wood (1980a) and CSICISH/QCICIDH (1991).
10 Wiersma argues that, at least for psychological impairments, it is nearly impossible to distinguish between the 'background' disease condition and the manifestations of the disease, the impairment (1986: 6); see also the sustained discussion of this issue in Coles (1987) with regard to developmental and learning disabilities.
11 See Canguilhem (1988, esp. ch. 6, and 1989).
12 See Minow (1990).
13 I am here relying on a characterization of positive freedom that parallels recent treatments of *autonomy*; see, e.g., Lindley (1986) and G. Dworkin (1988). The 'freedom to' and 'freedom from' distinction is usually credited to Berlin (1977; 'Two Concepts of Liberty').
14 An earlier attempt to make this distinction was made by Garrad where 'impairment' is defined as 'an anatomical, pathological or psychological disorder which may be described in diagnostic or symptomatic terms,' and a disability is given as 'limitation of performance in one or more activities which are generally accepted as essential basic components of daily living' (1974: 142).

15 One documented example of this is reported in Fross et al. (1980). Groups of children, with comparable degrees of pulmonary dysfunction caused by asthma, reported significantly different degrees of incapacitation and interference with daily life; these differences seemed to be attributable to the children's responses to the disease.

16 Thus, I.K. Zola has suggested that there may be more than meets the eye to the apparently straightforward factual issue of measuring the number of people with disabilities: 'By trying to find strict measures of disability or focussing on "severe" "visible" handicaps we draw dividing lines and make distinctions where matters are very blurry and constantly changing. By agreeing that there are 20 million disabled or 36 million, or even that half the population are in some way affected by disability, we delude ourselves into thinking there is some finite, no matter how large, number of people. In this way, both in the defining and in the measuring, we try to make the reality of disease, disability, and death problematic, and in this way make it at least potentially someone else's problem. But it is not, and can never be. Any person reading the words on this page is at best momentarily able-bodied. But nearly everyone reading them will, at some point, suffer from one or more chronic disease and be disabled, temporarily or permanently, for a significant portion of their lives' (1982: 242).

17 Colverz and Robine (1986: 19) argue that the French *handicap* implies an initial condition of insufficiency that one tries to overcome. For a more recent exchange, see CSICISH/QCICIDH (1990).

18 Colverz and Robine (1986: 20–1) and Haber (1985: 28–9). Wiersma (1986), while not denying the importance of a notion like handicap, suggests that the ICIDH definition of 'disability' might be expanded to include what he calls 'social disabilities,' a class of non-abilities that explicitly involve a person's functioning within social roles. For slightly different reasons Grimby, Finnstam, and Jette (1988) recommend that handicap be removed from the ICIDH and replaced by an expanded notion of disability. It is obvious, though, that the only effect of pursuing either of these suggestions would be to submerge handicaps into the class of disabilities, which would produce unnecessary confusion.

19 This is indeed evident in the document itself as soon as the discussion of examples begins. Once the 'obstacles' confronting particular individuals are set out in detail, there is nothing left to be added under the heading 'handicap situation.'

20 See Bickenbach (1991).

21 See studies of the disadvantages associated with poliomyelitis in Halstead and Weichers (1985), Kaufert and Kaufert (1984), and Kaufert, Kaufert, and Locker (1987). For social and institutional responses to people with rheumatoid arthritis, see Locker (1983). See also earlier work by J. Townsend in Townsend (1967, 1979), Harris (1971), Blaxter (1976), Shearer (1981), Strauss (1975), and discussion and citations in Bury (1987).

22 Kessler (1971)

23 See Nagi (1965, 1969).

24 In some of his later writings, Nagi has seemed to be far more willing to accept the interactive character of handicaps; he has written that 'Disability is determined by the interaction of limitations in function ... with factors of a situational and environmental nature. In the case of work disability, the latter factors include work requirements, attitudes and practices of employers, and general conditions of the labor market. Equity in decisions requires that these variables be given appropriate weights' (1981: 41).

25 Office des personnes handicapées du Québec (1984: 35–8)

Chapter 3

1 See Le Disert (1987, 255–6) for a discussion of the 'colère des Dieux' attitude towards disablement.

2 See Malthus (1958).

3 See, for example, Antonck and Livneh (1988).

4 Sontag (1979, 1988), and Kidel (1988), Scarry (1985), Gilman (1985, 1988), Kleinman (1988), Le Disert (1987), and Stiker (1982); in the related area of mental disease, see Foucault (1965, 1973) and Scull (1979).

5 Trevelyan (1967: 359)

6 See R.C. Fox (1977), Mechanic (1973), Conrad and Schneider (1980), and Kohlberg (1981), for the medicalization of unemployment; Gilman (1985, 1988), for the medicalization of sexuality; Donzelot (1979), for the medicalization of the family; and in general Illich (1976), Illich et al. (1977), and Ladd (1982).

7 The most prominent early critiques of the medicalization of psychiatric medicine and mental health care were those of Cooper (1971), Laing (1967), Moore (1975), Murphy (1976), and perhaps most well known of all, Szasz (1961, 1970a, 1970b).

8 Albert, Munson, and Resnik (1988: 158); the authors themselves argue for a slightly modified form of 'biomedical realism.'

9 I am relying here on G. Engel's statement of the thesis (1977: 130).

10 This phrase, now in standard use, comes from Dubos (1961).

11 Essentialism is characterized in this way by Uffe Juul Jensen in Jensen (1984) and critically considered in Engelhardt (1984).

12 See, for example, the critical assessment of the medical model of disease in Mishler (1981), 9–15.

13 For an interesting example of this research see Zola (1966) and in general Mishler (1981) and Jaco (1979).

14 See Boorse (1975, 1977); for a similar position, see Wulff (1976), ch. 4, 'The Concept of Disease.'

15 Examples of such theories of health have appeared from time to time; see, for example, Guttmacher (1979), Ladd (1982), Whitbeck (1981), and Porn (1984). The most sophisticated and complete account of this sort is offered in Nordenfelt (1987). For related arguments see Engelhardt (1986), Brown (1977), and Agich (1983).

16 An example of this worry, mentioned above, was that some federally regulated companies were circumventing the Canadian government's employment equity law and deceptively improving their hiring record by adopting very broad definitions of 'disability' so that people who wear glasses, have a minor speech impediment, or suffer lower back pain were counted as disabled.

17 Stone (1984), 26–8 and ch. 2, 'The Origins of the Disability Concept'

18 In particular see Stiker (1982).

19 Le Disert (1987), 256

20 Family Benefits Act Regulation 318, section 1(b). Compare the Social Security Act 42 U.S.C. section 423(d) (1), which states that a 'disability' is 'an inability to engage in any substantial gainful activity by reason of any medically determinable physical or mental impairment which can be expected to result in death or has lasted or can be expected to last for a continuous period of not less than 12 months.'

21 The Code of Justinian, Book XI, Title XXV: 'Concerning Sturdy Beggers,'; and compare Book XI, Title XXVI; see Le Disert (1987), 257 and citations.

22 Cassidy (1943), 148. It is noteworthy, however, that this rationale was not raised in the Marsh Report itself, primarily because of its focus on health insurance. Thus, Marsh writes that 'Certification of sickness ... should proceed desirably from the health insurance system' (1975: 144).

23 Advisory Council on Social Security *Permanent and Total Disability, a Report to Senate Committee on Finance*, 80th Congress, 2nd session, 1946, Senate Document 1621

24 Cited in Stone (1984), 120
25 See Gritzer and Arluke (1985).
26 American Medical Association (1988)
27 Social Security Act, 'Listing of Impairments,' 20 CFR, 404, Subpart P, Appendix 1; cf. U.S. Department of Health, Education and Welfare (1979).
28 Pryor (1990b)
29 Kessler (1931)
30 American Medical Association (1988), 5–6
31 For similar complaints about the *Guides* see Berkowitz, Johnson, and Murphy (1976), Blaxter (1976), Heinemann (1976), Albrecht and Levy (1981), Stone (1981), Wright (1983), Berkowitz and Burton (1987), and Liachowitz (1988).
32 *The Permanent Disability Rating Schedule* in use in Ontario is set out in Gilbert (1989), 34–7. By way of comparison see the *Guidelines for the Evaluation of Permanent Impairment* which were proposed by the Medical Services Division of the Ontario Workers' Compensation Board; see also Burton (1986).
33 Workers' Compensation Act R.S.O. (1990) c. W.11
34 Ontario, Social Assistance Review Commission (1988)
35 Pension Assessment Appeals Leading Case Strategy Decision No. 915 (Panel Chairman, S.R. Ellis; Toronto, Research and Publications Department, Workers' Compensation Appeals Tribunal, May 1987); all subsequent quotations come from this publication.
36 Gliedman and Roth (1980), esp. 37–8, 411–12; see also Zola (1977), Wendell (1989), Albrecht and Levy (1981), and DeJong (1983), 14–16.
37 Parsons (1961), 439–47, and (1972); see also the discussion of the sick role as it applies to mental illness, in Radden (1985), 18–19.
38 See Ryan (1977).
39 See Kidel (1988).
40 Connors (1985), 100
41 See Osmond and Siegler (1974); also Pellegrino (1979), 258–61.
42 DeJong (1983), 14–16; see E. Berkowitz (1987), ch. 6.
43 'Prenatal Screening Is Criticized,' *Globe and Mail*, 1 November 1990
44 The papers in which the 'medical perspective' on disablement is discussed are Hahn (1982, 1983, 1984a, 1984b, 1985, 1987).
45 Hahn (1984a), 8
46 Hahn (1987); this claim is somewhat stronger than Hahn's earlier observation that 'little or no consideration is given to the potential of improving personal circumstances through changes in laws or social policy' (1984a: 8).

47 Hahn (1982), 386
48 Hahn (1987), 181–2
49 Stone (1984), 116–17
50 Ibid., 128
51 Recently, the citizens of the state of Oregon were asked to consider a series of questions that were used to generate a ranking of 1,600 medical procedures that health officials could use to determine the funding priorities for Medicaid-paid services (see 'New Health Test: The Oregon Plan,' by Timothy Egan in the *New York Times*, 3 May 1990).
52 Pryor (1990a), 797–801 and (1990b)
53 Prior (1990b), 976
54 Ibid., 968–9
55 Pryor (1990b) and (1990a), 844–7
56 An indication of the extent to which the medical interpretation of accommodating needs can overcome even common sense can be found in the list of 'prescribed medical devices and equipment' in the Income Tax Act Regulations governing allowable medical expenses. The first such 'medical device' is a wig, as would be used by someone suffering hair loss after chemotherapy. Obviously the wig is not an impairment need but a disability or, more likely, a handicap need.
57 This is the terminology adopted by David Braybrooke (1987), ch. 2.

Chapter 4

1 Stone (1984)
2 See Rawls (1971), 267–8 for a discussion of this problem.
3 Michael Oliver suggests that Stone's analysis presumes an essentially Weberian account of the contradictions inherent in capitalism (1990: 40–2).
4 See Liachowitz (1988), 19–44 for her discussion of the merging of veterans' pensions with rehabilitation therapy programming.
5 P. Fortescue Fox (1917)
6 Kessler (1931)
7 Nagi (1969)
8 See, for example, Kjonstad (1984), Blaxter (1976), and National Rehabilitation Association (1975).
9 See Haber and Smith (1971), as well as Haber (1967, 1973, 1985); cf. Berkowitz, Johnson, and Murphy (1976), 3–4, 7–23.
10 See the discussion in Berkowitz and Burton (1987), 6–13.
11 The story of the professional legitimization of rehabilitation is admirably told in Gritzer and Arluke (1985).

12 See Knudson (1957) and the classic text by Howard Rusk (1971); see also the discussion in Fendoglio (1974).

13 Two symposia give a clear idea of the tenor and direction of this ongoing debate: 'Social Science Perspectives to Vocational Rehabilitation,' in *Rehabilitation Literature* (1984), vol. 45, in particular, the articles by Stubbins, Stubbins and Albee, Goldberg, and Trieschmann; and 'Ethical and Policy Issues in Rehabilitation Medicine,' in Caplan, Callahan, and Haas (1987). See also Bury (1979, 1987) and Purtilo (1981).

14 See the texts by Bauer (1989), Goodwill and Chamberlain (1988), and Sinaki (1987).

15 I am relying here on the survey found in Gresham and Labi (1984).

16 See, for example, Kaufert (1983) and Keith (1984).

17 See Jette (1984).

18 See the remarks by Nancy Crewe (1987).

19 Among the many treatments of vocational assessment are Power (1984), Cornes and Bochel (1987), Neff (1980), and Roessler and Greenwood (1987).

20 One of the most extensive recent discussions of evaluation can be found in Fuhrer (1987).

21 Canada, House of Commons Standing Committee on the Status of Disabled Persons (1990), 1; also Abella (1984)

22 Berkowitz, Johnson, and Murphy (1976), 13, my emphasis; cf. Conley (1965).

23 Haveman, Halberstadt, and Burkhauser (1984) and Burkhauser and Haveman (1982)

24 Nagi (1987)

25 See the general remarks in Haveman, Halberstadt, and Burkhauser (1984), ch. 2.

26 This is one of the main results of the classic economic analysis of 'tragic choices' in Calabresi and Bobbit (1978).

27 For the general 'national efficiency' argument and its role in the development of the welfare state, see Barr (1987), ch. 2 and Bill Jordan (1987), 115–28.

28 See Conley (1965) and Liachowitz (1988), 19–44.

29 See the discussion in Torjman (1988).

30 See Guest (1980), 39. The Quebec Workers' Compensation Act of 1909, though earlier, was not truly a form of social insurance, since it was not compulsory and allowed for the defence of contributory negligence.

31 Still the clearest discussion can be found in Marsh (1975), first pub-

lished in 1943. For the U.S. development see Stone (1984), 47–9 and Friedman and Ladinsky (1967).

32 This is one of the suggestions found in Pryor (1990b), 783.
33 Workers' Compensation Act R.S.O. (1990), c. W .11
34 Weiler (1986)
35 For examples of this approach, see Ison (1978), Stapleton (1986), and Pryor (1990a).
36 Ontario, Social Assistance Review Commission (SARC) (1988)
37 Beveridge (1942)
38 See Marsh (1975) and Guest (1980), ch. 10.
39 Canada Pension Plan Act R.S.C (1985), c. C.8
40 See Torjman (1988), 41 for this criticism.
41 See Andersen (1966), Barr (1976), and Beveridge (1942).
42 Rejda (1988), 348
43 Beveridge (1942), 6
44 General Welfare Assistance Act R.S.O. (1990), c. G.6
45 Family Benefits Act R.S.O. (1990), c. F.2
46 R.R.O. (1980) Reg. 318 s. 1(3) (c)
47 Liebman (1976)
48 Vocational Rehabilitative Services Act R.S.O. (1990), c. V.5
49 Ontario, SARC (1988)
50 (1978) 20 O.R. (2d) 698 (Divisional Court)
51 This argument can be found in the recent treatment of American social security by Marmor, Mashaw, and Harvey (1990).
52 See Joan Brown (1984) for the early studies.
53 Rogers (1987)
54 Stone (1984), ch. 1
55 See Leonard (1986); for a recent, and very plausible, attempt to counter the economic objections to a right to work for people with disabilities, see Kavka (1992). The more standard position is voiced by Goodin (1990), who argues that people who have become incapacitated have the social duty to drastically alter their 'unrealistic' aspirations to enter the workforce. For a collection of papers on this issue, see Gillroy and Wade (1992).
56 For the constitutional argument, see Cover (1988) and, more generally, Rubin (1984).
57 Such is the judgment of Samuel A. Rea (1981).
58 Johnson (1979)
59 Barr (1987), 241
60 I am using the terminology and examples found in Haveman, Halberstadt, and Burkhauser (1984), 32–4.

61 This is ably shown in the analysis of Erlanger and Roth (1985).
62 See Haveman, Halberstadt, and Burkhauser (1984), 58–9, 164–9 for the claim that the efficiency argument will never be important for such programming.
63 Haveman, Halberstadt, and Burkhauser state that 'economic efficiency and cost considerations play little if any role in this civil rights justification for government intervention on behalf of the handicapped' (1984: 42).
64 Abella (1984), 17
65 Posner (1973)
65 The *locus classicus* of this argument is Okun (1975); see also Thurow (1980).
67 Kuttner (1984)
68 For an example of this criticism, see Hahn (1984a), 9.
69 See, for example, David Thomas (1982) and Zola (1982).

Chapter 5

1 Law (1987)
2 Berger and Lockman (1965) are responsible for this notion.
3 An interesting history of this development, focusing on the Vocational Rehabilitation Act of 1973 can be found in Scotch (1984).
4 Fraser (1984)
5 See Parsons (1961, 1972).
6 See the review in Gallagher (1972).
7 Friedson (1965) may have been the first to suggest this, although as early as 1948 Lee Meyerson thought it appropriate to say that 'there is general agreement ... that the major problems of the handicapped are not physical but social and psychological' (1971: 205). See also Barker (1948) and Gellman (1959).
8 Perhaps the classical, anthropological treatment of disablement as deviance, overambitiously crediting all stigmas to religious or magical ways of thinking, is Evans-Pritchard (1937); more recent treatments are Foster and Anderson (1978), Stiker (1982), Hellman (1984), and Murphy (1987).
9 See Goffman (1963), Eisenberg (1982), and Bogdan and Biklen (1981).
10 Wright (1983) and Constantina Safilios-Rothschild (1970)
11 Wright (1983), 11
12 Safilios-Rothschild (1970), 71; compare the discussion of the 'handicap role' in Gliedman and Roth (1980).

13 Goode (1984), Pfuhl (1986); see also Liska (1987), Farrell and Swigert (1988), and the earlier treatment in Schur (1971).
14 For example, the seminal study of the sociology of deviance in Becker (1963) concentrates on marijuana users and jazz musicians, two groups who 'break the rules.'
15 Haffter (1968)
16 See Bickenbach (1991).
17 Sagarin (1975), 201–14 and, to similar effect, Kriegel (1969), Birenbaum and Lesieur (1982), and Bogdan and Biklen (1981)
18 See, for example, Farrell and Swigert (1988).
19 There is, for example, a dispute between functionalists who argue that some forms of deviance have a positive and integrative effect on society and monists and neo-Marxist conflict theorists who insist that all forms of deviance creation are exploitative; see Jim Thomas (1982).
20 The earliest suggestions concerning labelling came in Tannenbaum (1938).
21 Becker (1963), 9; see also, generally Rosenberg, Stebbins, and Turowetz (1982).
22 Becker (1963), 31–4 and Schur (1971), 30, 52; for the case of mental illness see Goffman (1961), Scheff (1966), and David Mechanic (1966, 1969).
23 Rosenberg, Stebbins, and Turowetz (1982), 17
24 Schur (1971), 162
25 A recent summary of this criticism is found in Glassner (1982); see also Sagarin (1975), 129–44.
26 Scott (1969)
27 David Thomas (1982)
28 See, for example, Maître (1987); this approach is also used to good effect in the recent feminist accounts of the experience of handicap found in Browne, Connors, and Stern (1985), Deegan and Brooks (1985), and Fine and Asch (1988).
29 See the debate between Fred Davis (1961) and R.H. Turner (1972).
30 See Kleck, Ono, and Hastorf (1966) and Kleck (1968).
31 Davis (1961)
32 See Jones (1984), Page (1984), 1–24, and Minaire et al. (1987).
33 For surveys of results, see Duval (1982) and English (1977).
34 Wright (1983)
35 See Yuker, Block, and Young (1966), Shontz (1977), Roessler and Bolton (1978), Cruickshank (1971), and Herman, Zanna, and Higgins (1986).
36 For reviews, see Richardson et al. (1961), English (1971), Richardson

(1976), and Siller (1986); cf. Féard et al. (1987).

37 Siller (1986)

38 Siller (1986), 208

39 This is the view taken by Jim Thomas (1982), but cf. Schur (1980), who contends that even politicized deviance research is merely descriptive and not normative.

40 See Haber and Smith (1971), Gove (1976), and Smith (1975).

41 Finkelstein (1980)

42 See, in particular, Scotch (1984); also Bowe (1978, 1980), Anspach (1979), Feinblatt (1981), and Simmons (1982).

43 See Oliver (1984); also (1990), 117–18. For a history of the politicization of disablement, see Driedger (1989).

44 See Canada, Health and Welfare (1981) for some historical suggestions.

45 See Lepofsky and Bickenbach (1985).

46 See Frieden (1978), Stoddard (1978), Dejong (1979, 1983), Stoddard and Brown (1980), and Center for Independent Living (1982).

47 See Wolfensberger (1972).

48 Scotch (1984)

49 See generally, Crewe and Zola (1983), Sutherland (1981), and Oliver (1990), 118–23.

50 See Barker (1948), Meyerson (1971), and Sidney Jordan (1971); Barker, however, uses the analysis to stress the need for the burden of 'adjustment' to fall on people with disabilities.

51 See Wright (1983) in her discussion of status in ch. 2 and Safilios-Rothschild (1970) in ch. 3.

52 See Gliedman and Roth (1980) and Roth (1985), 41 where the debate concerning the appropriateness of the minority analysis is said to be 'largely over.'

53 See Padden and Humphries (1988) and Sacks (1989).

54 Oliver (1990)

55 Ibid., 105–6, 121–2

56 See Hahn (1982, 1983, 1984a).

57 Hahn (1987), 182

58 Kallen (1982, 1989)

59 Kallen (1989), xi

60 Ibid., 50

61 David Thomas (1982), 18

62 Canada, Parliamentary Special Committee on the Disabled and the Handicapped (1981), Canada, Parliamentary Committee on Human

Rights (1985), and Ontario SARC (1988)

63 Bill C-78, An act to amend certain acts with respect to persons with disabilities (first reading, 5 May 1992)

64 Americans with Disabilities Act of 1990 P.L. No. 101–336, 104 Stat. 327 (1990); and see Canada, House of Commons Standing Committee on the Status of Disabled Persons (1990), 14–15.

65 Canada, Parliamentary Special Committee on the Disabled and the Handicapped (1981), 4

66 See Universal Declaration of Human Rights, United Nations General Assembly resolution 217A (III) (10 December 1948); Declaration on the Rights of Mentally Retarded Persons, United Nations General Assembly resolution 2856 (XXVI) (20 December 1971); and Declaration on the Rights of Disabled Persons, United Nations General Assembly resolution 3447 (XXX) (9 December 1975).

67 For the notion of 'manifesto rights,' see Feinberg (1980), 153.

68 See Scotch (1984) and Funk (1987), both of whom described these developments in detail.

69 347 U.S. 483 (1954)

70 See Liachowitz (1988), 37–41.

71 The most recent version of the act is at 29 U.S.C., Sections 7001–796 (Supp. V, 1981).

72 An exhaustive review of the issues raised by section 504 is found in Wegner (1983); I follow Wegner's breakdown of the issues.

73 For a helpful survey of the state legislation, focusing on the legislative definition of 'handicap,' see O'Connor (1988).

74 For this ongoing tension see O'Connor (1988) and Parry (1988).

75 Rehabilitation, Comprehensive Services and Developmental Disabilities Amendments of 1978 P.L. 95-602, section 122 (a) (6) (c) 92 Sta. 2985

76 Bickenbach (1991)

77 29 U.S.C., sections 791–3

78 See Cook (1987); and generally see Herr, Arons, and Wallace (1983).

79 Wegner (1983), 405–6

80 See the partial adoption of the view that a failure to provide accommodation is a form of discrimination in *Southeastern Community College v. Davis* 442 U.S. 397 (1979) and *School Board of Nassau County, Florida v. Arline* 107 S.Ct. 1123 (1987). Both cases argue for a case-by-case approach to reasonable accommodation expressly in order to avoid the effects of stereotyping.

81 See *Harvard Law Review* (1984).

82 28 C.F.R., sections 39.105(a) and 39.160(d)

83 See the review in Cook (1987) and Wegner (1983), 445–51.
84 *Griggs v. Duke Power Co.* 401 U.S. 424 (1971)
85 P.L. 101–336, 42 U.S.C.A. (West Supp. 1991)
86 42 U.S.C. sec. 1981
87 Abella (1984); Canada Employment Equity Act R.S.C. 1985 (2d) Supp. c. 23 (cf. the Ontario NDP's (pre-election) proposed Ontario act, Bill 172); and L.R.Q. c. E 20.1
88 A strong advocate for this approach is Oliver (1990).
89 Gliedman and Roth (1980), esp. 37–8, 411–12
90 Ibid., 411–12
91 See, in general, Strauss and Corbin (1988) and King (1985).
92 See the discussion on coping, in Burish and Bradley (1983).
93 See, in particular, Hahn (1985, 1987).
94 Hahn (1987), 182
95 Rains, Kitsuse, Duster, and Friedson (1975); and cf. Bartel and Guskin (1971) where it is suggested that 'handicapped persons' are created by the 'rationalized' pity of physicians, psychologists, and education and rehabilitation experts.
96 Burgdorf (1980), 11
97 Canada, House of Commons Standing Committee on the Status of Disabled Persons (1990), 2
98 Padden and Humphries (1988), 44
99 Kenneth Jernigon at the 1985 convention of the National Federation of the Blind; quoted in Gartner and Joe (1987), 2
100 The term, and a great deal of thought about the problem, can be found in Minow (1990).
101 Goffman (1963), 114
102 Liggett (1988); and cf. Anspach (1979), 765, who argues that although political activism is 'phenomenologically troublesome' for the 'normal' because it does not fit the common-sense image of the pathetic, docile, and pitiable persons with a disability, it need not be ineffective.
103 The *locus classicus* of the principle is found in Wolfensberger (1972); as for excesses in the name of the principle, see Perrin (1982).
104 Thus, in the quality-of-life assessment instrument known as PASS, Wolf Wolfensberger and L. Glenn have sought to assess service care for people with mild to profound developmental disabilities in terms of the 'normality' of setting in which the services are provided; see Wolfensberger and Glenn (1973).
105 In part as a response to the misuse of the principle of normalization, Wolfensberger (1983) has proposed that it be replaced by the principle

of 'social role valorization,' the principle that people with disabilities should be valued as they are, special needs and all.

106 David Thomas writes that the 'heroic handicapped' individual poses a problem since it is thought by 'normals' that 'if such achievements are possible for some, then all that can be holding back other equally handicapped people is lack of ability or insufficient motivation' (1982: 5). Compare Zola and the dual message of success stories: people with disabilities can achieve much; but 'if we fail, it is our problem, our personality defect, our weakness' (1982: 204–5).

Chapter 6

1 See generally English (1977) and Siller (1986).
2 For this discussion see Le Disert (1987), 255–6 and Stiker (1982) *passim* and summarized in Stiker (1987).
3 Gould (1981)
4 Rose, Lewontin, and Kamain (1984)
5 See Urbach (1987), 444–8; the Old Testament often speaks of impairments, usually contagious diseases, as being God's expression of displeasure for transgression, e.g., Deuteronomy 28:20, 28:22, and 28:35; see Stiker (1987).
6 On the changling in history, see Haffter (1968).
7 See Gellman (1959), Fiedler (1978, 1984), Gilman (1988), Verville (1981), and Thurer (1981).
8 See Orzack (1971), Foucault (1965), and Szasz (1961, 1970a, 1970b).
9 Sontag (1979, 1988)
10 Sontag (1979), 55–6
11 In *Traynor v. Turnage, Administrator, Veterans' Administration et al.* 485 U.S. 535 (1988) the petitioners were denied educational assistance benefits after being honourably discharged from the armed services on the grounds that their disability – alcoholism – was the result of 'wilful misconduct.' A bare four to three majority of the Supreme Court held that it was reasonable for the Veterans Administration to adopt as an administrative rule the conclusive presumption that alcoholism was the result of wilful misconduct. And see *Greene v. Union Pacific Railroad and Co.* 548 F. Supp. 3 (1981) (obesity is not a handicap since it is not 'immutable').
12 Gilman (1988), 4
13 For a statement and discussion of the 'just world' hypothesis, see Lerner and Miller (1978), and more generally Jones (1984), ch. 2.
14 For the complex and subtle shifts in views on disablement from Jew-

ish to Christian thought, see Stiker (1982) and (1987), 169–70.

15 Roberts (1990), 70–8

16 Augustine, *City of God*, Book XVI, ch. 8

17 Stone (1984) and Golding and Middleton (1982), ch. 2, 'God's Poor and the Devil's'; and generally Garraty (1972) and Corrigan and Corrigan (1979).

18 Parry and Parry (1979); and for the impact of the COS on developments in Canada, see Simmons (1982).

19 This is described by Satamurti (1979).

20 Liachowitz (1988), ch. 4, 'Disability and Charity: Rehabilitation for Civilians'

21 See the discussion in Waltzer (1983), 72–3.

22 Oliver (1990), esp. ch. 6

23 For studies of the stigma associated with welfare in the UK see Golding and Middleton (1982).

24 Frankena (1973), 47

25 In the Quran the verb for alms*giving* has as its primary meaning to thrive by the blessing of God and become purer. Roberts (1990), 70.

26 See the recent study by Reich (1990), 278–9.

27 Waltzer (1983), 92

28 Reich (1991), 278–9

29 Barry (1965), ch. 3 makes this point clearly.

30 Beveridge (1942)

31 I rely for this example and for much of what follows on Braybrooke (1987).

32 The phrase comes from Fried (1978), 67.

33 This is David Braybrooke's definition of 'course-of-life needs' (1987: 29).

34 This is a common definition that is based on John Rawls's characterization of 'primary social goods' as goods that every rational person is presumed to want; see Rawls (1971), 62 and Daniels (1985), 26.

35 See Waltzer (1983), 65, 75–6.

36 This literature is vast; see references in Braybrooke (1987), 20–1 and 179.

37 See Titmuss (1968) and more recently Bill Jordan (1987), 98.

38 See Torjman (1988) for a review.

39 Braybrooke (1987)

40 The views of Amartya Sen on this question are primarily contained in Sen (1980, 1982, 1984a, 1984b, 1985, 1990).

41 This debate is the topic of Ignatieff (1984).

42 This is discussed in Bill Jordan (1987), 19–30.
43 See Vlastos (1962) and discussions in Waltzer (1983), 75 and 82 and Braybrooke (1987), 133–58.
44 For this classical scheme, see Finnis (1980), ch. 3. More modern treatments of justice tend to focus on one of these three and treat the other two as subsidiary.
45 I am following here the classical work of Atiyah and Cane (1987), 472–76.
46 See Murphy and Coleman (1984), 174–84.
47 See, for example, Ontario's The Compensation for Victims of Crime Act R.S.O. (1990) C.24.
48 Cover (1988)
49 The best account of this can be found in Stapleton (1986); see also Atiyah and Cane (1987), 415–36 and Calabresi (1970). The argument has been forcefully made by Ison (1977), 'As a system of reparation for personal injury, tort liability is hopeless compared with almost any conceivable alternative.'
50 This analysis is found in Burton (1983); cf. Weiler (1986).
51 Pryor (1990a, 1990b)
52 This approach usually contains provision for a guaranteed minimum income; see Ison (1978) and Palmer (1973).
53 See, for example, Lewis (1981) and Pryor (1990a, 1990b).
54 See Stapleton (1986), 158–77 for a survey of some other options.
55 Atiyah and Cane (1987), 443
56 See Barr (1987), 69–74 for examples.
57 Rawls (1971)
58 Okun (1975) is the prominent source of this belief.
59 Pigou (1952), 10
60 For two admirable reviews of the conceptual problems brought on by 'welfarism,' first as a standard of living, and second as an explication of the object of equality, see Sen (1986) and Ronald Dworkin (1981a, 1981b).
61 Sen (1984a), 307, 309

Chapter 7

1 The dilemma is explored in various contexts, including disablement, in Minow (1990).
2 For Aristotle's treatment of equality, in the sense of proportionality, see Aristotle (1925).

3 Minow (1990)
4 The clearest development of this is presented by Rae et al. (1981).
5 Canada, Parliamentary Committee on Human Rights (1985)
6 *Dennis v. U.S.* 341 U.S. 494 (1951), quoted by Mr Justice McIntyre in *Andrews v. Law Society of B.C.* (1989) 56 D.L.R. (4th) 1.
7 Canadian Charter of Rights and Freedoms, Part I of the Constitution Act of 1982
8 For a Canadian account, see Harp and Hofley (1980).
9 For a helpful review, see Grabb (1990), ch. 7; see also Brian Turner (1986).
10 See Brian Turner (1986), 25–26 and Gellner (1979).
11 See Rae and Yates (1981).
12 This is the somewhat whimsical calculation found in Rae and Yates (1981), 133.
13 It is mysterious how this confusion can persist in the case of disabilities; but it does. In Fraser Institute (1983), for example, the authors quote Kurt Vonnegut, Jr's short story 'Harrison Bergeron' which describes a future society where people are truly 'equal': the Handicapper-General ensures that nobody is smarter, stronger, better-looking, or quicker than anyone else. People with normal eyesight are required to wear glasses with thick, wavy lenses. The point of including this story, one presumes, is to show the error of affirmative action programming. The 'paranoia about equality' that this story represents is considered by Professor Constance B. Backhouse, Chair, Board of Inquiry in *Re Roberts and Ministry of Health*, unreported.
14 Ronald Dworkin (1977b)
15 There are many expressions of the presumptive account, but I have selected the wording found in Isaiah Berlin's famous essay (1980).
16 The 'similarly situated' legal test is usually attributed to Tussman and tenBroek (1949); for a standard critique of it in Canadian law, see David Baker (1987).
17 On the 'emptiness' of formal equality, see Lucas (1971) and Westen (1982).
18 See Mr Justice McIntyre in *Andrews v. Law Society of B.C.* [1989] 2 W.W.R. 289, 301, where he suggests that if applied 'literally' it could be used to justify the Nuremberg Laws of Hitler. See Lepofsky and Schwartz (1988) and the level-headed reply in Gibson (1990), 70–5.
19 Bayefsky (1985), 3–11
20 This is Robert A. Veatch's claim about what he calls 'ontological equality' (1986: 121–3).

21 Ronald Dworkin (1977a), speaking of John Rawls's basis for justice as fairness in Rawls (1971); see similar characterizations by Vlastos (1962), Williams (1962), and Finnis (1980), 162–3 and 173–5.

22 See Brudner (1986) who makes this suggestion.

23 Ibid., 469, 496–7

24 One of the best treatments of this distinction in legal terms can be found in ch. 1 of Vizkelety (1987).

25 See the treatment of this political phenomenon in Beitz (1989); 58–67.

26 Thus, for example, John Baker (1987), 26–30 suggests that any form of social superiority is a violation of equality of respect.

27 McCluskey (1988)

28 Ibid., 880

29 See Vizkelety (1987), 89–96.

30 Ibid., 99–104

31 See *Andrews v. Law Society of B.C.* (1989) 56 D.L.R. (4th) 1, Gibson (1990), 117–22, and Lepofsky and Bickenbach (1985).

32 Madame Justice Wilson, writing for the court in *R. v. Turpin* (1989) 69 C.R. (3d) 97 said: 'It is only when one of the four equality rights has been denied with discrimination that the values protected by s. 15 are threatened and the court's legitimate role as the protector of such values comes into play.'

33 Abella (1984), 2–3

34 This basic distinction is most clearly described in Rae et al. (1981), ch. 4. For a Canadian human rights case where this issue is discussed see *Cameron v. Nel-Gor Castle Nursing Home* (1984) 5 C.H.R.R. D/2170, D/2180.

35 Understandably, this claim is usually made by egalitarianists who argue that the first two senses of equality of opportunity are not true principles of equality, since they either guarantee or countenance social inequalities. See John Baker (1987), ch. 5, Nielsen (1985), and Norman (1987).

36 Much of this is speculative, since our courts have still to interpret these phrases, but see Bayefsky (1985), 12–25 and Gibson (1990), 62–6; cf. Michelman (1969), who tries to argue that equality of opportunity includes an 'absolute assurance' that the minimum needs of all will be met.

37 See Judith Welch Wegner's treatment of section 504 of the Rehabilitation Act (1983: 437–42).

38 Thus, C.E. Baker (1983), 959, 963–4 argues that guarantees of re-

sources and opportunities flow directly from equality of respect.

39 Wegner identifies this problem (1983: 439).

40 I am following here the classic liberal statement found in Rawls (1971), 65–6, 72–3. Rawls's own distributive scheme includes a 'fair equality of opportunity' principle but he modifies it in ways irrelevant to the present discussion.

41 Daniels (1985)

42 Ibid., 108

43 Daniels (1985) believes he can distinguish impairments and disabilities in this fashion because he relies on a strongly 'realistic' account of health and disease that makes it possible to unambiguously characterize transcultural 'disfunctioning.'

44 See Brian Barry (1989), 222–4.

45 See MacKinnon (1987), 32–45.

46 See the discussion of equality in these terms in Lucas (1971) and Engelhardt (1982, 1986).

47 See Collignon (1986).

48 This is how Ronald Dworkin characterizes the problem (1981a).

49 See McCluskey (1988) and Scales (1988).

50 This view of social egalitarianism is part of the analysis of the rights of equal citizenship found in Karst (1983).

51 See Fiss (1976) and Michelman (1987).

52 *Andrews v. Law Society of B.C.* (1989) 56 D.L.R. (4th) 1

53 *U.S. v. Carolene Products Co.* 304 U.S. 144, at 153 fn. 4 (1938) and *San Antonio Independent Schools Dist. v. Rodriquez* 411 U.S. 1, 28 (1973); see also the application of this level of 'suspect classification' to (mental) disablement in *Cleburne Living Center Inc. v. City of Cleburne* 473 U.S. 432 (1985).

54 Michelman (1987), 95

55 This is certainly the approach taken by Judith Welch Wegner (1983: 442–5).

56 See Stapleton (1986), who argues that there are no intrinsic reasons for this preference, although there may be attitudinal reasons that will guarantee it in the future.

57 Tawney (1931)

58 Waltzer (1983)

59 Or more precisely, welfarism is the 'view that the goodness of a state of affairs can be judged entirely by the goodness of the utilities in that state' (Sen 1980: 195); see also Sen (1979).

60 Ronald Dworkin (1981a), 186

61 Rawls (1971), 60–5
62 Ronald Dworkin (1981b)
63 See Sen (1986) for examples.
64 See Ronald Dworkin (1981a), *passim*, and discussion of welfare maximization above.
65 Sen describes this as a problem of 'informational inadequacy' (1980).
66 Sen (1984a), 312
67 Ronald Dworkin (1981b), 288
68 Ibid., 307
69 Ibid., 313
70 Ibid., 315
71 Ibid., 314–15: 'we may say that someone who cannot play basketball like Wilt Chamberlain, paint like Piero, or make money like Geneen, suffers from an (especially common) handicap.'
72 See Sen (1980, 1982, 1984a, 1984b, 1985, 1986, 1990).
73 Sen (1982), 29–30
74 Sen (1986)
75 Sen (1990), 114
76 Sen (1984a), 315–16
77 Sen (1980), 160
78 Canada, House of Commons Standing Committee on the Status of Disabled Persons (1990)
79 tenBroek (1966), 867–8

References

Abella, Judge Rosalie S. (1984) *Equality in Employment: A Royal Commission Report*. Ottawa: Canadian Government Publishing Centre

Advisory Council on Social Security (1946) *Permanent and Total Disability: A Report to Senate Committee on Finance*, 80th Congress, 2nd Session, Senate Document 1621

Agich, George J. (1983) 'Disease and Value: A Rejection of the Value-Neutrality Thesis.' *Theoretical Medicine* 4: 27

Albert, Daniel A., Ronald Munson, and Michael D. Resnik (1988) *Reasoning in Medicine: An Introduction to Clinical Inference*. Baltimore: Johns Hopkins University Press

Albrecht, Gary L. (ed.) (1976) *The Sociology of Physical Disability and Rehabilitation*. Pittsburgh: University of Pittsburgh Press

Albrecht, Gary L. (ed.) (1981) *Cross National Rehabilitation Policies: A Sociological Perspective*. Beverly Hills: Sage Publications

Albrecht, Gary L., and Judith A. Levy (1981) 'Constructing Disabilities as Social Problems,' in Gary L. Albrecht (ed.)

Alexander, Karl L. (1976) 'Disability and Stratification Processes,' in Gary L. Albrecht (ed.)

American Medical Association (1988) *Guides to the Evaluation of Permanent Impairment*, 3rd ed., Alan Engelberg (ed.). Chicago: American Medical Association

Anderson, Bent (1966) *Work or Support: An Economic and Social Analysis of Substitute Permanent Employment*. Paris: Organisation for Economic Co-operation and Development

Anspach, Renee R. (1979) 'From Stigma to Identity Politics: Political Activism among the Physically Disabled and Former Mental Patients.' *Social Science and Medicine* 13: 765

Antonck, Rochard G., and Hanooch Liveneh (1988) *The Measurement of Attitudes toward People with Disabilities*. Springfield, Ill.: Charles C. Thomas

Aristotle (1925) *Ethica Nicomachea* and *Politica*, W.D. Ross (trans.). Oxford: Oxford University Press

Atiyah, P.S., and Peter Cane (1987) *Accidents, Compensation and the Law*, 4th ed. London: Weidenfeld and Nicolson

Augustine (1972) *The City of God*. David Knowles (ed.). Harmondsworth: Penguin

Baker, C.E. (1983) 'Outcome Equality or Equality of Respect: The Substantive Content of Equal Protection.' *University of Pennsylvania Law Review* 131: 933

Baker, David (1987) 'The Changing Norms of Equality in the Supreme Courts of Canada.' *The Supreme Court Law Review* 9: 497

Baker, John (1987) *Arguing for Equality*. London: Verso

Barker, R.C. (1948) 'The Social Psychology of Physical Disability.' *Journal of Social Issues* 4: 29

Barr, Nicholas (1987) *The Economics of the Welfare State*. London: Weidenfeld and Nicolson

Barry, Brian (1965) *Political Argument*. New York: Humanities Press
– (1989) *Theories of Justice*. Berkeley; Cal.: University of California Press

Barry, J.R. (1971) 'Behavioral Classification of the Physically Disabled.' *Psychological Aspects of Disability* 18: 136

Bartel, M., and S. Guskin (1971) 'A Handicap as a Social Phenomenon,' in William M. Cruickshank (ed.)

Bauer, Doreen (1989) *Foundations of Physical Rehabilitation*. New York: Churchill Livingstone

Bayefsky, Anne F. (1985) 'Defining Equality Rights,' in Anne F. Bayefsky and Mary Eberts (eds.)

Bayefsky, Anne F., and Mary Eberts (eds.) (1985) *Equality Rights and the Canadian Charter of Rights and Freedoms*. Toronto: Carswell

Becker, Howard (1963) *Outsiders: Studies in the Sociology of Deviance*. New York: Free Press

Beitz, Charles R. (1989) *Political Equality*. Princeton, NJ: Princeton University Press

Berger, Peter L., and Thomas Luckman (1965) *The Social Construction of Reality: A Treatise on the Sociology of Knowledge*. Garden City, NJ: Doubleday

Berkowitz, Edward D. (1985) 'Social Influences on Rehabilitation Planning: Introductory Remarks,' in Leonard G. Perlman and Gary F. Austin (eds.)

- (1987) *Disabled Policy: America's Programs for the Handicapped*. New York: Cambridge University Press

Berkowitz, Monroe (1984) 'Benefit-Cost Analysis in Rehabilitation Medicine,' in Carl V. Granger and Glen E. Gresham (eds.)

Berkowitz, Monroe, and John F. Burton Jr (1987) *Permanent Disability Benefits in Workers' Compensation*. Kalamazoo, Mich.: W.E. Upjohn Institute for Employment Research

Berkowitz, Monroe, and M. Anne Hill (1986) 'The Labor Market: An Overview,' in Monroe Berkowitz and M. Anne Hill (eds.)

Berkowitz, Monroe, and Anne M. Hill (eds.) (1986) *Disability and the Labor Market*. Ithaca, NY: ILR Press

Berkowitz, Monroe, William G. Johnson, and Edward H. Murphy (1976) *Public Policy toward Disability*. New York: Praeger

Berlin, Isaiah (1977) 'Two Concepts of Liberty,' in *Four Essays on Liberty*. Oxford: Oxford University Press

- (1980) 'Equality,' in *Concepts and Categories*. Oxford: Oxford University Press

Beveridge, Sir William (1942) *Social Insurance and Allied Services*. New York: Macmillan

Bickenbach, Jerome E. (1991) 'AIDS and Physical Disability,' in Christine Overall and William P. Zion (eds.) *Perspectives on AIDS*. Toronto: Oxford University Press

Birenbaum, Arnold, and Henry Lesieur (1982) 'Social Values and Expectations,' in M. Rosenberg, R. Stebbins, and A. Turowetz (eds.)

Blaxter, Mildred (1976) *The Meaning of Disability: A Sociological Study of Impairment*. London: Heinemann

Bogdan, Robert, and Douglas Biklen (1981) 'Handicapism,' in Allen D. Spiegel and Simon Podair (eds.)

Boorse, Christopher (1975) 'On the Distinction between Disease and Health.' *Philosophy and Public Affairs* 5: 49

- (1977) 'Health as a Theoretical Concept.' *Philosophy of Science* 44: 542

Bowe, Frank (1978) *Handicapping America: Barriers to Disabled People*. New York: Harper and Row

- (1980) *Rehabilitating America: Toward Independence for Disabled and Elderly People*. New York: Harper and Row

Braybrooke, David (1987) *Meeting Needs*. Princeton, NJ: Princeton University Press

Breslow, L. (1972) 'A Quantitative Approach to the WHO Definition of Health: Physical, Mental, and Social Well-being,' *International Journal of Epidemiology* 1: 347

Brown, Joan (1977) *A Hit-and-Miss Affair: Policies for Disabled Peopled in Canada*. Ottawa: Canadian Council of Social Development
– (1984) *The Disability Income System*. London, Ont.: Policy Studies Institute
Brown, Robert (1977) 'Physical Illness and Mental Health.' *Philosophy and Public Affairs* 7: 17
Browne, Susan E., Debra Connors, and Nancy Stern (eds.) (1985) *With the Power of Each Breath: A Disabled Women's Anthology*. Pittsburgh: CLEIS Press
Brudner, Alan (1986) 'What Are Reasonable Limits to Equality Rights?' *Canadian Bar Review* 64: 469
Burgdorf, Robert L. (ed.) (1980) *The Legal Rights of Handicapped Persons: Cases, Materials, and Text*. Baltimore: Paul H. Brookes
Burish, Thomas G. (ed.) (1983) *Coping with Chronic Disease*. New York: Academic Press
Burish, Thomas G., and Laurence A. Bradley (1983) 'Coping with Chronic Disease: Definitions and Issues,' in Thomas G. Burish (ed.)
Burkhauser, Richard V., and Robert Haveman (1982) *Disability and Work: The Economics of American Public Policy*. Baltimore: Johns Hopkins University Press
Burton, John F. (1983) 'Compensation for Permanent Partial Disabilities,' in John D. Worrell (ed.) *Safety and the Workplace: Incentives and Disincentives in Workers' Compensation*. Ithaca, NY: ILR Press
– (1986) 'The Role of the Permanent Disability Rating Schedule in the Ontario Workers' Compensation Program,' Appendix A of Paul Weiler, *A Report for the Ontario Workers' Compensation Board*. Ottawa: Ministry of Labour
Bury, Michael R. (1979) 'Disablement in Society: Towards an Integrated Perspective.' *International Journal of Rehabilitation Research* 2: 34
– (1987) 'Social Aspects of Rehabilitation.' *International Journal of Rehabilitation Research* (Supplement 5) 10: 25
Calabresi, Guido (1970) *The Cost of Accidents*. New Haven, Conn.: Yale University Press
Calabresi, Guido, and Philip Bobbitt (1978) *Tragic Choices*. New York: W.W. Norton
Callahan, Daniel (1982) 'The WHO Definition of "Health,"' in Tom L. Beauchamp and LeRoy Walters (eds.) *Contemporary Issues in Bioethics*, 2nd ed. Belmont, Cal.: Wadsworth
Canada, Health and Welfare Canada (1981) *Disabled Persons in Canada*. Ottawa: Minister of Supply and Services Canada
Canada, House of Commons Standing Committee on Human Rights and

the Status of Disabled Persons (1990) *A Consensus for Action: The Economic Integration of Disabled Persons*. Ottawa: House of Commons

Canada, House of Commons Standing Committee on Human Rights and the Status of Disabled Persons (1990) *Minutes of Proceedings and Evidence*, Issue No. 42. Ottawa: House of Commons

Canada, House of Commons Standing Committee on Justice and Legal Affairs (1985) *Equality for All*. Ottawa: Queen's Printer

Canada, Parliamentary Special Committee on the Disabled and the Handicapped (1981) *Obstacles*. Ottawa: Minister of Supply and Services Canada

Canada, Statistics Canada (1988) *The Health and Activity Limitation Survey – User's Guide*. Ottawa: Statistics Canada

Canguilhem, Georges (1988) *Ideology and Rationality in the History of the Life Sciences*. Cambridge, Mass.: MIT Press

– (1989) *The Normal and the Pathological*. New York: Zone Press

Caplan, Arthur L., Daniel Callahan, and Janet Haas (1987) 'Ethical and Policy Issues in Rehabilitation Medicine.' *Hastings Center Report* 17: 1

Cassidy, Harry M. (1943) *Social Security and Reconstruction in Canada*. Toronto: Ryerson

Center for Independent Living (1982) 'Independent Living The Right to Choose,' in M.G. Eisenberg, C. Griggins, and R.J. Duval (eds.) *Disabled People as Second-Class Citizens*. New York: Springer

Chamberlain, Anne (1988) 'The Rehabilitation Team and Functional Assessment,' in C. John Goodwill and M. Anne Chamberlain (eds.)

Coles, Gerald (1987) *The Learning Mystique: A Critical Look at 'Learning Disabilities.'* New York: Pantheon

Collignon, Frederick C. (1986) 'The Role of Reasonable Accommodation in Employing Disabled Persons in Private Industry,' in Monroe Berkowitz and Anne M. Hill (eds.)

Colverz, Alain, and Jean Marie Robine (1986) 'Problems Encountered in Using the Concepts of Impairment, Disability, and Handicap in a Health Assessment Survey of the Elderly in Upper Normandy.' *International Rehabilitative Medicine* 8: 18

Conley, Ronald W. (1965) *The Economics of Vocational Rehabilitation*. Baltimore: Johns Hopkins University Press

Conners, Debra (1985) 'Disability, Sexism and the Social Order,' in Susan E. Browne, Debra Connors, and Nancy Stern (eds.)

Conrad, Peter, and Joseph W. Schneider (1980) *Deviance and Medicalization: From Badness to Sickness*. St. Louis: C.V. Mosby

Cook, Timothy M. (1987) 'The Scope of the Right to Meaningful Access and the Defense of Undue Burdens under the Disability Civil Rights Laws.' *Loyola of Los Angeles Law Review* 20: 1471

Cooper, David (1971) *Psychiatry and Anti-Psychiatry*. New York: Ballantine

Cornes, P., and H.M. Bochel (1987) 'Fitness for Work: Medicolegal Assessment of Residual Disability and Employment Handicap.' *International Journal of Rehabilitation Research* (Supplement 5) 10: 309

Corrigan, Philip, and Val Corrigan (1979) 'State Formation and Social Policy until 1871,' in Noel Parry, Michael Rustin, and Carole Satyamurti (eds.)

Coughlan, Anthony (1988) 'Psychological Aspects of Disability,' in C. John Goodwill and M. Anne Chamberlain (eds.)

Cover, Robert M. (1988) 'Social Security and Constitutional Entitlement,' in Theodore R. Marmor and Jerry L. Mashaw (eds.)

Crewe, Nancy M. (1987) 'Assessment of Physical Functioning,' in Brian Bolton (ed.) *Handbook of Measurement and Evaluation in Rehabilitation*, 2nd ed. Baltimore: Paul H. Brookes

Crewe, Nancy M., et al. (eds.) (1983) *Independent Living for Physically Disabled People*. San Francisco: Jossey-Bass

Cruickshank, William M. (ed.) (1971) *Psychology of Exceptional Children and Youth*, 3rd ed. Englewood Cliffs, NJ: Prentice-Hall

CSICIDH/QCICIDH (1990) 'Comments on the Proposition of Revision of the Handicap Concept.' *ICIDH International Network*

– (1991) 'The Handicap Creation Process.' *ICIDH International Network*

Daniels, Norman (1985) *Just Health Care*. Cambridge: Cambridge University Press

Davies, Brian Meredith (1988) 'Social Factors in Disability,' in C. John Goodwill and M. Anne Chamberlain (eds.)

Davis, Fred (1961) 'Deviance Disavowal: The Management of Strained Interaction by the Visibly Handicapped.' *Social Problems* 9: 120

Deegan, Mary Jo, and Nancy A. Brooks (1985) *Women and Disability: The Double Handicap*. New Brunswick, NJ: Transaction Books

DeJong, Gerben (1979) 'Independent Living: From Social Movement to Analytic Paradigm.' *Archives of Physical Medicine and Rehabilitation* 60: 438

– (1983) 'Defining and Implementing the Independent Living Concept,' in Nancy M. Crewe et al. (eds.)

Donaldson, Susanne W., Conlin C. Wagner, and Glen E. Gresham (1980) 'A Unified ADL Evaluation Form,' in Brian Bolton and Daniel W. Cook (eds.) *Rehabilitation Client Assessment*. Baltimore: University Park Press

Donzelot, Jacques (1979) *The Policing of Families*. New York: Pantheon

Driedger, Diane (1989) *The Last Civil Rights Movement*. London: Hurst

Dubos, Rene (1961) *Mirage of Health.* New York: Anchor

Duckworth, Derek (1983) *The Classification and Measurement of Disablement.* London: Department of Health and Social Security

– (1984) 'The Need for a Standard Terminology and Classification of Disablement,' in Carl V. Granger and Glen E. Gresham (eds.)

Dunt, D.R., J.M. Kaufert, R. Corkhill, A.L. Creese, S. Green, and D. Locker (1980) 'Technique for Precisely Measuring Activities of Daily Living.' *Community Medicine* 2: 120

Duval, Richard J. (1982) 'Psychological Theories of Physical Disability: New Perspectives,' in M.G. Eisenberg, C. Griggins, and R.J. Duval (eds.) *Disabled People as Second-Class Citizens.* New York: Springer

Dworkin, Gerald (1988) *The Theory and Practice of Autonomy.* Cambridge: Cambridge University Press

Dworkin, Ronald (1977a) 'Taking Rights Seriously,' in *Taking Rights Seriously.* Cambridge, Mass.: Harvard University Press

– (1977b) 'Reverse Discrimination,' in *Taking Rights Seriously.* Cambridge, Mass.: Harvard University Press

– (1981a) 'What Is Equality? Part 1: Equality of Welfare.' *Philosophy and Public Affairs* 10: 185

– (1981b) 'What Is Equality? Part 2: Equality of Resources.' *Philosophy and Public Affairs* 10: 283

Eisenberg, Myron G. (1982) 'Disability as Stigma,' in M.G. Eisenberg, C. Griggins, and R.J. Duval (eds.) *Disabled People as Second-Class Citizens.* New York: Springer

Emanuel, Han, Eric H. De Gier, and Peter A.B. Kalker Konijn (eds.) (1987) *Disability Benefits: Factors Determining Application and Awards.* Greenwich, Conn.: JAI Press

Engel, George (1977) 'The Need for a New Medical Model: A Challenge for Biomedicine.' *Science* 196: 129

Engelhardt, H. Tristram Jr (1982) 'Health Care Allocations: Responses to the Unjust, the Unfortunate and the Undesirable,' in Earl E. Shelp (ed.) *Justice and Health Care.* Dordrecht: Reidel

– (1984) 'Clinical Problems and the Concept of Disease,' in L. Nordenfelt and B.I.B. Lindahl (eds.)

– (1986) *The Foundations of Bioethics.* New York: Oxford University Press

English, R. William (1971) 'Correlates of Stigma toward Physically Disabled Persons.' *Rehabilitation Research and Practice Review* 2: 1

– (1977) 'The Application of Personality Theory to Explain Psychological Reactions to Physical Disability,' in Joseph Stubbins (ed.) *Social and Psychological Aspects of Disability.* Baltimore: University Park Press

Erlanger, H., and W. Roth (1985) 'Disability Policy: The Parts and the Whole.' *American Behavioral Scientist* 28: 320

Evans-Pritchard, E. (1937) *Witchcraft, Oracles and Magic amongst the Azande.* Oxford: Clarendon Press

Farrell, Ronald A., and Victoria Lynn Swigert (1988) *Social Deviance*, 3rd ed. Belmont, Cal.: Wadsworth

Féard, S., J.-P. Deschamps, R. Guéguen, and J. Jacques (1987) 'Stéréotypes de valeurs de l'enfant handicapé chez l'enfant valide,' in Jean-Marc Alby and Patrick Sansoy (eds.) *Handicap, Vécu, Évalué.* Grenoble: La Pensée Sauvage

Feinberg, Joel (1980) 'The Nature and Value of Rights,' in *Rights, Justice and the Bounds of Liberty.* Princeton, NJ: Princeton University Press

Feinblatt, Arlene (1981) 'Political Activism among Physically Disabled Individuals.' *Archives of Physical Medicine and Rehabilitation* 62: 360

Fendoglio, John A. (1974) 'The Severely Disabled – A Rehabilitation Challenge,' in A Beatrix Cobb (ed.) *Special Problems in Rehabilitation.* Springfield, Ill.: Charles C. Thomas

Fiedler, Leslie A. (1978) *Freaks, Myths, and Images of the Secret Self.* New York: Simon and Schuster

– (1984) 'The Tyranny of the Normal.' *Hastings Center Report* 14: 40

Fine, Michelle, and Adrienne Asch (eds). (1988) *Women with Disabilities: Essays in Psychology, Culture, and Politics.* Philadelphia: Temple University Press

Finkelstein, Victor (1980) *Attitudes and Disabled People.* New York: World Rehabilitation Fund

Finnis, John (1980) *Natural Law and Natural Rights.* Oxford: Clarendon Press

Fiss, Owen (1976) 'Groups and the Equal Protection Clause.' *Philosophy and Public Affairs* 5: 107

Foster, G., and B. Anderson (1978) *Medical Anthropology.* New York: Knopf

Foucault, Michael (1965) *Madness and Civilization: A History of Insanity in the Age of Reason.* New York: Vintage

– (1973) *The Birth of the Clinic: An Archaeology of Medical Perception.* New York: Pantheon

Fox, R.C. (1977) 'The Medicalization and Demedicalization of American Society,' in J. Knowles (ed.) *Doing Better and Feeling Worse: Health Care in the United States.* New York: W.W. Norton

Fox, R. Fortescue (1917) *Physical Remedies for Disabled Soldiers.* London: Baillière, Tindal, and Cox

Frankena, William (1973) *Ethics*, 2nd ed. Englewood Cliffs, NJ: Prentice-Hall

Fraser, Robert T. (1984) 'An Introduction to Rehabilitation Psychology,' in Charles J. Golden (ed.)

Fraser Institute (1983) *Discrimination, Affirmative Action and Equal Opportunity*. Vancouver, BC: Fraser Institute

Fried, Charles (1978) *Right and Wrong*. Cambridge, Mass.: Harvard University Press

Frieden, Lex (1978) 'IL: Movement and Programs.' *American Rehabilitation* 3: 6

Friedman, Lawrence, and Sack Ladinsky (1967) 'Social Change and the Law of Industrial Accidents.' *Columbia Law Review* 67: 50

Friedson, Eliot (1965) 'Disability as Social Deviance,' in Marvin B. Sussman (ed.)

Fross, K.H., J.F. Dirks, R.A. Kinsman, and N.F. Jones (1980) 'Functionally Determined Invalidism in Chronic Asthma.' *Journal of Chronic Disease* 33: 485

Fuhrer, Marcus J. (1987) 'Overview of Outcome Analysis in Rehabilitation,' in Marcus J. Fuhrer (ed.) *Rehabilitation Outcomes: Analysis and Measurement*. Baltimore: Paul Brookes

Funk, Robert (1987) 'Disability Rights: From Caste to Class in the Context of Civil Rights,' in Alan Gartner and Tom Joe (eds.)

Gallagher, Eugene B. (1972) 'Lines of Reconstruction and Extension in the Parsonian Sociology of Illness,' in E. Gartly Jaco (ed.)

Garrad, J. (1974) 'Impairment and Disability: Their Measurement, Prevalence and Psychological Cost,' in D. Lees and S. Shaw (eds.) *Impairment, Disability and Handicap*. London: Heinemann

Garraty, John (1972) *Unemployment in History*. New York: Harper and Row

Gartner, Alan, and Tom Joe (eds.) (1987) *Images of the Disabled, Disabling Images*. New York: Praeger

Gellman, W. (1959) 'Roots of Prejudice against the Handicapped.' *Journal of Rehabilitation* 25: 4

Gellner, Ernst (1979) 'The Social Roots of Egalitarianism.' *Dialectic and Humanism* 4: 27

Gilbert, Douglas G. (1989) *A Guide to Workers' Compensation in Ontario*. Aurora, Ont.: Canada Law Book

Gibson, Dale (1990) *The Law of the Charter: Equality Rights*. Toronto: Carswell

Gillroy, John Martin, and Maurice Wade (eds.) (1992) *The Moral Dimensions of Public Policy Choice*. Pittsburgh: University of Pittsburgh Press

Gilman, Sander (1985) *Difference and Pathology: Stereotypes of Sexuality, Race, and Madness*. Ithaca, NY: Cornell University Press

– (1988) *Disease and Representation*. Ithaca, NY: Cornell University Press

Glassner, Barry (1982) 'Labeling Theory,' in M. Rosenberg, R. Stebbins, and A. Turowetz (eds.)

Gliedman, John, and William Roth (1980) *The Unexpected Minority: Handicapped Children in America*. New York: Harcourt Brace, Jovanovich

Goffman, Erving (1961) *Asylums*. New York: Anchor

– (1963) *Stigma: Notes on the Maintenance of Spoiled Identity*. Englewood Cliffs, NJ: Prentice-Hall

Goldberg, Richard T. (1984) 'Vocational Rehabilitation: A Psychological Perspective.' *Rehabilitation Literature* 45: 345

Golden, Charles J. (ed.) (1984) *Current Topics in Rehabilitation Psychology*. New York: Grune and Stratton

Golding, Peter, and Sue Middleton (1982) *Images of Welfare: Press and Public Attitudes to Poverty*. Oxford: M. Robertson

Goode, Erich (1984) *Deviant Behavior*, 2nd ed. Englewood Cliffs, NJ: Prentice-Hall

Goodin, Robert (1990) 'Stabilizing Expectations.' *Ethics* 100: 532

Goodwill, John (1988) 'The Doctor's Assessment of the Disabled Person.' in C. John Goodwill and M. Anne Chamberlain (eds.)

Goodwill, John, and Anne Chamberlain (1988) 'Aims of Rehabilitation,' in C. John Goodwill and M. Anne Chamberlain (eds.)

Goodwill, C. John, and M. Anne Chamberlain (eds.) (1988) *Rehabilitation of the Physically Disabled Adult*. London: Croom Helm

Gould, Stephen Jay (1981) *The Mismeasure of Man*. New York: W.W. Norton

Gove, W. (1976) 'Societal Reaction Theory and Disability,' in Gary L. Albrecht (ed.)

– (ed.) (1980) *The Labeling of Deviance: Evaluating a Perspective*, 2nd ed. New York: Wiley

Grabb, Edward (1990) *Theories of Social Inequality*, 2nd ed. Toronto: Holt, Rinehart and Winston

Granger, Carl V. (1984) 'A Conceptual Model for Functional Assessment,' in Carl V. Granger and Glen E. Gresham (eds.)

Granger, Carl V., and Glen E. Gresham (eds.) (1984) *Functional Assessment in Rehabilitation Medicine*. Baltimore: Williams and Wilkins

Gresham, Glen E., and Maria L.C. Labi (1984) 'Functional Assessment Instruments Currently Available for Documenting Outcomes in Rehabilitation Medicine,' in Carl V. Granger and Glen E. Gresham (eds.)

Grimby, Gunnar, Jane Finstam, and Alan Jette (1988) 'On the Application of the WHO Handicap Classification in Rehabilitation.' *Scandinavian Journal of Rehabilitation Medicine* 20: 93

Gritzer, Glenn, and Arnold Arluke (1985) *The Making of Rehabilitation: A*

Political Economy of Medical Specialization. Berkeley: University of California Press

Guest, Dennis (1980) *The Emergence of Social Security in Canada.* Vancouver: University of British Columbia Press

Guttmacher, Sally (1979) 'Whole in Body, Mind and Spirit: Holistic Health and the Limits of Medicine.' *Hastings Center Report* 9: 15

Haber, Lawrence D. (1967) 'Identifying the Disabled: Concepts and Methods in the Measurance of Disability.' *Social Security Bulletin* 30: 17

– (1973) 'Some Parameters for Social Policy in Disability: A Cross-National Comparison.' *Health and Society* 51: 319

– (1985) 'Trends and Demographic Studies on Programs for Disabled Persons,' in Leonard Perlman and Gary F. Austin (eds.)

Haber, Lawrence D., and Richard T. Smith (1971) 'Disability and Deviance: Normative Adaptations of Role Behavior.' *American Sociological Review* 36: 87

Haffter, C. (1968) 'The Changeling: History and Psychodynamics of Attitudes to Handicapped Children in European Folklore.' *Journal of the History of the Behavioral Sciences* 4: 55

Hahn, Harlan (1982) 'Disability and Rehabilitation Policy: Is Paternalistic Neglect Really Benign?' *Public Administration Review* 42: 385

– (1983) 'Paternalism and Public Policy.' *Society* 20: 36

– (1984a) *The Issue of Equality: European Perceptions of Employment for Disabled Persons.* New York: World Rehabilitation Fund

– (1984b) 'Reconceptualizing Disability: A Political Science Perspective.' *Rehabilitation Literature* 45: 362

– (1985) 'Changing Perception of Disability and the Future of Rehabilitation,' in Leonard Perlman and Gary F. Austin (eds.)

– (1987) 'Civil Rights for Disabled Americans: The Foundation of a Political Agenda,' in Alan Gartner and Tom Joe (eds.)

Halstead, L., and D. Weichers (eds.) (1985) *Late Effects of Poliomyelitis.* Miami, Fla.: Symposia Foundation

Hamilton, K.W. (1950) *Counseling the Handicapped in the Rehabilitation Process.* New York: Ronald Press

Harp, J., and J.R. Hofley (eds.) (1980) *Structural Inequality in Canada.* Scarborough, Ont.: Prentice-Hall

Harris, A.L. (1971) *Handicapped and Impaired in Great Britain.* London: Office of Population Censuses and Surveys, HMSO

Haveman, Robert, Victor Halberstadt, and Richard V. Burkhauser (1984) *Public Policy toward Disabled Workers: Cross-National Analyses of Economic Impacts.* Ithaca, NY: Cornell University Press

Hellman, C. (1984) *Culture, Health and Disease.* Bristol: John Wright

Herman, C. Peter, Mark P. Zanna, and E. Tory Higgins (1986) *Physical Appearance, Stigma, and Social Behavior.* Hillsdale, NJ: Lawrence Erlbaum

Herr, Stanley S., Stephen Arons, and Richard E. Wallace (1983) *Legal Rights and Mental-Health Care.* Toronto: Lexington Books

Ignatieff, Michael (1984) *The Needs of Strangers.* New York: Penguin

Illich, Ivan (1976) *Medical Nemesis.* New York: Pantheon

– (ed.) (1977) *Disabling Professions.* London: Marion Boyars

Ison, Terence G. (1977) 'The Politics of Reform in Personal Injury Compensation.' *University of Toronto Law Journal* 22: 385

– (1978) *Human Disability and Personal Income.* Kingston, Ont.: Industrial Relations Centre Reprint Series, No. 42

Jablensky, A., R. Schwarz, and T. Tomov (1980) 'WHO Collaborative Study on Impairments and Disabilities Associated with Schizophrenic Disoders: A Preliminary Communication – Objectives and Methods.' *Acta Psychiatrica Scandinavica* 62: 152

Jaco, Gartly E. (ed.) (1979) *Patients, Physicians, and Illness: A Sourcebook in Behavioral Science and Health,* 3rd ed. New York: Free Press

Jensen, Uffe Juul (1984) 'A Critique of Essentialism in Medicine,' in L. Nordenfelt and B.I.B. Lindahl (eds.)

Jette, Alan M. (1984) 'Concepts of Health and Methodological Issues in Functional Assessment,' in Carl V. Granger and Glen E. Gresham (eds.)

Johnson, William G. (1979) 'Disability, Income Support and Social Insurance,' in Edward Berkowitz (ed.) *Disability Policies and Government Policies.* New York: Praeger

– (1986) 'The Rehabilitation Act and Discrimination against Handicapped Workers: Does the Cure Fit the Disease?' in Monroe Berkowitz and M. Anne Hill (eds.)

Jones, Edward E. (1984) *Social Stigma: The Psychology of Marked Relationships.* New York: W.H. Freeman

Jordan, Bill (1987) *Rethinking Welfare.* Oxford: Basil Blackwell

Jordan, Sidney (1971) 'The Disadvantaged Group: A Concept Applicable to the Physically Handicapped,' in Edward Sagarin (ed.)

Kallen, Evelyn (1982) *Ethnicity and Human Rights in Canada.* Agincourt, Ont.: Gage

– (1989) *Label Me Human: Minority Rights of Stigmatized Canadians.* Toronto: University of Toronto Press

Karst, Kenneth L. (1977) 'Foreword: Equal Citizenship under the Fourteenth Amendment.' *Harvard Law Review* 91: 1

– (1983) 'Why Equality Matters.' *Georgia Law Review* 17: 245

Kaufert, J.M. (1983) 'Functional Ability Indices Measurement Problems in

Assessing Their Validity.' *Archives of Physical Medicine and Rehabilitation* 64: 260

Kaufert, Joseph M., and Patricia A. Kaufert (1984) 'Methodological and Conceptual Issues in Measuring the Long-Term Impact of Disability: The Experience of Poliomyelitis Patients in Manitoba.' *Social Science and Medicine* 19: 609

Kaufert, Joseph M., Patricia A. Kaufert, and David Locker (1987) 'After the Epidemic: The Long-Term Impact of Poliomyelitis,' in David Coburn, Carl D'Arcy, George M. Torrance, and Peter New (eds.) *Health and Canadian Society: Sociological Perspectives,* 2nd ed. Markham, Ont.: Fitzhenry and Whiteside

Kavka, Gregory S. (1992) 'Disability and the Right to Work,' in Ellen Frankel Paul, Fred D. Miller, Jr., and Jeffrey Paul (eds.) *Economic Rights.* Cambridge: Cambridge University Press

Keith, Robert Allen (1984) 'Functional Assessment Measures in Medical Rehabilitation: Current Status.' *Archives of Physical Medicine and Rehabilitation* 65: 74

Kessler, Henry (1931) *Accidental Injuries.* Philadelphia: Lea and Febiger
– (1970) *Disability – Determination and Evaluation.* Philadelphia: Lea and Febiger

Kidel, Mark (1988) 'Illness and Meaning,' in Mark Kidel and Susan Rowe-Leete (eds.) *The Meaning of Illness.* London: Routledge

King, Kathlean (ed.) (1985) *Long-Term Care.* Edinburgh: Churchill Livingston

Kjonstad, A. (1984) 'Assessment of Disability,' in A. Carmi, E. Chigier, and S. Schneider (eds.) *Disability.* Berlin: Springer-Verlag

Kleck, Robert (1968) 'Physical Stigma and Nonverbal Cue Emitted in Face-to-face Interaction.' *Human Relations* 31: 19

Kleck, Robert, Hiroshi Ono, and Arbert H. Hastorf (1966) 'The Effects of Physical Deviance and Face-to-Face Interaction. *Human Relations* 19: 325

Kleinman, Arthur (1988) *The Illness Narratives: Suffering, Healing and the Human Condition.* New York: Basic Books

Knudson, A.C.C. (1957) 'Philosophy, Operation, and Effectiveness of Physical Medicine and Rehabilitation,' in Harry A. Pattison (ed.)

Kohlberg, Jon Evind (1981) 'Conceptions of Social Disability,' in Gary L. Albrecht (ed.)

Kriegel, L. (1969) 'Uncle Tom and Tiny Tim: Some Reflections on the Cripple as Negro.' *American Scholar* 38: 412

Kuttner, Robert (1984) *The Economic Illusion.* Philadelphia: University of Pennsylvania Press

Labi, Maria L.C., and Glen E. Gresham (1984) 'Some Research Applications of Functional Assessment Instruments Used in Rehabilitation Medicine,' in Carl V. Granger and Glen E. Gresham (eds.)

Ladd, John (1982) 'The Concepts of Health and Disease and Their Ethical Implications,' in Bart Gruzalski and Carl Nelson (eds.) *Value Conflicts in Health Care Delivery*. Cambridge, Mass.: Ballinger

Laing, R.D. (1967) *The Politics of Experience*. New York: Ballantine

Law, C.M. (1987) 'The Disability of Short Stature.' *Archives of Disease in Childhood* 62: 855

Le Disert, Dominique (1987) 'Entre la peur et la pitié: Quelques aspects socio-historiques de l'infirmité.' *International Journal of Rehabilitation Research* 10: 253

Leonard, Jonathan (1986) 'Labor Supply Incentives and Disincentives for Disabled Persons,' in Monroe Berkowitz and Anne M. Hill (eds.)

Lepofsky, M. David, and Jerome E. Bickenbach (1985) 'Equality Rights and the Physically Handicapped,' in Anne F. Bayefsky and Mary Eberts (eds.)

Lepofsky, M. David, and H. Schwartz (1988) 'An Erroneous Approach to the Charter's Equality Guarantee.' *Canadian Bar Review* 67: 115

Lerner, R.M., and D. Miller (1978) 'Just World Research and the Attribution Process: Looking Back and Ahead.' *Psychological Bulletin* 85: 1030

Lewis, R. (1981) 'No-Fault Compensation for Victims of Road Accidents: Can it Be Justified?' *Journal of Political Science* 10: 161

Liachowitz, Claire H. (1988) *Disability as a Social Construct: Legislative Roots*. Philadelphia: University of Pennsylvania Press

Liebman, Lance (1976) 'The Definition of Disability in Social Security and Social Security Income: Drawing the Bounds of Social Welfare Estates.' *Harvard Law Review* 89: 833

Liggett, H. (1988) 'Stars are Not Born: An Interactive Approach to the Politics of Disability.' *Disability, Handicap and Society* 3: 271

Lindley, Richard (1986) *Autonomy*. Atlantic Highlands, NJ: Humanities Press International

Liska, Allena E. (1987) *Perspectives on Deviance*, 2nd ed. Englewood Cliffs, NJ: Prentice-Hall

Locker, David (1983) *Disability and Disadvantage: The Consequences of Chronic Illness*. London: Tavistock

Lucas, J.R. (1971) 'Against Equality,' in H. Bedau (ed.) *Justice and Equality*. Englewood Cliffs, NJ: Prentice-Hall

MacKinnon, Catharine A. (1987) *Feminism Unmodified*. Cambridge, Mass.: Harvard University Press

Maître, Jacques (1987) 'Construction de la norme et construction du handi-

cap,' in Jean-Marc Alby and Patrick Sansoy (eds.) *Handicap, Vécu, Évalué.*
Grenoble: La Pensée Sauvage

Malthus, T.R. (1958) *An Essay on Population.* Reprint of the 1872 edition.
London: Dent

Marmor, Theodore R., and Jerry L. Mashaw (eds.) (1991) *Social Security:
Beyond the Rhetoric of Crisis.* Princeton, NJ: Princeton University Press

Marmor, Theodore R., Jerry L. Mashaw, and Philip L. Harvey (1990)
America's Misunderstood Welfare State. New York: Basic Books

Marsh, Leonard (1975) *Report on Social Security for Canada.* Toronto: University of Toronto Press

McCluskey, Martha T. (1988) 'Rethinking Equality and Difference: Disability Discrimination in Public Transportation.' *Yale Law Journal* 97: 863

Mechanic, David (1966) 'Response Factors in Illness: The Study of Illness
Behavior.' *Social Psychiatry and Psychiatric Epidemiology* 11: 1

– (1969) *Mental Health and Social Policy.* Englewood Cliffs, NJ: Prentice-Hall

– (1973) 'Health and Illness in Technological Societies.' *Hastings Center
Studies* 1: 7

Meyerson, L. (1971) 'Physical Disability as a Social Psychological Problem,'
in Edward Sagarin (ed.)

Michelman, Frank (1969) 'The Supreme Court, 1968 Term – Forward: On
Protecting the Poor through the Fourteenth Amendment.' *Harvard Law
Review* 83: 7

– (1987) 'The Meanings of Legal Equality,' in F.E. McArdle (ed.) *The Cambridge Lectures, 1985.* Montreal: Editions Yuon Blais

Minaire, P., J. Cherpin, J.-L. Flores, and D. Weber (1987) 'Handicap de
situation et étude fonctionnelle de population,' in Jean-Marc Alby and
Patrick Sansoy (eds.) *Handicap, Vécu, Évalué.* Grenoble: La Pensée
Sauvage

Minow, Martha (1990) *Making All the Difference: Inclusion, Exclusion, and
American Law.* Ithaca, NY: Cornell University Press

Mishler, Elliot G. (1981) 'Viewpoint: Critical Perspectives on the Biomedical Model,' in Elliot G. Mishler, Lorna R. Amarasingham, Stuart T.
Hauser, Ramsey Liem, Samuel D. Osherson, and Nancy E. Waxler (eds.)
Social Contexts of Health, Illness, and Patient Care. Cambridge: Cambridge
University Press

Moore, M.S. (1975) 'Some Myths about Mental Illness.' *Archives of General
Psychiatry* 32: 1483

Murphy, Jeffrie (1976) 'Psychiatric Labelling in Cross-Cultural Perspective.'
Science 191: 1019

Murphy, Jeffrie, and Jules Coleman (1984) *The Philosophy of Law.* Totowa,
NJ: Rowman and Allanheld

Murphy, R. (1987) *The Body Silent*. London: Dent

Nagi, Saad Z. (1965) 'Some Conceptual Issues in Disability and Rehabilitation,' in Marvin B. Sussman (ed.)

– (1969) *Disability and Rehabilitation: Legal, Clinical and Self-Concepts and Measurement.* Columbus: Ohio State University

– (1979) 'The Concept and Measurement of Disability,' in Edward Berkowitz (ed.) *Disability Policies and Government Policies*. New York: Praeger

– (1981) 'Disability Concepts and Implications for Programs,' in Gary L. Albrecht (ed.) *Cross-National Rehabilitation Policies: A Sociological Perspective*. Beverly Hills, Cal.: Sage Studies in International Sociology

– (1987) 'Decision Criteria and the Question of Equity and Incentives,' in Han Emanuel, Eric H. De Gier, and Peter A.B. Kalker Konijn (eds.) *Disability Benefits: Factors Determining Application and Awards*. Greenwich, Conn.: JAI Press

National Rehabilitation Association (1975) *Definitions of Pathology, Impairment, Functional Limitation and Disability – Implications for Practicer, Research, Program and Policy Development and Service Delivery*. New York: National Rehabilitation Association

Neff, Walter S. (1980) 'Vocational Assessment – Theory and Models,' in Brian Bolton and Daniel W. Cook (eds.) *Rehabilitation Client Assessment*. Baltimore: University Park Press

Nielsen, Kai (1985) *Equality and Liberty*. Totowa, NJ: Rowman and Allanheld

Nordenfelt, Lennart (1987) *On the Nature of Health: An Action-Theoretic Approach*. Dordrecht: Reidel

Nordenfelt, Lennart, and B.I.B. Lindahl (eds.) (1984) *Health, Disease and Causal Explanation in Medicine*. Dordrecht: Reidel

Norman, Richard (1987) *Free and Equal*. Oxford: Oxford University Press

Note (1984) 'Employment Discrimination against the Handicapped and Section 504 of the Rehabilitation Act: An Essay on Legal Evasiveness.' *Harvard Law Review* 97: 997

O'Connor, Maureen (1988) 'Defining "Handicap" for Purposes of Employment Discrimination.' *Arizona Law Review* 30: 633

Okun, Arthur (1975) *Equality and Efficiency: The Big Tradeoff*. Washington, DC: Brookings Institute

Oliver, Michael (1984) 'The Politics of Disability.' *Critical Social Politics* 11

– (1990) *The Politics of Disablement*. London: Macmillan

Ontario, Social Assistance Review Commission (1988) *Transitions*. Toronto: Publications Ontario

Orzack, Louis H. (1971) 'Social Changes, Minorities, and the Mentally

Retarded,' in Edward Sagarin (ed.) *The Other Minorities*. New York: Ginn

Osmond, Humphry, and Miriam Siegler (1974) *Models of Madness, Models of Medicine*. New York: Macmillan

Padden, Carol, and Tom Humphries (1988) *Deaf in America: Voices from a Culture*. Cambridge, Mass.: Harvard University Press

Page, Robert (1984) *Stigma*. London: Routledge and Kegan Paul

Paicheler, Henri (1987) 'Deficiencies, personnes handicapées et societé,' in Jean-Marc Alby and Patrick Sansoy (eds.) *Handicap, Vécu, Évalué*. Grenoble: La Pensée Sauvage

Palmer, G. (1973) 'Compensation for Personal Injury: A Requiem for the Common Law of New Zealand.' *American Journal of Comparative Law* 21: 1

Parry, John (1988) 'New Medical Meanings of #504 – the Federal Handicapped Persons Civil Rights Provision.' *Mental and Physical Disability Law Reporter* 12: 234

Parry, Noel, and Jose Parry (1979) 'Social Work, Professionalism and the State,' in Noel Parry, Michael Rustin, and Carole Satyamurti (eds.)

Parry, Noel, Michael Rustin, and Carole Satyamurti (eds.) (1979) *Social Work, Welfare and the State*. London: Edward Arnold

Parsons, Talcott (1961) *The Social System*. Glencoe, Ill. Free Press

– (1979) 'Definitions of Health and Illness in the Light of American Values and Social Structure,' in E. Gartly Jaco (ed.)

Pattison, Harry A. (ed.) (1957) *The Handicapped and their Rehabilitation*. Springfield, Ill.: Charles C. Thomas

Pellegrino, Edmund D. (1979) 'The Sociocultural Impact of Twentieth-Century Therapeutics.' in Morris J. Vogel and Charles E. Rosenberg (eds.) *The Therapeutic Revolution*. Pittsburg: University of Pennsylvania Press

Perlman, Leonard, and Gary F. Austin (eds.) (1985) *Social Influences in Rehabilitation Planning: Blueprint for the 21st Century*. Alexandria, Va.: National Rehabilitation Association

Perrin, Burt (1982) 'Misconceptions about the Principle of Normalization.' *Mental Retardation* 32: 39

Pfeiffer, Jan (1986) 'Functional Evaluation of Cerebral Palsy using the ICIDH.' *International Rehabilitation Medicine* 8: 11

Pfuhl, E. (1986) *The Deviance Process*, 2nd ed. Belmont, Cal.: Wadsworth

Pigou, A.C. (1952) *The Economics of Welfare*. London: Macmillan

Porn, I. (1984) 'An Equilibrium Model of Health,' in L. Nordenfelt and B.I.B. Lindahl (eds.)

Posner, Richard (1973) *The Economic Analysis of the Law*. Boston: Little, Brown

Power, Paul W.A. (1984) *A Guide to Vocational Assessment*. Baltimore: University Park Press

Pryor, Ellen Smith (1990a) 'Compensation and a Consequential Model of Loss.' *Tulane Law Review* 64: 783

– (1990b) 'Flawed Promises: A Critical Evaluation of the American Medical Association's *Guides to the Evaluation of Permanent Impairment*.' *Harvard Law Review* 103: 964

Purtilo, Ruth (1981) *Justice, Liberty, Compassion: 'Humane' Health Care and Rehabilitation*. New York: World Rehabilitation Fund

Québec, Office des personnes handicapées du Québec. (1984) *On Equal Terms*. Québec: Office des personnes handicapées

Radden, Jennifer (1985) *Madness and Reason*. London: George Allen and Unwin

Rae, Douglas, and Douglas Yates (1981) *Equalities*. Cambridge, Mass.: Harvard University Press

Rains, P., J. Kitsuse, T. Duster, and E. Friedson (1975) 'The Labeling Approach to Deviance,' in N. Hobbs (ed.) *Issues in the Classification of Children*. San Francisco: Jossey-Bass

Rawls, John (1971) *A Theory of Justice*. Cambridge, Mass.: Harvard University

Rea, Samuel A. (1981) *Disability Insurance and Public Policy*. Toronto: University of Toronto Press

Reich, Robert B. (1991) *The Work of Nations*. New York: Knopf

Rejda, George E. (1988) *Social Insurance and Economic Security*, 3rd ed. Englewood Cliffs, NJ: Prentice-Hall

Richardson, Stephen A. (1976) 'Attitudes and Behavior towards the Physically Handicapped.' *Birth Defects: Original Articles Series* 12: 15

Richardson Stephen A., et al. (1961) 'Cultural Uniformity in Reaction to Physical Disability.' *American Sociological Review* 26: 241

Roberts, Robert (1990) *The Social Laws of the Qoran* Atlantic Highlands, NJ: Humanities Press

Roessler, Richard, and Brian Bolton (1978) *Psychosocial Adjustment to Disability*. Baltimore: University Park Press

Roessler, Richard, and Reed Greenwood (1987) 'Vocational Evaluation,' in Brian Bolton (ed.) *Handbook of Measurement and Evaluation in Rehabilitation*. Baltimore: Paul Brookes

Rogers, Cheryl (1987) 'The Employment Dilemma for Disabled Persons,' in Alan Gartner and Tom Joe (eds.)

Rose, Steven, R.C. Lewontin, and Leon J. Kamin (1984) *Not in Our Genes.* Harmondsworth: Penguin

Rosenberg, M., R. Stebbins, and A. Turowetz (eds.) (1982) *The Sociology of Deviance.* New York: St. Martin's Press

Roth, William (1985) 'The Politics of Disability: Future Trends as Shaped by Current Realities,' in Leonard G. Perlman and Gary F. Austin (eds.)

Rubin, J. (1984) 'Economic Constraints on the Effectiveness of Litigation and Legislation for the Disabled.' in A. Carmi, E. Chigier, and S. Schneider (eds.) *Disability.* Berlin: Springer-Verlag

Rusk, Howard (1971) *Rehabilitation Medicine,* 3rd ed. St Louis: Charles V. Mosby

Ryan, W. (1977) *Blaming the Victim.* New York: Pantheon

– (1982) *Equality.* New York: Vintage Books

Sacks, Oliver (1989) *Seeing Voices.* Berkeley, Cal.: University of California Press

Safilios-Rothschild, Constantina (1970) *The Sociology and Social Psychology of Disability and Rehabilitation.* New York: Random House

– (1976) 'Disabled Persons' Self-Definitions and Their Implications for Rehabilitation,' in Gary L. Albrecht (ed.)

Sagarin, Edward (1975) *Deviants and Deviance.* New York: Praeger

Sagarin, Edward (ed.) (1971) *The Other Minorities: Nonethnic Collectivities Conceptualized as Minority Groups.* Toronto: Ginn

Satamurti, Carole (1979) 'Care and Control in Local Authority Social Work,' in Noel Parry, Michael Rustin, and Carole Satyamurti (eds.)

Scales, Ann (1988) 'The Emergence of Feminist Jurisprudence: An Essay.' *Yale Law Journal* 95: 1375

Scarry, Elaine (1985) *The Body in Pain.* New York: Oxford University Press

Scheff, Thomas (1966) *Being Mentally Ill.* Chicago: Aldine

Schur, E. (1971) *Labeling Deviant Behavior: Its Sociological Implications.* New York: Harper and Row

– (1980) *Politics of Deviance: Stigma Contests and the Uses of Power.* Englewood Cliffs, NJ: Prentice-Hall

Scotch, Richard K. (1984) *From Goodwill to Civil Rights.* Philadelphia: Temple University Press

Scott, Robert A. (1969) *The Making of Blind Men.* New York: Russell Sage Foundation

Scull, Andrew (1979) *Museums of Madness.* London: Allen Lane/Penguin

Sen, Amartya (1979) 'Welfarism and Utilitarianism.' *Journal of Philosophy* 76: 463

- (1980) 'Equality of What?' in S. McMurrin (ed.) *The Tanner Lectures on Human Values*. Cambridge: Cambridge University Press
- (1982) *Choice, Welfare and Measurement*. Cambridge, Mass.: MIT Press
- (1984a) 'Rights and Capabilities,' in *Resources, Values and Development*. Oxford: Basil Blackwell
- (1984b) 'Goods and People,' in *Resources, Values and Development*. Oxford: Basil Blackwell
- (1985) *Commodities and Capabilities*. Amsterdam: North-Holland
- (1986) 'The Standard of Living,' in S. McMurrin (ed.) *The Tanner Lectures on Human Values*. Cambridge: Cambridge University Press
- (1987) *On Ethics and Economics*. Oxford: Basil Blackwell
- (1990) 'Justice: Means versus Freedoms.' *Philosophy and Public Affairs* 19: 111

Shearer, A. (1981) *Disability: Whose Handicap?* London: Basil Blackwell

Shontz, Franklin C. (1977) 'Physical Disability and Personality: Theory and Recent Research,' in Joseph Stubbins (ed.) *Social and Psychological Aspects of Disability*. Baltimore: University Park Press

Siller, Jerome (1986) 'The Measurement of Attitudes toward Physically Disabled Persons,' in C. Peter Herman, Mark P. Zanna, and E. Tory Higgins (eds.) *Physical Appearance, Stigma, and Social Behavior*. Hillsdale, NJ: Lawrence Erlbaum

Simmons, H.G. (1982) *From Asylum to Welfare*. Toronto: National Institute for Mental Retardation

Sinaki, Mehrsheed (ed.) (1987) *Basic Clinical Rehabilitation Medicine*. Toronto: B.C. Decker

Sinaki, Mehrsheed, and G. Keith Stillwell (1987) 'Current Concepts and Practical Aspects of Physical Medicine and Rehabilitation,' in Mehrsheed Sinaki (ed.)

Smith, Richard T. (1980) 'Societal Reaction and Physical Disability: Contrasting Perspectives,' in Richard R. Gove (ed.)

Sokolow, J., et al. (1959) 'Disability.' *Archives of Physiotherapy and Medical Rehabilitation* 40: 421

Sontag, Susan (1979) *Illness as Metaphor*. New York: Vintage
- (1988) *AIDS and Its Metaphors*. New York: Farrar, Straus and Giroux

Spiegel, Allen D., and Simon Podair (eds.) (1981) *Rehabilitating People with Disabilities into the Mainstream of Society*. Park Ridge, NJ: Noyes Medical Publications

Stapleton, Jane (1986) *Disease and the Compensation Debate*. Oxford: Clarendon Press

Stiker, Henri-Jacques (1982) *Corps Infirmés et Sociétés*. Paris: Aubier Montaigne
– (1987) 'Catégories organisatrices des visions du handicap,' in Jean-Marc Alby and Patrick Sansoy (eds.) *Handicap, Vécu, Évalué*. Grenoble: La Pensée Sauvage
Stoddard, Susan (1978) 'Independent Living: Concept and Programs.' *American Rehabilitation* 3: 2
Stoddard, S., and B. Brown (1980) 'Evaluating California's Independent Living Centers.' *American Rehabilitation* 5: 18
Stone, Deborah A. (1981) 'The Definition and Determination of Disability in Public Programs,' in Gary L. Albrecht (ed.)
– (1984) *The Disabled State*. Philadelphia: Temple University Press
– (1988) *Policy Paradox and Political Reason*. Glenview, Ill.: Scott, Foresman
Strauss, Anselm L. (1975) *Chronic Illness and the Quality of Life*. St Louis: Charles V. Mosby
Strauss, Anselm L., and Juliet M. Corbin (1988) *Shaping a New Health Care System*. San Francisco: Jossey-Bass
Stubbins, Joseph (1984) 'Vocational Rehabilitation as Social Science.' *Rehabilitation Literature* 45: 375
Stubbins, Joseph, and George W. Albee (1984) 'Ideologies of Clinical and Ecological Models.' *Rehabilitation Literature* 45: 349
Sussman, Marvin B. (ed.) (1965) *Sociology and Rehabilitation*. Washington, DC: American Sociological Association
– (1969) 'Dependent Disabled and Dependent Poor: Similarity of Conceptual Issues and Research Needs.' *Social Science Review* 43: 439
Sutherland, A. (1981) *Disabled We Stand*. London: Souvenir Press
Szasz, T.S. (1961) *The Myth of Mental Illness*. New York: Harper and Row
– (1970a) *The Manufacture of Madness*. New York: Harper and Row
– (1970b) *Ideology and Insanity*. New York: Doubleday
Tannenbaum, Frank (1938) *Crime and Community*. Boston: Ginn
Tawney, R.H. (1931) *Equality*. London: George Allen and Unwin
tenBroek, Jacobus (1966) 'The Right to Live in the World: The Disabled in the Law of Torts. *California Law Review* 54: 841
Thomas, David (1982) *The Experience of Handicap*. London: Methuen
Thomas, Jim (1982) 'New Directions in Deviance Research,' in M. Rosenberg, R. Stebbins, and A. Turowetz (eds.)
Thurer, Shari (1981) 'Disability and Monstrosity: A Look at Literary Distortions of Handicapping Conditions,' in Allen D. Spiegel and Simon Podair (eds.)

Thurow, Lester (1980) *The Zero-Sum Society*. New York: Basic Books

Titmuss, R.M. (1968) *Commitment to Welfare*. London: Allen and Unwin

Torjman, Sherri Resin (1988) *Income Insecurity: the Disability Income System in Canada*. Toronto: G. Allen Roeher Institute

Townsend, Peter (1967) *The Disabled in Society*. London: GLAD

– (1979) *Poverty in the United Kingdom*. London: Allen Lane

Trevelyan, G.M. (1967) *English Social History*. Harmondsworth: Penguin

Trieschmann, Roberta (1984) 'Vocational Rehabilitation: A Psychological Perspective.' *Rehabilitation Literature* 45: 345

Turner, Bryan (1986) *Equality*. Chichester: Tavistock

Turner, R.H. (1972) 'Deviance Avowal as Neutralization of Commitment.' *Social Problems* 19: 308

Tussman, J., and J. TenBroek (1949) 'The Equal Protection of the Law.' *California Law Review* 37: 341

Urbach, Ephraim E. (1987) *The Sages*. Cambridge, Mass.: Harvard University Press

U.S. Department of Health, Education and Welfare (1979) *Disability Evaluation under Social Security: A Handbook for Physicians*. Washington, DC: United States Government Printing Office

U.S. Department of Health and Human Services (1991) *International Classification of Disease*, 9th ed. Washington, DC: United States Government Printing Office

Veatch, Robert A. (1986) *The Foundations of Justice*. New York: Oxford University Press

Verville, Richard E. (1981) 'The Disabled, Rehabilitation, and Current Public Policy,' in Allen D. Spiegel and Simon Podair (eds.)

Vickers, Jill (1983) 'Majority Equality Issues of the Eighties.' *Canadian Human Rights Yearbook*

Vizkelety, Beatrice (1987) *Proving Discrimination in Canada*. Toronto: Carswell

Vlastos, Gregory (1962) 'Justice and Equality,' in Richard Brandt (ed.) *Social Justice*. Englewood Cliffs, NJ: Prentice-Hall

Waltzer, Michael (1983) *Spheres of Justice*. New York: Basic Books

Wegner, Judith Welch (1983) 'The Antidiscrimination Model Reconsidered: Ensuring Equal Opportunity without Respect to Handicap under Section 504 of the Rehabilitation Act of 1973.' *Cornell Law Review* 69: 401

Weiler, Paul C. (1986) *Permanent Partial Disability: Alternative Models of Compensation*. Toronto: Ministry of Labour

Wendell, Susan (1989) 'Toward a Feminist Theory of Disability.' *Hypatia* 4: 104

Westen, Peter (1982) 'The Empty Idea of Equality.' *Harvard Law Review* 95: 537

Whitbeck, Carol (1981) 'A Theory of Health,' in A.L. Caplan, H.T. Engelhardt Jr., and J.J. McCartney (eds.) *Concepts of Health and Disease: Interdisciplinary Perspectives.* Reading, Mass.: Addison-Wesley

Wiersma, D. (1986) 'Psychological Impairments and Social Disabilities: On the Applicability of the ICIDH to Psychiatry.' *International Rehabilitation Medicine* 8: 3

Williams, Bernard (1962) 'The Idea of Equality,' in Peter Laslett and W.G. Runciman (eds.) *Philosophy, Politics and Society*, 2nd series. Oxford: Basil Blackwell

Wolfensberger, Wolf (1972) *The Principle of Normalization in Human Service.* Toronto: National Institute on Mental Retardation

– (1983) 'Social Role Valorization: A Proposed New Term for the Principle of Normalization.' *Mental Retardation* 21: 234

Wolfensberger, Wolf, and L. Glenn (1973) *Program Analysis of Service Systems (PASS): A Method for Quantitative Evaluation of Human Services: A Field Manual.* Toronto: National Institute on Mental Retardation

Wood, Philip H.N. (1975) *Classification of Impairments and Handicaps.* WHO/ICD9/Rev. CONF/75.15

– (1980a) 'The Language of Disablement: A Glossary Relating to Disease and Its Consequences.' *International Rehabilitation Medicine* 2: 86

– (1980b) 'Appreciating the Consequences of Disease: The International Classification of Impairments, Disabilities, and Handicaps.' *WHO Chronicle* 376

– (1989) 'A Man's Reach Should Exceed His Grasp.' *International Disability Studies* 11: 1

Wood, Philip H.N., and Elizabeth M. Badley (1978a) 'Setting Disablement in Perspective.' *International Rehabilitation Medicine* 1: 32

– (1978b) 'An Epidemiological Appraisal of Disablement,' in A.E. Bennett (ed.) *Recent Advances in Community Medicine.* Edinburgh: Churchill Livingstone

– (1980) *People with Disabilities – Towards Acquiring Information Which Reflects More Sensitivity to Their Problems and Needs.* Monograph No. 12 International Exchange of Information in Rehabilitation Project. Washington, DC: U.S. Department of Education

– (1984) 'Contribution of Epidemiology to Health Care Planning for People with Disabilities,' in Carl V. Granger and Glen E. Gresham (eds.)

World Health Organization (1958) *The First Ten Years of the World Health Organization.* New York: WHO

- (1980) *International Classification of Impairments, Disabilities and Handicaps: A Manual of Classification Relating to the Consequences of Disease.* Geneva: WHO
Wright, Beatrice A. (1983) *Physical Disability – A Psychosocial Approach*, 2nd ed. New York: Harper and Row
Wulff, H. (1976) *Rational Diagnosis and Treatment.* Oxford: Basil Blackwell
Yuker, H.E., J.R. Block, and J.H. Young (1966) *The Measurement of Attitudes toward Disabled Persons.* Albertson, NY: Human Resources Center
Zola, Irving K. (1966) 'Culture and Symptoms: An Analysis of Patients' Presenting Complaints.' *American Sociological Review* 31: 615
- (1977) 'Healthism and Disabling Medicalization,' in Ivan Illich (ed.)
- (1982) *Missing Pieces: A Chronicle of Living with a Disability.* Philadelphia: Temple University Press

Index

39–40. *See also* Vocational rehabilitation

Rehabilitation Act (U.S.), 9, 151, 164–70

Re Mroskowski and Director of V.R.S. Branch (Canada), 119

Respect (policy goal), 3–4, 14, 199; and biomedical model, 91–4; and economic model, 107–8, 129–30; and equality, 235–6; and normative basis, 225–6; and social-political model, 155–8, 173

Rights: absolute/defeasible, 186; and disablement theory, 184–8; and economic reasoning, 128, 133–4; and equality, 163–72, 241–2, 245–56; fair treatment, 162–3; legal, 227–8, 245–9; moral, 163; and politicization, 151–2, 156, 157–8; positive/negative, 186; and social-political model, 162–72, 179–80; and welfare miximization, 215

Robine, Jean Marie, 273nn. 17, 18

Rose, Steven, 190

Roth, William, 154, 172–3

Royal Commission on New Reproductive Technologies (Canada), 83–4

Rule of law, 12, 179, 204, 241–2

Rusk, Howard, 58, 96–7

Safilios-Rothschild, Constantina, 142, 154

Scott, Robert, 145

Sen, Amartya, 202–3, 219–20, 265–8

Sen argument, 202–3

Sexual impairments, 87–8, 191

Short stature, 53, 136–7, 139–40, 154

Sickness and the sick role, 27–8, 36, 38, 81–4, 141–2, 172

Siller, Jerome, 147–8

Social activism, 137, 150–8, 160–2, 171–2, 284n. 102

Social assistance programs: and biomedical model, 70–3; and economic model, 115–19, 120, 122–3, 124–6, 131; and need, 201; stigma of, 194, 197

Social Assistance Review Commission (Ontario), 11, 79, 159

Social disadvantage. *See* Handicap

Social environment: creating handicaps, 47–53, 58–60, 136–7, 138–9, 141–9; and economic model, 94–6, 103, 126–31; and handicapping, 152–5, 178; and social-political model, 140–1, 159

Social insurance programs, 112–15, 120, 122, 124, 209–13

Social policy analysis, 4–7, 43–4, 105, 184–5, 198, 202–4, 230–1

Social security programs, 119–21, 122–5, 126, 130–1. *See also* Social assistance programs; Social insurance programs

Social Security Administration (U.S.), 76, 95

Social Security Disability Insurance (U.S.), 70, 75–6

Socially constructed disadvantages, 136–7, 138–40, 141–9

Social-political model: definition of, 13–15, 135–81; distortions of, 172–81; effects on policy, 162–72, 175–81, 234; evolution of, 136–41; focus on social environment, 140; and handicap, 138–40; and minority-rights analysis, 152–8, 167, 171–2; normative basis of, 179–81, 222; politicalization of,

Welfarism, 202–3, 215, 218–19, 260–5, 290n. 59
Wellman, Mark, 178
'Whole person impairment,' 74–8, 85–9, 130
Wiersma, D., 272n. 10, 273n. 18
Wood, Philip H.N., 23–4, 26–8, 30–1, 35, 44, 59, 95
Work disability. *See* Employability
Workers' compensation: and biomedical model, 70–3, 74–81; and

compensation, 209–12; and disability classification, 43, 74–5; and economic model, 108–12
Workers' Compensation Board (Ontario), 79–81, 86
'Worthy poor,' 71–3, 94, 116–18, 193–4
Wright, Beatrice A., 142, 146, 154

Zola, I.K., 273n. 16, 285n. 106